MW01245395

Beyond Despair:
Tender Care

Pain of the Past or Devastation Today—
Restoration by God's Wondrous Ways!

The LORD said, "I have indeed seen the affliction of my people....
I have heard them crying out.... I know their sorrows....
I am concerned about their suffering.
So I ... come ... to rescue them." (Exodus 3:7-8)

Erin Worthley

Cover design by Rhea Beaudry.

(**Author's Note**: When necessary, names have been changed to ensure privacy. Throughout this book, all names of [and referring pronouns to] God are capitalized, while references to satan are lowercased; exceptions to this will be in exact scriptural quotations where I do not have the freedom to make these distinctions. Biblical passages inferred but not directly quoted will usually not contain "see" by their notation [e.g., see John 3:16]. When I cite verbatim from Scripture, I use quotation marks or set the quote apart in an indented paragraph. Some passages are italicized to place focus on their meaning; such emphasis is mine and not in the original quotation.)

Published by

OTC Publishing
12650 Larch St NW
Coon Rapids, MN 55448
(763)757-8102
Printed in the United States of America

ENDORSEMENTS

I have had the privilege of being Tom and Erin's pastor for the past eight years and have served on Garden of Grace Ministries' Board of Directors for six years. I have witnessed firsthand the wonderful healing and victory that Christ has bought to them. I can highly recommend this book because these principles have worked in their lives and the lives of countless people to whom Erin has ministered. It will quickly become obvious that the Scriptures play a huge role in Erin's ministry. Not only does she use the Bible for guidance and wisdom, but under the Holy Spirit's guidance, she uses Scripture as a weapon to destroy the lies of the enemy and bring healing and liberty to the people in her care. Part 2: The study of "Exodus: Model of Restoration" is alone worth the price. This book will serve as a great resource to help pastors, counselors, and prayer partners provide tender, yet effective, care for those seeking new levels of freedom.

—Pastor Bob Pullar
Living Waters Church, Elk River, MN

God has given Erin many insights, truths, and prayer strategies from Scripture, which spoke powerfully to us. Because God's heart is for the healing of nations, her anointed wisdom will be of great value in our ministry to see the gates of individuals, cities, and nations open to God and the gates of the enemy closed. This book will help many to discover their destiny and freedom in Christ.

—Ken and Carrie Beaudry, Apostolic Servants
Pray Elk River/Kenneth Beaudry Ministries

Erin Worthley is a woman I admire greatly, and her book reflects her awesome giftings and personality. Having ministered with Erin in prayer counseling sessions, I know that she is real and dynamic. She is also an amazing listener. When she asks a question, she actually listens to the answer, something that reflects Jesus in her. Because of her ability to listen, her book is full and flavorful and informative without being "preachy". From the very introduction, I felt invited into a very personal space that displayed honesty, pain, and hope. She shares the glory parts, as well as the gory parts of her life in Christ.

—Alice Sharping, Missionary
Every Nation Ministries

DEDICATION

Most mornings, while sipping coffee, my husband and I like to view the garden from our bedroom window. One day, in August, 2004, we both noticed what looked like a fast growing weed among our colorful impatiens. Upon closer examination, I realized it was going to be a sunflower, so I decided to give the out-of-place plant a chance to grow.

When I eventually got around to picking the blossom, I noticed that God had created a phenomenal sunflower, three blooms, blended together as one. As I admired the oddity, the Lord gave me a prophetic revelation:

Symbolically, I saw the three flowering heads as Tom and I, miraculously one under the headship of Christ. Like dancing sunflowers facing the morning sun, we have turned to face the Sun of Righteousness to lighten our darkness. The heavenly Father is blessing our marriage because we have chosen His path of righteousness. Like the maturely seeded heart of a sunflower, God's root of love has resulted in our being surrounded by petals of His golden beauty and hearts filled with the Good Seed, Jesus.

The following word from Malachi 4:2 (AMP) was brought to my remembrance:

But unto you who revere and worshipfully fear My name shall the Sun of Righteousness arise with healing in His wings and His beams, and you shall go forth and gambol like calves [released] from the stall and leap for joy.

God has been true to His promises—the Master Mender has made Tom and me truly united in Christ.

I gratefully dedicate this book to Jesus Christ, the Son of God, Whose gentle and humble heart brings transforming love, mercy, rest, restoration, and unity to all who come unto Him.

ACKNOWLEDGMENTS

I would like to honor all in God's bouquet of golden blooms who made this book a reality. I express my deepest thanks to those whose continual fruitfulness in God's Garden of Grace has blessed me significantly:

♥ To Tom, my husband and friend, for all his love and for shouldering the many household chores; and especially for opening the door to his dark memories so others may open their hearts to Christ's light. Great men humble themselves before God: My husband is a giant of a man.

♥ To our children, grandchildren, and extended family for their warm hearts of forgiveness and for their willingness to be a testimony of God's tender care.

♥ To Rhea Beaudry, God's eagle-eye proofreader and God's sweet fragrance in my life; a best friend, who gave me wise words of critique; plus she contributed the meaningful photo for the book's cover. I'll always be grateful for her steadfast encouragement, brilliant assistance, and loving support.

♥ To my faithful pastors: Bob Pullar, Dave Weigel, Grant Hill, and Frank Masserano (the staff of International Ministerial Fellowship) for their wisdom, love, and covering prayers.

♥ To Garden of Grace Ministries' Board of Directors and Intercessors (Leon and Rhea Beaudry, Robert and Mary Blood, Jeff and Chris Hill, and Bob and Marci Pullar) for their vital support and care. When I was struggling to find the right title, Jeff recommended Beyond Despair: Tender Care; I will be forever indebted for his anointed suggestion.

♥ To Michael Schwab for his tender care and being God's gracious prophetic voice in our trying times.

♥ To Paul Mielke for selflessly building an updated computer with the needed software for the ministry, after I shared with him that I was going to write a book using my 1995 Macintosh.

♥ To Kirk Carlson, Gary Finseth, Kim Oberg, Eric and Janet Staupe, and the many others God provided at just the right time, for their needed computer skills and advice.

♥ To Dianne Annis and Alice Sharping for skillfully proof-reading the manuscript and giving me encouraging and helpful feedback.

♥ And to Christopher Soderstrom, my talented, encouraging friend for professionally editing and formatting my manuscript. His challenging questions stretched me to do my best and helped me to add additional history and annotations that bridged my writing gaps.

ABOUT THE AUTHOR

Meet Erin Worthley, a living testimony to God's healing heart. After graduating from college in 1962, Erin enjoyed many years of teaching in public schools. She is also a licensed minister with International Ministerial Fellowship.

Her passion is comforting others the way she has received hope. She has more than thirty years' experience writing and teaching Bible lessons, facilitating small groups, and speaking at retreats, seminars, and other special events. In 1987 she organized and directed Beacon of Hope, an inner-healing ministry for survivors of abuse and other wounds. Her Beacon of Hope services included teaching weekly from her written material, overseeing small-group facilitators, and leading a support group.

Erin is the founder (1989) and executive director of a counseling and prayer ministry that recognizes Jesus Christ as the Living River of Life. Garden of Grace Ministries is a nonprofit, nondenominational organization whose main mission is to bring recovery, hope, and restoration to wounded hearts. Erin is gifted in her ability to lead others into God's shining grace, freeing them to grow in the light of His splendor. Her desire is that all who feel like dry, trampled weeds will bloom like sunflowers in a well-watered garden. A treasure of wisdom has come through her family's struggles with pain and shame.

Erin and her husband, Tom, love to share about the Lord's healing grace. Since 1999, through their church, Living Waters, in Elk River, Minnesota, they've been overseeing a care group in their home. Their marriage itself is a testimony to God's faithfulness, because of His love, March 2007 is their jubilee celebration of fifty years! Tom and Erin's two children are married, and the family's rich blessings continue with five grandchildren.

CONTENTS

ENDORSEMENTS
DEDICATION
ACKNOWLEDGEMENTS
ABOUT THE AUTHOR
PREFACE
INTRODUCTION: A Trumpet of Hope   13

PART 1.   WOUNDED WARRIOR: HIS HEALING HEART

1.   A Lost Diamond—A Treasure from God   19
2.   A Spiral of Darkness: A Ray of Light   29
3.   A Garland of Beauty for Ashes   39
4.   Tom's Testimony of Tender Care   51
5.   God, the Caring Gardener   59

PART 2.   EXODUS: MODEL FOR RESTORATION

6.   A Story Never to be Forgotten   65
7.   Preparation for Victory   73
8.   The Dawning of Hope   83
9.   Deliverance from Despair   91
10. Roadmap to Freedom   99
11. Precepts from History   109
12. Keys to Breakthrough   125
13. Battle Strategies   137
14. Victory Fulfilled   145
15. New Beginnings   155

PART 3.   REMEMBERING GOD'S WONDROUS WAYS

16. Foresight Through Hindsight   169
17. Consider His Goodness and Glory   181
18. Pivotal Points of my Restoration   193
19. Embracing Your Inheritance   209

APPENDIX
INFORMATION
ENDNOTES

PREFACE

Brief biographies that note names, places, some distinctions, and a few family facts seem so safe. Even the sentence in the preceding biography that "a treasure of wisdom has come through [my] family's struggles with pain and shame" shrouds a buried past. For God's light to shine more brightly, my veil of pride must be removed.

My husband Tom and I choose to share our story in this book. It speaks of Calvary's love. It's a testimony of God's grace and forgiveness. Jesus Christ restores broken people who have been in bondage—whether bringing about Israel's deliverance from Egypt's pharaoh, thousands of years ago, or healing our marriage, which was shattered by Tom's third-degree criminal sexual conduct. This betrayal was devastating. While the picture of our pain varies, no wounds are too deep for a faithful God to reach.

The Bible recorded Israel's wandering ways; the local newspaper published our embarrassing troubles. The headlines felt like lethal darts of shame that added to my misery. I remember praying and hoping that no one would read the scandalous news, but they did. Thankfully the good Lord said no to my childish request. The next day, a neighbor left a card in our mailbox, letting us know they were praying for us. With tears, I went over and shared with her my anguish. A cup of tea, a listening ear, and a caring touch were like God's arms of grace reaching out and wrapping around me. Her warmth allowed me to grieve, and some of the hornets of disgrace lost their sting. God was comforting me as a tenderhearted warrior would soothe the screams of a battle-scarred child.

Recovery is a process, and even as I write this book, I struggle. Even though I sometimes feel like a brand-new car, under the hood are minor marks of a major collision and with my record of damage, even expert mechanical repairs seem dubious. I can understand the leeriness of those who have heard our story. Anxiety rises within me. *Am I opening a casket of judgment? Will my scars become like an oozing infection?* Without God's comfort, doubts would flow forth in a flood of fear.

Recently, He quieted my heart by using a nightmare as an inner gateway to my emotions. In my dream I was sleeping, and I heard a deafening crack of timbers that woke me up. The whole house shook, and a river of gravel, surging through the roof like a deadly lava flow, miraculously stopped before it reached me. God's unseen hand had stopped the havoc. My overwhelming terror turned to peace. I sensed His protection. He would do the impossible!

I awakened disoriented; it had felt so real. The dream's devastation seemed to mirror my own pit of despair. I asked Jesus for help and pictured my scars going into His nail-pierced hands. In my heart, I perceived that God was changing what felt like a mark of shame into a Medal of Honor that proclaimed, "Redeemed!"

As I was pondering on this encouraging thought, I noticed the eight-inch red tulips I'd stenciled as a border near the top of our bedroom walls. A gentle whisper seemed to say, "Count them!" I did, feeling rather foolish, until I saw with my spiritual eyes a revelation of God's glory. Suddenly, *I envisioned the flowers, coupled to each other by a linking leaf, as seventy-two magnificent angels whose connecting, outstretched wings formed a hedge of beauty all around me!* This disclosure assured my heart that the Lord of Hosts would continue to turn my misery of memories into a garden of grace, destroying all the imaginations that seemed to me as a swarm of killer bees.

A prayer of surrender also lifted the oppression and brought me peace.

Dear Lord Jesus,
Worries, like black flies, can land so quickly on my mind. Please help me to see the futility of my hands slapping at them. I am willing to be stretched and leave my comfortable nest. Only your hand, God, has the skill to carry me through all the uncertainties of writing this book.

—I trust You, Erin

I choose to depend on the Lord by believing that He is bigger than my fears. He can do all things, and "I *know* that my Redeemer lives" (Job 19:25). God, my Comforter, has carried me through the unimaginable! Like Moses and the Israelites, I sing of His wonders: "The LORD is my strength and my song.... The LORD is a warrior.... Pharaoh's chariots and his army he has hurled into the sea" (Exodus 15:2–4).

I am bursting, like a ripe sunflower, to share the many seeds of gentle care planted in the very core of my being. These seemingly insignificant grains of life have grown into mature, fruitful plants yielding treasures of wisdom that nothing can erode and no one can steal. For all captives of discouragement, *Beyond Despair: Tender Care* is a proclamation of freedom and a declaration of restoration by God's wondrous ways!

Erin Worthley
Elk River, Minnesota

A Trumpet of Hope

The Israelites groaned in their slavery and cried out,
and their cry for help because of their slavery went up to God.
God heard their groaning and he remembered his covenant....
God looked ... and was concerned about them. (Exodus 2:23–25)

Blow a trumpet in Zion; Sound an alarm on my holy hill. (Joel 2:1)

As in the days of Moses, the Lord's war trumpet is now thundering over the whole world...

"LET MY PEOPLE GO!"

When the cries of the redeemed ascend to the heavens, the Good Shepherd hears and blows His freedom trumpet that roars, "*Release!*" To His bruised lambs who are terrorized by the taunting of the mockers, it is a rally trumpet, *a shophar of jubilee!* This holy declaration will be like the biblical decree of liberty that was proclaimed throughout the land every fiftieth year for the Israelites (see Leviticus 25).

The Bible prophetically proclaims,

O Sing to the Lord a new song, for He has done marvelous things; His right hand and His holy arm have wrought salvation for Him. The Lord has made known His salvation; His righteousness has He openly shown in the sight of the nations. He has [earnestly] remembered His mercy and loving-kindness, His truth and His faithfulness toward the house of Israel; all the ends of the earth have witnessed the salvation of our God. With trumpets and the sound of the horn make a joyful noise before the King, the Lord! Before the Lord, for He is coming to judge [and rule] the earth; with righteousness will He judge [and rule] the world, and the peoples with equity. (Psalm 98:1–3, 6, 9 AMP)

God sounded a trumpet when He was about to bring change. For example, a ram's horn was blown to gather the exiles for the rebuilding of Jerusalem's broken walls: Nehemiah announced, "Whenever you hear the sound of the trumpet, join us there. Our God will fight for us!" (Nehemiah 4:20).

This is the day—now is the time—for God's family to proclaim restoration by His wondrous ways. The Fountain of Life is bubbling up from the profound inner spring of His beloved. God's trumpet call is freeing His bride to flow in prophetic words, intercession, songs, teachings, poetry, dancing, books, movies, drama, and other creative ways like a river of life to the world. *This living stream is God's proclamation of emancipation!* He desires "all men to be saved and come to a knowledge of the truth" (1 Timothy 2:4); He is rebuilding broken hearts and broken dreams. The season of God's promised harvest for human hearts has come!

Beyond Despair: Tender Care is a part of this flowing testimony of God's tender care for His bleating lambs; a trumpet for the brokenhearted. I will share scriptural promises that became treasures of truth discovered in my pit of darkness, as well as disclose nuggets of golden wisdom gleaned from the book of Exodus. The Lord provided a way out of bondage for the Israelites, but freedom didn't come by a wand wave or by positive thinking. True to His character, the heavenly Father took time to skillfully prepare and partner with His children, especially one son, Moses. The Exodus chronicle is an accurate, historical adventure that imparts hope to the hurting, providing models for both ministry and recovery.

~~~~~~~~~~

My husband Tom also testifies about God's mercy and faithfulness while he was in prison; first besieged by hopelessness, then overcome and restored by love. The heavenly Father's light and truth broke through his oppression and deception. The sin that had landed this man of God behind iron bars felt unforgivable. His shame was overwhelming and familiar, a heavy burden from earlier years. From his schooldays, Tom Worthley's nickname had been "Worthless." His self-perception as a failure who could never measure up had lingered and festered throughout his life. In *confinement*, the Lord changed Tom's pain to gain.

His story will be stirring for all who struggle with the shame of moral failure, addictions, and incarceration. We desired that our story will be an encouragement for the many who have the ambivalent anguish of a loved one behind bars. Life may become like an overwhelming obstacle course with many hoops which have to be hurdled.

During my healing process, the Exodus account became a pattern for my renewal as I discovered that the Israelites' struggles in Egypt mirrored my troubles. God lifted their yokes of injustice; similarly He lifted mine. God's encouraging words to His people in Egypt became restoring words to me, speaking life to my crushed spirit: *"I have surely seen the oppression of My people who are in Egypt, and have heard their cry because of their taskmasters, for I know their sorrows. So I have come down to deliver them"* (3:7–8 NKJV). Because God gave me His treasures in my sea of pain, with joy I am able to comfort others the way I was consoled and lifted up.

The book beautifully paints a picture of our loving Lord Who is both the Gentle Lamb and the Almighty Lion, shining through the millennia of recorded history. This writing is a preparation for saints so that they will be able to minister with greater confidence and skill to the wounded (as both lamb and lion).

In the Exodus story, God is described as a tender Mother Eagle, Who catches her eaglets on her wings before they might crash, and as a powerful Father Eagle, Who could make even Pharaoh a prey of weakness. God said, "You yourselves have seen what I did to Egypt, and how I carried you on eagles' wings and brought you to myself" (19:4). This is the inspiration for the book's cover, which pictures father eagle watching protectively while mother eagle hovers lovingly over their family.

The Exodus narrative is a guide for anyone who desires to effectively comfort and counsel the brokenhearted. Moses and his family particularly provide inspiration for faithful leadership. It is a paradigm for healing the despairing, discovering strategies for setting captives free, and imparting hope to those who have lost all expectancy for divine breakthrough.

~~~~~~~~~~

Beyond Despair: Tender Care is written to comfort wounded souls who:

- have been traumatized in their formative years
- have experienced the tyranny of injustice
- have suffered loss and remain frozen in sorrow and grief
- have cried out with silent screams and feel invisible
- have been judged and taunted into hopelessness
- have a wounded spirit and thoughts of self-hatred
- have hidden behind the masks of performance, but still feel empty
- have shame and can't accept God's forgiveness
- have turned to addiction to numb their pain
- have been emotional harassed and feel overwhelmed
- have a shattered marriage and feel disheartened
- have been betrayed and feel devastated by a loved one.

Beyond Despair: Tender Care is also written for pastors, prayer ministers, and caregivers who:

- strive to understand the deeply wounded, God's crippled lambs
- feel frustrated with those who seem stuck in pain and addiction
- preach the Good News to discouraged hearts who can't seem to hear it
- desire to reach despairing ones who feel worthless or invisible
- need keys for opening doors to freedom for the captive
- struggle with shame and a fractured life because of moral failure.

It is my fervent desire that the brokenhearted, the lonely, the imprisoned and the weary will realize their inheritance in Christ through heartwarming personal testimonies and through the moving story of Israel's miraculous deliverance. My heart is to impart a revelation of God's awesome love!

Part 1

WOUNDED WARRIOR: HIS HEALING HEART

Chapter 1

A Lost Diamond—A Treasure From God

O Lord, truly I am your servant....
You have freed me from my chains. (Psalm 116:16)

O afflicted one, storm-tossed, (and) not comforted,
Behold ... I will make your gates of carbuncles [crystal],
and all your walls of precious stones. (Isaiah 54:11–12 RSV)

When Tom and I lived in Kenner, Louisiana during the 1960's, we became acutely aware of hurricane havoc: we survived Hilda, Betsy, and Camille. In 2005, I empathetically watched Katrina's devastations on television; some New Orleans residents felt safe in their homes until the protective levees broke, flooding houses with contaminated water. Overwhelmed by loss, they began to feel defenseless against the surmounting danger and mayhem.

Similarly, I was battered when my personal "storm of the century" hit in 1994. During my storm-tossed season, I felt as if a curse of chaos had swept in like an ill wind. All external, protective walls from my father, husband, and church were suddenly breached, leaving me in disarray. Grieving, I wailed, "I can't take one more loss!"

With hindsight, I now realize that God had faithfully prepared, protected, and strengthened my spirit for the coming trials. He *didn't* leave me orphaned. So that I can yield clearer perspective into my story of deep despair, I want to share some particulars from my difficult formative years.

My sisters were born at the outset of the Great Depression; I arrived at its tail end. I felt like the pickle in the middle when my brother was born and metaphorically ushered in World War II! From my perspective, Murrell was the brilliant firstborn; Kathy was vivacious and beautiful; I attempted to be the helpful one; my brother, Tom, was the hilarious, favored son. Today, in fun, he refers to us as his "ugly sisters," and we still adore him!

While childhood teasing *was* spiteful at times, my brother became my best buddy. The woods behind our home in Edina, Minnesota, provided magnificent adventure. We built tree houses, crawled around in underground forts, and dueled with swords made from cattails. He brought excitement into my life and sunshine into my soul, but not all was bliss in the Towne family.

Broken Beginnings

During the three years before my brother's birth, the family frequently spent weekends at our Lake Edwards cottage. Although I have scant memories of being very young, I do sense this vacation place was not idyllic for me. From an eighteen-month-old viewpoint, the lakeshore had giant weeds and a mucky bottom that stuck to my feet. I still remember spotting an icky bloodsucker anchored between my toes. Amidst my screams, Mother quickly pulled it off, leaving wounds inside and out. After that, only if I was held would I go near the lake. A petrifying panic plagued me if I was put down in the water; I knew my mother resented having to deal with my fears. As a vocal, strong-willed toddler, I felt her disapproval when she asked why I couldn't be a big girl like my sisters and enjoy the water.

My most difficult ordeal during my earliest years remained a repressed memory until after Mother's death, when I was in my forties. Most of my life I had a foreboding, a dread around her, and an inordinate need to please her. I felt I could never live up to her expectations. Buried in the storehouse of my heart were deeply ingrained childhood attitudes and actions that had set me on a deceptive path of performance, self-protection, and destruction.

While I was seeking wholeness, Jesus revealed to me hurtful moments that continued throughout my childhood. With the Holy Spirit's guidance, I saw myself as a child being violently shaken by my mother. For a moment I felt confusion, then terror. I sensed that the brutality stopped when I became limp. I saw Christ tenderly holding me, and I was able to grieve the loss of basic trust and well-being. He validated my pain and spoke restoring, comforting words to my wounded heart.

By acknowledging the specifics of my abuse, I gained understanding into why I struggled with feeling safe around Mother, whom I grew to love. I was able to forgive her. In His light and truth, the Spirit gently confronted my twisted ways and perceptions. Repenting of my sinful responses to my mother, I was set free to walk in renewing truth. I know Christ's love covered and healed my wounded spirit, and I am grateful that He continues to bring transformation and cleansing to my inner person.

When I told my sisters about the violence, Kathy shared that she had once seen the cruelty from the top of our basement stairway. Frightened by what she saw, she had quietly shut the door and walked away. My sisters then revealed some painful times from their childhood. The family's code of silence was finally broken!

The War Years

Memories of my father during my toddler years are warm and inviting. I remember a daddy who was elated to have me around. Oddly, I can still recollect a favorite ritual I had with him. As he sat very still on our davenport, I would stand behind him and repeatedly comb his hair. Eventually, he would look into my face and rave delightfully about the results. I relished his praises!

The Second World War suddenly changed our home when Daddy joined the army in 1941. He left behind his wife, a year-old son, and three daughters—three, ten, and twelve. I felt orphaned when he answered America's call to arms, and the four years he served our country seemed like an eternity to me. Even though I was the youngest daughter, I felt an abrupt void in my life; I missed his comforting presence. (The photo was taken shortly before Dad was shipped overseas.)

With an aching heart, I spent hours crouched in front of our living room radio hoping to connect with my father. Childishly, I assumed that any man talking on a program was Daddy. Even though I was disappointed that he never quietly listened to me, I persistently tried to bond with him by sharing all the day's events that were important to me—Billy the Bully's teasing, the tooth fairy forgetting to change a tooth into a dime, or anything else significant in my world. But most of all, I told him I missed him and wanted him to come home. Even though Mother assured me Daddy was listening, I eventually quit in frustration, probably realizing the constant radio chatter wasn't him.

~~~~~~~~~~

One alleged bad habit was that I loved to sing songs, though only my brother tolerated them. As an adult, I now understand that my original "Wash with the Washrag" (sung over and over) sounded like the cawing of a sick bird. When I was a child, however, the rejection of my song felt like a rejection of me. In spite of their rebuffs, I believe I enjoyed a benefit from my sisters' ensuing protestations: I was noticed! I likely reasoned that some attention, however negative, was better than being disregarded.

Mother's days were filled with sewing, cooking, or taking care of my brother, which left little time for me. When her sister, Aunt Lillian, came occasionally to help, she brought boxes of fabric and her sewing machine. The two of them would sew for days on end in the basement corner. To reach them, I maneuvered through piles taller than me by following a narrow path. When I found them, neither was very glad to see me and told me not to bother them. Feeling rejected, I would usually seek out my best friend,

Terryl, who lived several doors down. I felt welcomed by her family; they also had plenty of treats and toys.

Another occasion that added to my bewilderment, one that left both Mother and me badly shaken, happened as she was racing up to Brainerd on Highway 169. Somehow my brother spilled his milk on the backseat floor, and since I was the oldest child in the car, Mother expected me to clean the mess. I was trying to wipe it up when the door suddenly flung open—somehow I tumbled out of her old Ford like a rag doll. I remember feeling I was dying as I finally ended up in a mud puddle beside the road. Miraculously, to Mother's relief, I was alive with no broken bones, but I wasn't spared years of subsequent nightmares.

~~~~~~~~~~

Frightening air raids added to my fears and loneliness. Their loud sirens warning "all lights out!" were sometimes a trigger for me to wet my bed or throw up. After pulling down a dark bathroom shade, my mother would clean me in the dim light. By her sighs, I knew she wasn't happy with me. I felt naughty. Evading shame, I eventually learned to cover my messes with numerous towels hidden in my sheets. I especially missed my father's care during stressful times.

Almost as scary as the sirens were my "yellow sisters"; I didn't understand that they were extremely sick with hepatitis, at that time known as "yellow jaundice." Part of their care was Fanny Farmer chocolate and special food prepared by Aunt Lillian. They loved the candy, but threw away most of Lillian's concoctions, gleefully tossing them like bombs from a small upstairs deck to our yard below. Lillian, pleased because their plates were clean, gave them more chocolates. The system worked quite well until the fateful day they hurled tomato aspic that landed on Auntie's head. Her scream rang throughout the neighborhood as the gelatin oozed through her hair, making her look like a bloody mess.

Mother tried her best, but life was taxing with four rambunctious children. Unending stress finally landed her in the hospital. Auntie Florence, Daddy's sister, watched over us through Mother's hysterectomy and again as she recuperated from a nervous breakdown. I was happy when Auntie came; she combed my hair and put a pretty ribbon in it. I valued the simple, tender care my mother had been unable to give me.

Pain Acknowledged

While Daddy was gone, my home was in constant chaos, unpredictable with endless accidents, air raids, sicknesses, and emotional meltdowns. I tried hard not to add to my mother's pain, but I sensed she didn't see me as "the helpful one." No matter how hard I tried to please her, I always felt I was a nuisance to be tolerated. Many times she said to me, "Stop it! You are hurting my ears!"

I couldn't understand why I continually felt unwanted by her. I sometimes doubted my feelings. Maybe, I reasoned, I was just too sensitive.

Years later, when I became a mother, she admitted her negative responses to me. After I asked some probing questions about my childhood, she told me that I constantly got on her nerves. Apparently, I had learned to walk at seven months by pushing my baby buggy. Up and running, I was into everything. She shared that, as a toddler, I had hated going to sleep; instead, I would incessantly shake my crib across the wooden floor. While she was telling me how difficult I made her life, I felt blamed for wearing her out with my excessive energy.

I was not surprised at what she relayed to me. From her, I have no memories of comforting hugs or a warm "I love you." To myself, I sadly noted that she never conveyed even one moment in which she felt joy in my existence or appreciated my little girl antics. I would need to choose whether to stay like a buried, bitter acorn—or become God's mighty oak of life.

Better Days

I was thrilled when Daddy *finally* came home. He had survived the Battle of Normandy; I'd survived the battle of neglect. Daddy had dodged the bullets of the Nazis, but I hadn't been as successful in trying to duck my bullets of shame, rejection, and fear.

The family needed an adjustment period to get reacquainted with our hero. Because my brother had been only a baby when Daddy left, he was afraid of this strange man. On the other hand, I clung to him, couldn't get enough of his attention. It felt so good to be with my daddy again! He had returned to a broken family, all isolated into separate worlds, doing our own thing.

Discovering that our out-of-control days had ended was a rude awakening for my brother and me. On summer mornings, we had loved getting up at sunrise to run around wildly, yelling and chasing our Scottie dog. When Dad confronted our unruly behavior with a spanking, we tested his resolve for about four more days. We had always been able to wear down Mother, but Dad wisely stood firm.

Knowing we probably couldn't totally avoid another smarting encounter, we invented our own spanking salve. In a jar we combined toothpaste, rubbing alcohol, perfume, and hand lotion, which we then applied as needed. Our secret solution smelled terrible and looked worse, but we were totally convinced that it smoothed away our pain. Eventually we learned to honor Dad's authority, our strong wills intact but definitely subdued.

~~~~~~~~~~

Even with my father's stabilizing presence, I continued to dislike myself and felt restless. Stormy days frightened me—I had heard that Jesus was coming in the clouds with thunder and lightning to take some people back to heaven. Being more of a sour pickle than a sweet one, I was sure I would be excluded. At age nine I told my mother about my fears of being left behind, and with her help I invited Jesus Christ into my heart, asking Him to forgive all my sins. I found peace, and Jesus found a buried, unpolished diamond He treasured.

All in all, my childhood years had laid a foundation that felt confusing: love, yet shame; acceptance, yet rejection; faith, yet fear. Neither parent was all good or all bad. My mother imprinted upon my heart creativity, adventure, and humor; my father imparted dignity, grace, truth, discipline, courage, and a faith I could emulate. Best of all, both pointed me to my Savior.

Teenage Years

From my earliest recollections, First Baptist Church of Minneapolis was an integral part of our lives, and over the years, the stories of the Bible were written all over my heart. As an adolescent, church provided an inviting place to hang out, and on Sunday evenings I rode the streetcar downtown to attend youth group, where I enjoyed fellowship and was challenged to mature in my Christian walk. In the fall of 1955, my life changed in more ways than I could ever have imagined: here I met my future husband.

When a friend of Tom's family discerned that he needed spiritual guidance, he invited Tom to a Sunday evening church meeting. Tom gladly accepted because this mentor was a former professional football player. Several other girls and I, noticing the good-looking newcomer, descended on Tom like bees to honey and invited him to our post-service gathering. My heart's intent was not spiritual—I aimed at being the queen bee who aced out her rivals for a prize date. I won the challenge!

I was a seventeen-year-old who thought I'd found my Prince Charming, the one who would take away all my inner pain. Tom was impressive and always full of encouraging words for me; we could talk on the phone for hours. He was fun, nurturing, and a truth-seeker—I was drawn to his willingness to pray and study the Bible with me. When I asked God if he was the man I should marry, I felt the answer was yes, but only if I would love Tom with the unfailing love of Christ, love that "bears all things, believes all things, hopes all things, endures all things" (1 Corinthians 13:4–8). *God's love ... Prince Charming ... no problem!*

Eighteen months after meeting, Tom and I were wed. Unfortunately, primarily because of baggage from the past that we each brought into the marriage, King Perfect and Queen Bee soon became more like stinging hornets than starry-eyed teenagers! Mutual judgments stung all our vulnerable places. We lived as wounded children, reliving the pain from our broken beginnings. Throughout this book I'll share more about how the Lord has faithfully wrought transformation in our lives, displaying His goodness and glory at countless pivotal times. In what were once our many dark places, Jesus Christ became our Beacon of Light. *His love did not fail!*

~~~~~~~~~~

Many years later I would come to realize that a part of me was emotionally stuck with feelings of rejection from my formative years. While receiving prayer ministry, I was able to journal my emotions with a poem and a drawing, and I was able to see my misconceptions based on my childish conclusions. *I chose to forgive my family members, especially my mother, by releasing my pain to God.* He healed the wounds from my blemished background by revealing His deep love for me.

Oh God, can You really understand?
I feel small, broken, forgotten,
like a little chick still in a shell,
weak, isolated, hurting, and bound.
I hate my shell, I want to fly,
but flapping my wings makes me cry.
I'm stirred to move, yet stay still,
the unknown fills me with dread,
growing up seems oh so scary.
Daddies go to war, Moms go wanting.
I'm so confused, what should I do?
Oh God, can you really understand?

Yes, my child, My little one, I understand.
I, too, was small and vulnerable,
just a babe in Bethlehem.
My mother was mocked,
father confused, struggling with doubt.
The manger was hard,
the air was foul, the animals loud.
My spirit knew the curse of death,
the deceit of Herod was a dread,
as was the sudden Egypt flight.
Rejection, rejection all around!
Oh, my child, I knew the dry ground.
So come, my child, my precious chick,
let's break that fragile outer shell;
beneath My protective wings of love,
I'll be like your Everlasting Mother Hen.

Okay, Papa God, I'm coming.
I'm here, please fly with me.

God Finds Lost Diamonds

Now I soar like God's eagle—all because I know I am one with Christ Jesus in the heavenly realms (Ephesians 2:6). From God's magnificent perspective, I am able to perceive His wondrously restorative ways.

One event, especially etched on my heart, I shared in our 1993 Christmas newsletter. The timing was significant—God knew I needed this fresh in my memory as I headed into the formidable year of 1994. Reflecting on the awesomeness of Jesus Christ coming as *Immanuel*, "God with us," He Who restores, I recalled how these truths were forever planted within me. Jesus taught me through an experience with my sisters that I call "my living parable."

The episode began in summer 1991 when my sisters came to Minnesota for a vacation at our lake cabin. On the last day of our stay, both spent hours helping me with the never-ending chores; Murrell and I vacuumed, cleaned bathrooms, and organized the kitchen while Kathy stained the dock. They wanted to support Tom and me any way they could—our plate was full, particularly with taking care of a now-frail Dad, who lived with us. Late in the day, driving back to Minneapolis, Kathy discovered that the valuable diamond from her ring was missing. She felt devastated.

I knew we had to return and search. We scoured the entire haystack of our property looking for the "needle"; we even looked in the bathroom drain and the vacuum bag! Dust was flying everywhere, but no diamond, and with hopelessness we wondered if it had fallen into the lake when she was on the dock. We headed back home, discouraged, but before I left, with feeble faith, I prayed, "Jesus, I really feel bad. Please find that diamond for my sister."

Three *months* later, while doing dishes at the cabin, I glanced down by my feet: there was the glittering gem! I could hardly believe it—I'd previously searched everywhere in this area. As I reached down to pick it up, I felt the Lord whisper in my heart, *Erin, remember—in this lifetime there will be many losses, but always remember—I am the God Who restores!*

With tremendous joy I mailed the diamond to Kathy. The even greater delight was God's word, written upon my heart: "I am the God Who restores!"

God Himself rejoices when He finds His lost diamonds, His treasured people. In my mother's golden years, God and I were jubilant when she became His brilliant jewel. In 1982, when she passed away as one of His dear saints, she was no longer like a hard, unpolished stone of former years, but a transformed, sparkling diamond who blessed her family and a multitude.

> But the godly will flourish like palm trees
> and grow strong like the cedars of Lebanon.
> For they are transplanted into the LORD's own house.

They flourish in the courts of our God.
Even in old age they will still produce fruit;
they will remain vital and green.
They will declare, "The LORD is just!
He is my rock!
There is nothing but goodness in him!"
(Psalm 92:13–15 NLT)

Chapter 2

A Spiral of Darkness: A Ray of Light

There is nothing concealed that will not be disclosed....
What you have said in the dark will be heard in the daylight,
and what you have whispered in the ear in the inner rooms
will be proclaimed from the roofs. (Luke 12:2–3)

Unfortunately, diamonds do not always shine brightly, and the diamond in my wedding band never seemed to sparkle either. Under a jeweler's trained eye, a defect was discovered. In natural light my gem seemed dull, but under professionally magnified light its flaw was exposed.

Likewise, in God's intense light the imperfections and fractured places in our characters are disclosed, despite our best efforts to keep them concealed. Tom and I are no longer ashamed to expose our blemished history. Though my husband was the fallen Christian leader, the Refiner's fire also disclosed my prideful places. I did not welcome tumultuous times: No wife desires to see her beloved descend from a pinnacle of trust into a pit of darkness. In this chapter I'll share my perspective as the betrayed wife—how I survived and thrived.

It's easier to grasp God's guidance when looking back at events than while in the midst of the whirlwind. In addition to the Lord writing on my heart that He is the God of restoration, Jamie Buckingham's *Where Eagles Soar*, about venturing with God into tough places, left a major imprint for helping me through my heartbreak.[1]

In the book, Buckingham discloses an adulterous relationship. After his deacons confronted him, he asked his wife to come to their church and pick him up. After sharing his fears and his anguish, he writes: "She found me, the shepherd of the flock, crouched in a fetal position in a basement hallway, huddled against the landing of the stairs."

I was disappointed that there was nothing written about his wife's feelings and struggles. At the time I wondered how she ever made it through the betrayal. Nevertheless, even though I knew nothing about her broken heart and her journey back to wholeness; it was evident from the testimony of the Buckinghams' healed marriage that God graced them both with His winds of favor.

By learning how to soar with God's spirit, Jamie Buckingham became a widely read author and spiritual overseer of a church. His honest witness gave hope to men struggling with sexual issues and with vulnerability, and his graphic story showed two profound realities: the dire consequences of resisting God's presence in the heart's innermost recesses, and the almost indescribable inner change and growth that comes from finally yielding to Him.

~~~~~~~~~~

Like the Buckinghams, Tom and I were involved in Christian leadership. When our children were teenagers and young adults, we served as our church's lay leaders for youth. For years we had fifty to sixty-five young people pile into our home for a weekly gathering. Tom was a councilman for youth ministries and led a men's prayer group. Our home was always one of openhearted hospitality, a refuge for those who needed a place to be welcomed.

In 1989, I founded a prayer ministry to help those with hurting hearts and blemished beginnings. My deep desire was to bring freedom from the darkness of deception by applying the light of God's truth through counseling, prayer, and education. I didn't charge for the services, though many gave a grateful donation.

In 1991, Tom and Jake, his weekly prayer partner, asked to serve alongside me as counselors. Eagerly, I embraced the partnership of these talented men. It seemed similar to when I welcomed my Dad home after the war—I felt sought out. It seemed good for the ministry to have their spiritual covering and the added depth of their giftedness. Tom was a compassionate listener with a gentle heart, while Jake was a therapist who would add professional credibility and knowledge. While occasionally they would partner together, most of the time they saw clients separately. Many favorable reports from the bruised lambs to whom they ministered seemed to confirm their shepherding skills.

A Spiral of Darkness

Winds of oppression ushered in 1994. Tom and I both felt the stress. My frail, diabetic eighty-nine-year-old father had been living with us for the past eight years. This heroic war veteran was now facing another great battle—gangrene. Earlier he'd lost his left leg due to diabetic complications; now he faced a horrendous death if he didn't have his right leg amputated. On a cold, snowy January day, God helped him through the operation, and then the following months were filled with the strain of aftercare. Dad was so ill, in need of extensive care because of post-amputation issues.

Despite all the challenges and difficulties, we saw Dad always as our blessing, never a burden. He had spent the previous two years mostly confined to his room, but his mind was sharp and he still loved to challenge us to a card game. We deeply appreciated and cherished him. It was evident that he was God's friend.

Though Tom and I both continued to serve the ministry, we balanced and battled the pressure of a harried routine with the many emergencies of Dad's failing health. At times I've wondered *how* I could have been so deceived by Tom's behavior in the months that followed; the likely truth is that our hectic schedule, plus Dad's constant supervision and eventual death (in September of that year), probably clouded my discernment regarding ministry and marriage. As caregivers, we were experiencing *compassion fatigue and exhaustion.*

By spring it was noticeable that Tom and I were connecting less. I felt he had a closed door all the way around his heart that was shutting me out. Feeling desolate, I drew a picture of me with tears running down from my eyes; underneath my sorrowful face I wrote, "Why are you running away from me?" Tom responded with comfort, admitting that he was "on overload" but would try to do better. I felt consoled, and I buried my doubts; I prayed that God would continue to support and uphold us through the difficult days of caring for a dying family member.

Shortly after his ninetieth birthday, my beloved father died of heart failure in our home. Our family lost a wonderful man, a precious praying warrior. I felt exhausted and heart-burdened, and after this time there was a palpably growing heaviness over us that seemed beyond and additional to the natural grieving process. It felt like a hovering black cloud that prayer and praise couldn't lift.

In October, I told Tom that I felt cursed but didn't know why. I couldn't get past or see over the foreboding oppressiveness. Finally, at month's end, my "why" was answered when a brave woman (I'll call her Jane) called and asked if she could bring a mutual friend and meet with us. She shared that Tom had crossed sexual boundaries with her during counseling sessions.

When Tom wept and admitted she was telling the truth, I was stunned, horror-stricken. The bomb of betrayal shattered my heart. I immediately regretted my choice to trust my husband to minister with women alone. Feeling deep shame, I meekly validated Jane's pain. She had been dishonored and defiled by a man she had trusted for godly care.

With sorrowing hearts, we sought God's strength, comfort, wisdom and light to guide us through what seemed to me like a muddled maze full of monsters.

The chilly winds of Minnesota's November seemed to fill even the inside of our house with cold air. Sadness overwhelmed me like a spiral of darkness. Tom wanted to run to Alaska; I wanted to fall sleep and never wake up. Utterly overwhelmed, like an unstable, virus-riddled computer slated to crash, I nevertheless had an unseen hand nudging me to complete one small task after another. By God's strength alone, I was able to persevere.

With the greatest of difficulty, I purposefully resolved to uncover the full magnitude of Tom's deeds. I discovered that another woman counselee (whom I'll call Sally) also had been sexually violated by Tom. This disclosure felt like the unleashing of an earthquake into our home and throughout my heart.

God's Ray of Light

My son, do not make light of the Lord's discipline, and do not lose heart when he rebukes you, because the Lord disciplines those he loves, and he punishes everyone he accepts as a son. (Hebrews 12:5–6)

On November 13, 1994, I arranged a meeting, so that now Sally with her husband (whom I will call Carl) could confront Tom. I asked two caring friends, Michael and Julie, to be there with us also—they were trusted confidantes, vested in the ministry. As Sally and her husband began to share their anger and agony over what had happened, I felt overwhelming emotional shock; my mind could not handle all the agitating and startling feelings. God gave me the grace to run on autopilot, so I could remain the serene, empathetic president of the ministry in the face of this firestorm.

Even in this darkest and bleakest of places, God sent a beautiful ray of light, as though a lifeline was being extended to every person at this tragic gathering. After each had shared their sorrow, Michael gave a prophetic word he had received while praying for Tom and me. He was gracious, seasoned, straightforward, and poignant. Here is the written prophetic exhortation of this man of God, spoken to Tom that evening:

> We have come to restore. We refuse to gather with the mockers, those in the spiritual realm bent on your destruction. Before God, we know our hearts are right, our aim true. We've examined our motives in the light of the Holy Spirit. Truly, we have come to restore, though at first it will not seem so.
>
> Sitting before you this night is a wife several times betrayed. Not only have you given your affections to others, but you have pushed a ministry birthed in the bosom of God to the brink of destruction. A ministry founded in the caring heart of your wife Erin now teeters because of your actions. Despite the pain, the lies, the deception, she refuses to give up on you. God has given you a great gift in her, but you have chosen others, leaving her unopened under the Christmas tree.
>
> Sitting before you this night is [Sally], a tender reed now bent and trampled by you. She entrusted herself to you. She believed, like a child, that you knew what was best. You deceived her, taking advantage of her vulnerable state. Her welfare overlooked

in order to meet a need of yours, she sits confused. She agonizes now, maybe forever, over her responsibility in this matter. She has displayed incredible courage. She has not run. She is willing to own all that is hers. Despite being violated, she remains, resisting the hate that destroys relationships. Your pupil now comes to teach you the way of righteousness. Your victim now extends the same mercy she has known. Despite all that has happened, she too refuses to give up on you.

Sitting before you this night is [Carl], a man of exceptional character and inner strength, as proved by the fact that your jaw is not yet broken. Being a "man's man" yourself, Tom, surely you understand that it is in the nature of man to protect, at all cost, his wife and family. Sitting before you is a man wrestling with his primal instincts to lash out in defense of what is most precious to him. He has even submitted in prayer his rage to God, asking that it come in a proper way at a proper time. He has denied himself the right to retaliate. He has chosen instead God's way, putting in check the righteous anger he has toward you. He does all this for your sake because he, too, refuses to give up on you.

You must hear this. You must feel this. You must bear the weight of this wrongdoing. You must see from all perspectives the impact of your actions. You betrayed your wife. You deceived a vulnerable woman. You stole from another man something most precious to him. Realize that every sinful notion carried out has devastating consequences. See it; feel it; taste it; never forget it.

Finally, it is I who sit before you. I have never participated in a more difficult task. It feels funny because I've never been formally given the right to speak to you in such a way. I can say this, though: I love you and Erin very much. I'm committed to you both. You are one of the most impressive men I've ever met. I'm sure you've heard it before, but you have an incredible capacity to love. You project a vulnerability that suggests to people, "You are welcome here." You put people at ease immediately. You make people around you feel safe. These are essential components of a great counselor.

The problem is, you've used the great gifts God has given—the ones He's given to benefit others—to satisfy your own flesh. I'm sure you have known great frustration. You do not see yourself the way others see you. You minimize your ability to love, thinking, perhaps, "I can't hear God the way others do" or "I'm of little use to God. I can't help or heal anyone."

Let me remind you, my brother, that the gift you have—the gift of loving—is the greatest gift of all. Love is the only gift that remains until the end. The others—prophecy, physical healing, and the rest—are only temporary. God is showing me that love, and the ability to love deeply, bring healing to others in and of themselves. You don't have to be the most intelligent person. You don't have to be the wisest. You don't have to be able to interpret dreams. You don't have to be able to hear the audible voice of God to effect change in yourself and those around you. You just have to care deeply. You have to love; and you, my brother, love like no one I've ever met. Jesus left only two commands for us: to love Him with all our hearts, and to love our fellow man. When we do these things, healing and restoration follows.

We are here today in obedience to the command of Christ to love. We are not deceived. We are not fooled.

Now I will speak God's mind concerning you, Tom Worthley.

The Lord says, "Turn back, for I am the God Who makes a way where there is no way. I Myself am coming for you. I know where you're hiding. I know how lonely you've been there. Prepare yourself: I am coming. Prepare a place for Me in the place where you are. I see you, Tom, hiding behind the only green bush in the dry place. Listen carefully. Do not delay. Carry out my commands with all of your might. Roll over every rock you can move with your hands. Roll it over once, exposing the belly so long embedded in the earth. You will see vile things. Do not look long at them. Move quickly to the next rock, and the next. Do not turn back from what I've commanded you to do for any reason; for distractions will come. Do not look for my arrival. Toil with all of your might. I will come to you without your knowing, and I will observe for a time. If, when I come, I find you resting, then power will be given to every vile thing you have uncovered. It will be raised up to consume you. If, when I come, I find you soaked in sweat, working feverishly, then I, in full view of you, will destroy every vile thing. I will roll over the rocks you were unable to budge and remove forever the curse they have been to you. Know this: I am your God. I know your limits. You will not be pushed beyond what you are able to endure. I will call out your name. That will be my signal to you to stop what you are doing. On hearing it, turn to face your Maker.

This prophetic message to Tom was Father God's loving rebuke. When King David committed adultery and then murder, God sent Nathan with a word that brought conviction of sin; Mike was our Nathan, the Lord's man for the hour. I felt validated when he described me as my husband's unopened Christmas gift, and his word picture touched my broken heart. I felt that the Lord understood each person's pain in this awful situation—a holy God was angry and so was I.

~~~~~~~~~~

As everyone continued to tell of the considerable pain that Tom had caused, with great shame he validated our grief and answered all our questions. Still none of us were able to trust him completely. Tom consented to receive professional counseling, to stop counseling female clients, and to see his male clients only until he could find work outside the ministry. Because we felt we needed more information before exposing Tom's abuse to others, we agreed to meet again in a week. We knew this might not be possible because of prior commitments and the upcoming Thanksgiving holiday, but we all expressed the importance of a further meeting in which we would decide the next course of action to follow. As we concluded, we established that there would be *no cover-up of the moral failure.*

Later, Tom personally confessed to Jake who immediately resigned. As a friend and colleague, he too was deeply wounded and angered by all that had been uncovered. Tom regretted the fact that he had hurt so many. Another meeting was pointless!

Full Disclosure

Though all choices seemed to be like a living death, and choosing to fully expose Tom's indefensible behavior seemed like diving into an unknown riptide of terror, not making the leap would have been wrong and cowardly. I felt as though I were on a cliff's edge, overlooking swirling waters far below, the destroyer's battle drums beating with the rhythm of my impending plunge. I felt frozen, too vulnerable to make the phone calls to all of our clients, pastors, friends, family … anyone and everyone connected to the ministry. Tightly gripping God's hand, I finally jumped into the dark waters. With Him as my only hope and strength, I resolved to face all the mockers and all the consequences of absolute exposure.

It was a formidable task for a wife to undertake! I felt tiny, inadequate—like the little girl in my mother's car, one moment cleaning up another's spilled milk, the next being violently thrown into mud and gravel at a deadly pace, with lethal vehicles speeding all around. I had to remind myself: in the same way I'd survived that potential disaster as a child, I would survive as Father God continued to watch over me now.

Completely acknowledging the moral failure in our ministry to all whose lives were affected was a dreaded, fearsome prospect. How does one tell God's precious lambs that a shepherd has trampled upon their trust? Out of respect for the innocent, I prayed for wisdom to guide Tom and me in proper disclosure. To the police Tom willingly confessed all the facts, but others didn't need the defiling details.

We hated having to tell our children, who were then left with the difficult and embarrassing task of dealing with our grandchildren. So many were unjustly hurt. In the community of faith and the community at large, the news rushed outward like expanding waves from a meteor hitting still waters. Understandably, some shunned us as if we had leprosy. Others told me that I could do better and should divorce Tom. I began to understand why David hid the ghastly reality of his adultery with Bathsheba. The engulfing shame of sexual sin feels like an undertow of death; disclosure often doesn't feel like the path to life.

Besides his full confession to the local police, Tom submitted to church discipline, and we both sought counseling from a recommended Christian therapist. I needed a season for rest and healing, so I sadly closed the ministry and released its future into the hands of Jesus. Heartache for Jane, Sally, and their husbands added to my grief. Much like Joseph, who was sold into slavery, I was in a nightmarish place not of my choosing.

At times my anger seethed with sarcasm. I wanted to retaliate and hurt back. The thoughts that invaded my mind felt like jumping frogs. Why? Why? *Why* would my beloved husband wound so many? How could he betray the trust of God, the body of Christ, a faithful wife? When a man of God crosses the line from tender care to sexual abuse, the ramifications seem unending. I truly wondered if the shame and the pain would ever end.

Not Forsaken

In the midst of the storm, I found comfort when I read, *"The Lord will not reject His people; He will never forsake His inheritance"* (Psalm 94:4). God brought hope on Thanksgiving Day, 1994. I'll share about His consolation in the next chapter.

In December a severe virus laid me lower than a car with blown tires; I was exhausted, but gave what I had to support Tom whenever possible. Charges were pending, so a lawyer was retained. We were informed that before 1993 in Minnesota (and still in some other states), he probably wouldn't have been criminally charged, as he wasn't a psychotherapist or professional counselor. State legislation on criminal sexual conduct had been expanded to include clergy and others who counsel families.

The lawyer counseled us to leave our church so that Tom's presence would not be harassment to those he had injured. He told us that Tom should not have confessed the truth to the police, that this would damage his case. Legally he was probably right, but spiritually God's ways are different than man's. As Michael had revealed, Tom needed to leave no stone unturned. Although we vacillated at times, we believed that *only a ship of repentance sails into a harbor of healing.*

~~~~~~~~~~

In 1995, therapy, prayer, and love supported us during the many months of waiting for Tom to be formally charged. By May, with the approval of my new pastor and the organization through which I have my ministerial license, I began comforting others the way I was comforted. I felt like a weak and wounded warrior, but I trusted God to administer His care through me.

In September, Tom stood before the judge and pleaded guilty to two felony counts of third-degree criminal sexual conduct. He was sentenced to forty-eight months in prison; with "good time" he could be released in thirty-two months. He also was ordered to pay $11,800 in restitution and fines, then was immediately incarcerated—handcuffed and whisked off without any good-byes.

I headed for home with some family and friends. The gathering felt like a funeral. My world was shattered. I struggled with doubt, wondering how God could restore and redeem what felt like a living death. *When grief is overwhelming, previously cherished thoughts of hope fade like once-bright flowers that have dropped their petals.*

Even so, the agitation of my emotions didn't negate the truth that God was still with me: I was not forsaken. The Lord is gentle, merciful, and full of forgiving grace. We can be like a tree that's been cut down or broken by a storm, but if the roots are good, we will grow again. God's hand is not shortened. He always has a wondrous plan for recovery.

I prayed: *Dear Lord Jesus, help me to trust You when I feel terror.*

> I am forgotten by them as though I were dead;
>> I have become like broken pottery.
> For I hear the slander of many;
>> there is terror on every side;
>> they conspire against me and plot to take my life.
> But I trust in you, O LORD;
>> I say, "You are my God."
> My times are in your hands;
>> deliver me from my enemies
>> and from those who pursue me.
> Let your face shine on your servant;
>> save me in your unfailing love....
> In the shelter of your presence you hide [me].
>> (Psalm 31:12–16, 20)

Chapter 3

A Garland of Beauty for Ashes

[Jesus came] to grant for those who mourn in Zion—
to give them a garland instead of ashes. (Isaiah 61:3 rsv)

In my firestorm of fear, I wondered if God would restore our marriage. Would He grow a garden of grace out of the dirt of disgrace? The oppression was so overwhelming that I questioned if He could turn the ash heap of our actions into a garland of beauty. When adultery violated our union, I felt that Tom had trashed our love to ashes, our home to a place of mourning.

It's hard to understand how ashes, the messy, ugly residue, the left-over trash from a fire, could be changed into anything beautiful. It became easier for me to comprehend why ashes and sackcloth were biblical signs of mourning. For instance, after his many world-shattering losses, Job cried out in anguish. He perceived himself to be a cursed man, reduced to nothing; a man without purpose, leveled to dust and ashes (Job 30:19). The overwhelming heat in the furnace of affliction can reduce a heart to hopelessness. Grief hovers like blackness that will never leave. There were days my tears simply never stopped flowing.

So many have asked, "How did you make it? How did you recover? How did you forgive?"

My response is short: *"God!"* Then, I love to testify in detail about His wondrous ways of restoration. Sometimes He intervened miraculously, but predominantly the family of God was His garland of beauty. My special friends and family became a fragrant bouquet to me. At times I literally felt the prayers of the body of Christ uplifting me. My mind would suddenly clear of heaviness as if loving balm were being applied to me.

The body of Christ became His heart, mouth, hands, and feet. Their caring hearts brought redemptive life to me by praying, listening, protecting, providing, correcting, and sharing. I experienced God's kindness working through authorities, counselors, and pastors. *I knew I was not abandoned.*

A Garland of Love

On Thanksgiving Day, 1994, about three weeks after the breaches of trust had surfaced; God miraculously broke through with healing light at dawn.

My despondency was so pervasive I felt like the Philistines had shot a thousand arrows into me. Forlorn that morning, I was slouched on our living room couch. I couldn't sleep, my mind felt like a whirl of confusion, and my heart physically hurt. I wondered—was Tom living in regret or repentance? I struggled deeply to trust his words.

I was relieved that the disclosure of moral failure was almost complete, and that the afternoon family dinner had been moved from our house to the home of Tom's sister, Mary. I didn't have the energy to prepare any food. I felt overwhelmed with all my losses. My fifty-seventh birthday was the next day; thinking about it added to my depression. I wondered if the mourning and grief would ever lift.

Through tears I cried out to God that I felt like I'd been nailed to a cross and couldn't breathe. I felt all alone and sorely troubled. Suddenly, the chaos in my spirit lifted and I sensed His warm presence. In my imagination, I pictured Jesus on the cross with me; His broken heart was absorbing my pain and bitterness. I perceived that God was delivering me from the sting of a living death.

With Christ's light all around me, we went to a place of darkness like the furnace of hell. Christ revealed to me His love for the lost and imparted to me His heart for the poor, the sick, the destitute, the captive, the prisoners, the brokenhearted, the afflicted, the crushed in spirit. Paradoxically, in the darkness of the abyss, He imparted to me a vision of His glory. I saw a heavenly Father Who deeply cares; His heart is grieved over those who have lost their way. I knew He would redeem all I was enduring. He was calling me to a greater depth of love.

Then, in a blink of an eye, it seemed that Jesus and I were in heaven together on His throne of grace, and I felt like a little child finding comfort on her daddy's lap. He spoke truth into my heart by simply declaring, *"Because I live, you live!"* These words revitalized my life. Just as the Word in the beginning of time had created the universe when all was chaotic and black, His declaration of hope imparted light into my future: I too would be renewed and restored by His gentle grace. He reminded me of many scriptural realities, especially regarding His grief when a sinner wanders—He further revealed to me His heart for all who have drifted from truth. He disclosed how significant it is for a person to help turn precious ones from the error of their ways, serving to rescue them from destruction by the power of Calvary's love covering over their multitude of sins.

I remembered the biblical accounts of saints whose lives are celebrated. I recalled what my Lord had done for each of them. When God reminded me of my youthful agreement to love Tom with His love, I asked Him to forgive me for my pride, fear, and bitterness. I chose to forgive Tom with the same love with which God pardons me, and I invited God to heal my crushed spirit. I recalled good times with Tom, and I remembered his persevering care for my ailing father. *I felt embraced by Papa God's healing love as He touched my heart with the miracle of forgiveness.* I broke out in thanksgiving, thanking Him for being my anchor of hope.

~~~~~~~~~~

As I was basking in this phenomenal, life-changing encounter, Tom walked into the room, all bent over. When he vented to me about his horrible pain and requested prayer, I momentarily resented the intrusion—I wanted to stay on the mountaintop. However, my disdain and my hesitation soon turned to compassion. Who am I, but another very imperfect human being? I realized that Jesus' Spirit of gentleness had been imparted to me as I entered God's throne of grace.

Because God had removed logs of judgment from my eyes, I was able to clearly see the speck in Tom's and therefore respond with empathy and respect. Mercifully, Jesus ministered deliverance and forgiveness. Strongholds and soul ties were broken, gates to darkness were closed, bitter roots were removed, and Tom recommitted his life to Christ. As with Lazarus in the tomb, Tom had been like a stinking dead man, buried behind a stone of scorn; I was granted the privilege of unbinding his "grave clothes." God, in His mercy, gave us our greatest Thanksgiving Day gift, a garland of life, replacing what felt like ashes upon my head with a garland of beauty. He cleansed both of us in His living water with the promises of Isaiah 61:

> God comforts Tom and me in our mourning,
>   forgives us as we grieve over our sins,
>   bestows a garland of beauty,
>   removes our ashes of shame,
>   pours out the oil of gladness upon us,
>   gives us a garment of praise
>   instead of a spirit of despair.
> He calls us His oaks of righteousness,
>   His planting of the LORD,
>   for the display of His splendor.
> He will rebuild our ancient ruins
>   and restore the places long devastated.
> Instead of shame,
>   He will give us a double blessing,
>   and instead of disgrace,
>   we will rejoice in our inheritance.
> (vv. 2–4, 7, personalized)

I'll never forget what I felt, saw, and experienced on that Thanksgiving Day, on what I call my Breakthrough Day. Nevertheless, recovery was still a process. The inner healing of my painful memories and emotional wounds took years. New crises would arise and hammer away like a woodpecker at my vulnerable flesh. I trusted God, but, like Peter, my eyes would turn from Jesus and focus on the storm instead of on His strength. I struggled with fear of being deceived. I needed time to see changes in Tom's character. Forgiveness is a healing gift, but trust is a privilege that must be earned.

A Wonderful Counselor

Seeking help, we found a therapist whose ministry was like a gentle breeze from heaven; for nine months he provided a safe place to share our struggles and confessions. Until Tom went to prison, at each difficult turn in the road he stood beside us, imparting wisdom that brought healing to our damaged emotions.

I also found a personal counselor who listened and validated my pain. Because his spouse had spent time in prison, he could identify with my anguish. This comforter knew the agony of rejection and understood the affliction of a dysfunctional family.

I found it helpful to journal our conversations. Here is one example of how he helped me through the grieving process:

Counselor, sometimes the grief is so overwhelming, I wonder if the tears will ever stop. I don't understand myself. I cry harder when I hear words of kindness and encouragement than when I hear a rebuke.

I'm glad you're not numbing out, Erin, but are feeling grief and anger. It is healing grief. Because of your numerous losses and many mockers, when a heartening word is given, tears of appreciation flow. When I grieve, I cherish all my caring friends. Erin, there are days I weep so hard that my tears fall like rain and sometimes my anger sounds like thunder.

Tears bring some relief, but comfort at times is so fleeting. I have great friends, but their support is limited. I feel like I'm in a garden of agony like Gethsemane, where only an angel from God is able to minister to me, because my heart hurts so deeply.

Only Father God is able to heal a broken heart and a crushed spirit. I know—He healed mine. He has many ways of working.

You had a broken heart? How did your heart get healed? Please share your insights with me.

I learned a lot through my suffering. The Psalms were a comfort to me. They reveal that there is a time to weep and mourn. King David is an example to follow. David's journaling in the Psalms records both his feelings and his faith. He expresses his pain but then remembers the "Who, what, and when" of God. For example, when he felt like there wasn't any hope, he pictured God's shield of glory about him and he remembered that God in faithfulness lifts his head above the battle. His emotions helped him to identify what was in his heart, his humanity and neediness—but remembering God's truth filled his heart with faith. It is the word of truth bathed in His light that sets us free.

Hmm ... sounds like Psalm 3! Thanks for the wisdom. Emotions are a blessing, and identifying them helps me to connect with others and to God. They're like a window to my soul that assists me in surrendering my pain. I also need to see in my imagination a heavenly perspective; otherwise, I feel overwhelmed and get stuck in fear and regret. There are benefits in expressing the word of life, His truth, as well as my emotions. Sometimes I feel abandoned, but the Bible states plainly that I will never be forsaken by God. Yes, feelings are a part of recovery, but I need God's truth to enlighten my inner being. What else is helpful to you?

Remember that healing is a day-by-day impartation, but sometimes God does a miracle. Your recovery won't look just like mine or anyone else's. My heavenly Father raised me by His Spirit from the grave. It surely surprised all my friends! Your Father God has many wondrous ways to heal a hurting heart.

Are you surprised? The above dialogue was between me and the Ultimate Counselor, Jesus Christ, Whose still small voice consoled my heart! He is a gentle High Priest Who is able to sympathize with our weaknesses and frailties.

Have you ever considered the dysfunction of His spiritual family? Father God, as Israel's husband, wept and gave His wife a bill of divorce when she refused to repent of her adulteries (see Jeremiah 3:8–10). The Lord knows the thorns of the faithless. Our faithful Comforter not only eases our pain and sorrow, but convicts us of unrighteous behavior. Jesus hears and forgives when His children call from isolated places!

God's Garden Family

Other blooms of blessing appeared regularly in our mailbox in the form of cordial notes that brightened our days. One friend wrote this thought:

We can help ourselves by remembering that Christianity is not about perfect people doing perfect things and always living obedient lives. It is about forgiven people forgiving themselves and others and trusting God to change all of us.

Another letter addressed to me seemed like an encouraging note right from the heart of God:

> Dear Erin,
> Please forgive me that it's been so long since communicating with you—I guess I feel a bit protective of you, so I am cautious not to be intrusive. I think about you often and am very sorry for the pain you are going through at this time. Even though I can't understand your world of pain as you understand it, I do know what it is like to be in dark places of pain with no human answers. So in some small way I'd like to sit in the corner of your world so that, maybe, your world won't feel so empty and scary.
> I know that for the most part our relationship has been a lay counseling relationship and so do not expect to be more than someone who cares. I love you—it matters to me that you don't go through this alone—that you know I care.

Friends and family called from all over the country. Some who didn't even know what had happened shared that we were on their hearts and that they cared. One niece from South Carolina told us about a dream she had: She saw Tom and me like a shattered house in a tornado, but when the wind died down, *God's hands restored the house to greater glory!* We received it as a prophetic word that would help us and shield us from darts of doubt.

An Unexpected Blessing

Tom's stay in prison was itself an unexpected garland of beauty. When I first realized he would be incarcerated, for a moment my nasty vindictive flesh thought, *good, he deserves prison and I need a break! How many "cheatin' husbands" get their just desserts?* Those prideful feelings didn't last long, as the Spirit convicted me of my sinful desire for revenge. God showed me that on judgment day He wouldn't declare, "Erin, you are acceptable since your sins are forgivable, but Tom, you are unacceptable since your sins are totally unforgivable!." How foolish!

> If we claim that we experience a shared life with him and continue to stumble around in the dark, we're obviously lying through our teeth—we're not living what we claim. But if we walk in the light, God himself being the light, we also experience a shared life with one another, as the sacrificed blood of Jesus, God's Son, purges all our sin.

If we claim that we're free of sin, we're only fooling ourselves. A claim like that is errant nonsense. On the other hand, if we admit our sins—make a clean breast of them—he won't let us down; he'll be true to himself. He'll forgive our sins and purge us of all wrongdoing. (1 John 1:6–9 MSG)

Tom's incarceration was extremely humbling for me as well. Nonetheless, even though I hated the humiliation, if God was not ashamed to embrace Tom in prison, then I did not need to embrace shame.

Visitation memories are faint, but I do remember the distress of the long drive over to Stillwater; the dark walk from the parking lot to the front door; the waiting room filled with forlorn women, some with small children. I felt uncomfortable with the security check and the three barred automatic doors I had to pass through before greeting my husband. It was difficult to hear because we sat a distance across from each other, in a room filled with other prisoners and their visitors. I felt overwhelmed when I observed so many sad faces and squirmy youngsters.

Tom tried valiantly to be cheerful, but we were both hurting so deeply. Knowing that the prison housed some hardcore violent inmates, I was concerned when he shared his difficulties, especially about being attacked verbally by another inmate. Time would quickly fly past us, and parting was difficult. God gave me fortitude for the trip back home, but the first few months of visiting Tom felt more like ashes than beauty.

However, another "living parable" helped me through Tom's incarceration at the Minnesota Correctional Facility. One day, as I was driving east down State Highway 36, the words on the city sign announcing "Stillwater" leaped out at me. Many times I had driven past the marker, but this day was different: I heard *still water* whispered in my ear. Yes, Tom was at the Stillwater prison, but the significance wasn't either the town or the facility; Jesus was saying to me that this prison was the Good Shepherd's special place for Tom to drink deeply of healing. In prayer I agreed with the twenty-third Psalm while picturing God leading Tom to green pastures and *still water*. I felt comforted, and the word proved true.

By the orders of his sentencing judge, one year later, Tom was assigned to the Lino Lakes Correctional Facility, a medium security prison. Tom and I were now able to hold hands and visit weekly for two hours. How many wives have two hours of undivided attention from their spouses? Tom allowed me to process my pain, and we both worked through heart issues. I loved our healing dialogue. For us, prison turned out to be like a tasty sweet-and-sour sauce poured out on the meat of our relationship, a time for our lives to be enriched and nurtured with needed changes.

~~~~~~~~~~

Several months after Tom went to prison, I also received an encouraging word from our friend Michael, who had confronted Tom the year before. He shared with me a letter he had written to one of the pastors at the church where Tom had first received correction. In part of that communiqué, Michael noted my husband's repentance and his willingness to face the penalties for his crime.

> Tom Worthley broke before God. He emptied himself of every vile thing. He confessed with his mouth his wrongdoing. He sought out a counselor he had not previously known. He came forward with information we couldn't have otherwise known. He owned his stuff, refusing to introduce evidence that could have shifted responsibility from himself. He honorably spared the women the scrutiny of a trial. He stood in the white-hot lights of public scrutiny and refused to defend himself.

Like the prodigal son (Luke 15:11–32), Tom had humbled himself before his Father and asked for help. Father God embraced Tom as a beloved son, forgave him, and welcomed him to a feast of honor. Tom's changed life was a prized bloom in God's garland and a tremendous blessing for me!

A Banquet of Bounty

Another time the twenty-third Psalm brought a fresh revelation into my garland of beauty was Thanksgiving Day, 1996. I was preparing a turkey when grief flooded my heart. I felt like a sad, lonely lamb stranded on bare pasture. I had no desire to try celebrating another holiday without my husband—I was missing him so deeply. While I was absorbed in self-pity, Provider God whispered in my heart: *I have prepared a table before you. Why are you wondering if I can spread a table of joy before you* now?

Jolted by the rebuke, I imagined how foolish it would be for my guests to have to sit down to an empty table while I excused myself to kill a turkey and pick some cranberries—they would eventually leave and wonder about my sanity. If I as a mother take time to prepare a feast for my family and bless them with a beautifully decorated table arrayed with food, how much greater and more glorious is the Lord's banquet! It's not a bird on that table but His very life.

Like the Israelites, I had murmured, "Can God spread a table in this desert?" (Psalm 78:19). Daily He fed them manna from heaven and miraculously brought forth water from a desert rock. *He prepares a table in the wilderness for all who will look up and cry out.*

"Father God," I replied, "Forgive me for doubting your faithfulness, and help me to be contented with my daily provision."

At my feet, Barney, my apricot toy poodle, waited confidently for a treat. With a smile in my heart, I handed him a piece of cheddar cheese and asked God for an expectant faith that trusted in His goodness just like Barney trusted in mine.

Even my Barney was a part of God's prepared provision, His garland of beauty. In January 1994, when I was under the stress of Dad's illness, he had come as a dubious gift from my daughter, whose home was in an uproar from Barney's continuous barking and attacks on their new hunting dog. Even though it meant additional responsibility, we brought the little guy home so he wouldn't be put to sleep. After Dad died and Tom was imprisoned, Barney, with his fun antics, was a faithful friend from God's hand.

Courage Under Fire

Storms buffeted me continually during the winter of 1996; at first I could see almost nothing but destruction. An especially frightening tempest blew upon my home in the form of a civil lawsuit containing charges against the ministry, Tom, and me, in which a substantial monetary settlement was demanded. Although I knew on a rational level that I had not been negligent as ministry president, I acutely felt the full force of the accusations made against my character. This was a horrible furnace of affliction!

True to His character, God provided a banquet on the table of my heart just when I needed it most. As I was sorting out some of Dad's books, I came across a tattered Bible that his mother had given him for Christmas in 1927. Thumbing through it, I discovered on the last page a treasure she had written to her son, my father:

> *"And we know that to them that love God, all things work together for good, and to them that are called according to his purposes"* (Romans 8:28). Faith in this truth will help you to solve any problem—big or small. Cling to it with all your might. At all times and under all circumstances overcome evil with good. God will supply the wisdom and the occasion for a victory over darkness. Always know that your strength is equal to your courage, and I know of no one who has more courage than you, my son.

I rejoiced in my rich heritage of faith, and I liked the thought that God would work even the lawsuit for good. I experienced peace ... until I received from my lawyer ten pages of fifty invasive questions from the plaintiff's attorney. My uneasiness increased substantially when I was unable to reach my attorney by phone to obtain his counsel. My mind went blank. Just before an anxiety attack totally overshadowed me, a friend called and asked if I was all right.

Hearing my no, she interceded for me, and a cloud of confusion lifted. Afterward, when I again picked up the Interrogatories, the Holy Spirit asked me, *Erin, can you answer the first question?* I chuckled and wrote my name with ease. He softly helped me with each question and assured me when some needed to be answered later with my lawyer.

God had also given me another bloom of beauty while in the midst of the false charges. One friend, who'd been active in the youth group we'd led fifteen years before, sent me a letter of encouragement, sharing that I'd come to mind while she was having devotions. The Lord had spoken to her that He was with me! Her note included Psalm 37, reminding me to be still before the Lord and not to fret. My heart quieted, and my worries concerning the lawsuit subsided.

The lawsuit was dropped eight months later, with no money exchanged. God had exonerated my character! I found courage under fire by leaning on His everlasting arms.

~~~~~~~~~~

The Redeemer, Jesus Christ, bestowed one bloom after another upon me through the generosity and kindness of others. My siblings, who all lived in fantastic vacation places, welcomed me into their homes for fun and rest. Murrell would tell me to come with an empty suitcase, and then she would fill it with almost-new clothes for me. A professional hairdresser provided for all my hair needs. Others plowed my driveway. Some sent books or money. Some prayed with me and for me. Others shared a meal. Family members included me in their holidays.

The summer before Tom's discharge, special friends Tom and Jan stayed at our home. When the weight was becoming too heavy for me, these "garden friends" came with care, love, and prayers. They, like so many, were Christ's burden bearers who lifted my load of many cares. Another dear friend sent me a plaque declaring that God would never leave me nor forsake me.

The Lord was faithful to His word, spoken years earlier, after I found my sister's diamond: *Erin, remember—in this lifetime there will be many losses, but always remember—I am the God Who restores!* His garland of beauty never drooped or died: blessings of truth, salvation, forgiveness, hope, freedom, gentleness, glory, provision, counsel, health, grace, joy, peace, kindness, and love ... *His life* exchanged for the ashes of despair. He continued to grow a garden of grace out of the dirt of disgrace with innumerable blessings from family, friends, and even a dog named Barney. And I continued to grow stronger in Christ.

These trials are only to test your faith,
to show that it is strong and pure.
It is being tested as fire tests and purifies gold—
and your faith is far more precious to God than mere gold.
So if your faith remains strong after being tried by fiery trials,
it will bring you much praise and glory
and honor on the day when Jesus Christ is revealed to the whole world.
(1 Peter 1:7 NLT)

Chapter 4

Tom's Testimony of Tender Care

Here is a faithful saying: If we died with Him, we will also live with Him....
If we are faithless He will remain faithful,
for He cannot deny Himself. (2 Timothy 2:11, 13 NKJV)

Therefore, I tell you, her many sins have been forgiven—for she loved much.
But he who has been forgiven little loves little. (Luke 7:47)

Tom hates to write but loves to talk, so I recorded his reflections and recollections about his turbulent times. It was both hard and healing to revisit mutual anguish that happened so many years ago. Details and feelings tumbled out of Tom with an uncharacteristic flow. By baring his soul and exposing his flaws, my job of writing about his journey was made relatively easy—except my notes got stained by some occasional tears. Recalling and retrieving betrayal's stinging heartache did not make for enjoyable reminiscing. It seemed we were reconnecting the detached sections of a complex puzzle as we pieced together the painful parts of a broken life. God's grace skillfully led us through the process. The final outcome was a colorful mosaic that revealed His mercy and testified to His tender care.

Tom's Freedom Trail

On June 30, 1995, I was summoned for my first fearful court appearance, in which my felony charges were read in Sherburne County Courthouse, Elk River, Minnesota. On July 21, I appeared before the Honorable Judge Bruce R. Douglas and pled guilty to two charges of Criminal Sexual Conduct in the Third Degree; sentencing was September 1. Finally I had to face the full awfulness and consequence of my deeds.

Before long I was another new inmate at the maximum security Minnesota Correctional Facility—Stillwater. Everyone was placed for the first three days in quarantine after being tested for active tuberculosis; each prisoner had to be locked down for about twenty-two of twenty-four hours to determine the results.

As I sat forlorn in my cell, I felt like a captive in an alien land, stripped of all that was familiar. The foul air reeked, the walls were oppressive, and the bed was hard. During the day, the continuous clamor of voices droned in my ears, but the night noises sounded like hounds from hell. Men were swearing, moaning, calling out. I was terrified.

The initial reaction, on my first day, was to peer through my barred door to survey all that was beyond my cell. Across the hall, sunshine beamed through the opening of a window. As I gazed longingly to the outside, I gratefully spotted a picayune maple, surviving next to another building's stone wall. I wondered if in this cooped-up place I would pull through as well as that brilliantly arrayed tree had.

How had I gotten here? Respectable citizen! Prayer counselor! Loving father and husband! Christian! I felt hopeless; I couldn't stop the dreadful, persistent thought, *I must be nuts!* My own stupidity had dashed all my dreams. Inside I felt horrible, piling self-pity onto shaming doubts. I missed my family. I felt I was drowning in a sea of loneliness.

As I turned around to explore my six-by-nine foot space, I noticed a book on an open shelf under my desktop. It was a worn Bible missing its front cover, and on the exposed top page someone had written, "This is the answer for peace." To fill a void in my heart, I decided to open to Genesis. As I read, I could identify with Adam and Eve eating the forbidden fruit and hiding from God. My shameful offenses had brought me to this desolate place. I felt hope that maybe God would be merciful to me also as I acknowledged my self-seeking deeds. As I continued in Scripture, light slowly began to replace darkness in my spirit.

After reading the sixteenth book, Nehemiah, I felt some comfort. I began to see the possibility that God would maybe use the rubble of my past to restore my future (2:11–13; 4:8). I needed to surrender my defenses of self-protection and allow Him to rebuild with His protective walls. Could I trust Him to do that in this scary place?

On the third day I was released from quarantine; by this time I knew I had been like the Jews bound and exiled to Babylon. I had ignored the Lord's warnings, and my destructive, selfish ways had led me into captivity. I realized I was no better than some of the exiled spiritual leaders in Jeremiah's day, two of whom were put to death in Babylon for outrageously speaking lies in God's name while committing adultery (Jeremiah 29:20–24). Even though I was surely grateful to be living under God's covenant of grace, my inner life and my actions hadn't changed with lasting results before I had been confronted publicly and received severe consequences.

Forgiving *me* for violating God's heart and inflicting enormous pain upon so many was a struggle. I had initially chosen to agree with God's forgiveness, but heart healing took years. Shame dogged me like a hunter tracking his game. I had to remind myself consistently that the law of the old covenant wasn't being applied to me—that I live under the grace of God as revealed, exemplified, and fulfilled through the work of His Son, Jesus Christ. The Lord gave me a promise from Jeremiah 30:11:

> I am with you and will save you.... I will discipline you but only with justice; I will not let you go entirely unpunished.

He was true to His word. I recognized that I needed prison as a rod of correction. I believe I was no longer like a human shipwreck but a man in dry-dock needing major overhaul. Finding freedom in prison, my Babylon, was a journey with Him.

A Checkered Past

No one becomes a criminal or sex offender without a checkered past. Looking back at my life, I realized I had brushed off my bad behavior with convenient lapses of memory. In truth, I was a people pleaser who would tell Erin whatever I knew she wanted to hear and deal with the consequences later. Sometimes I was like an angry bear who would attack Erin when she dared to confront; I controlled my pain and hid my shame. Erin was my usual target because she didn't always agree with me. I knew how to manipulate so that all arguments ended in my favor. Even if I was dead wrong, I would quickly maneuver the discussion to be about her—"*You* don't trust me! *You* have a bad attitude! *You* are trying to control me! Hear *your* terrible tone of voice!"

The final rabbit out of my hat of accusations was, "I never measure up, so why don't you get a divorce!" Then I would retreat like a scared animal back into my burrow of isolation, my cave of addictions. Somehow I avoided the trap of pornography; however, alcohol, sports, and endless television programs became my chief protectors from emotional vulnerability. I resented any intrusions from Erin into my cave.

~~~~~~~~~~

In 1943, my father became a marine and was a part of the Pacific campaign as a maintenance technician. After the war ended, he worked as a private contractor for another two years in Fairbanks, Alaska. During the four years he was away, my small world seemed untroubled. I have no memories of the day he came home, but I do remember that chaos entered our house again.

I had received very little discipline as a child; when I did a misdeed, I covered it up by lying or manipulating someone else to take the blame.

For example, out of curiosity, I once cut up and ruined Mom's new vinyl bathroom curtains while playing with a razor blade, and then I paid my younger sister, Mary, a quarter to say she had done it. My mother was furious when she discovered the wreckage; Mary got spanked after confessing, and I secretly gloated over my cleverness. My doting grandmother certainly didn't help to turn me in the right direction by calling my deception "weaving dreams," as if there was nothing wrong with my behavior.

From my early days I had coped with the difficulties of an angry, alcoholic father through fantasy. I pictured myself as Superman, as the guy with all the girls, or as the athletic hero. I became like a champion chameleon who would change color and blend into my surroundings. With little sense of self, I would be whatever I perceived another wanted. Sometimes I was like my mother, who suffered in silence and sought peace at all cost. I also could suddenly switch and swing to an opposite mood—emulating my aggressive father. Delusional, I thought of myself as "a good person."

As I grew older, my childish ways of handling thoughts and emotions had followed me into adulthood. Gradually I had become a stiff-necked man who blew off cautions and warnings, living a secret life. For example, when I traveled for business, I frequently drank excessively and disgustingly boasted about riches that never existed. Because I never drank around my family or had alcohol in my home, I never considered myself an alcoholic. In 1975, after receiving my second DUI, I realized I was heading down the same path as my father. Because of shame and fear of losing my family, I reluctantly asked our pastor for guidance. Through prayer, he broke a major generational stronghold over my life, and I entered the Hazelden Chemical Dependency Treatment Center, then an aftercare program. After I found my sobriety, a genuine relationship with God began; it was an important first step toward wholeness.

Prison Life

The first visit with Erin in September of 1995 was exceedingly difficult. Sitting across from each other, we attempted to converse but couldn't; only tears flowed down our cheeks. I quickly tried to wipe mine away so none of the other inmates would see my vulnerability. I felt devastated that she had suffered so much because of my sins. In prison, I learned to appreciate the precious woman of God Erin is to me, a jewel to be treasured. I was finding the freedom to love my wife.

~~~~~~~~~~

By December I was accepted into a sex offender treatment program, which would continue with other phases after my transfer to a medium security prison the following fall. At both places I attended educational classes that aided development of therapeutic self-care skills, including reading and writing assignments and participation in various therapy groups. In my search for greater serenity, I eventually studied chemical dependency and addictive behavior, grief and loss issues, anger management, parental education, assertiveness training, communication skills, victim empathy, and cognitive restructuring. Part of my homework was journaling my thoughts daily and challenging my faulty thinking with truth.

I discovered that irrational core beliefs had dominated my life. For example, I had thought that if I got relationally close to Erin, she would then die and leave me like my mother did when I was a young man. Growing up in a troubled home, my mother was my source of security. After her death in 1966, I put a barrier around my heart to protect myself from the pain of such devastating loss. My irrational fears of intimacy had indeed caused Erin to stay like an unopened Christmas gift. She was kind, fun, a beautiful gift from God; but rather than enjoying her, I had chosen activities in which I could remain emotionally hidden. I had been afraid to reveal myself to others because I feared the agony of loss or painful rejection.

~~~~~~~~~~

The skills I learned to apply for healthy living brought me freedom from the domination of deception in my relationships. With God's help, I continued to challenge my defective thoughts as I proceeded toward healing and love.

On September 30, 1996, I received a certificate for successfully completing the Stillwater program and was finally transferred to medium security. At the Minnesota Correctional Facility—Lino Lakes, I fulfilled all requirements of Treatment Phases II and III by November of 1997, and was given another certificate of achievement. Since only a minority who start the sexual offender education program effectively finishes all suggested phases, I felt good that I was able to persevere this way. The classes were informative and therapeutic, but the homework was tedious at times; therapy groups were brutally honest and challenging. I learned I was not a nice guy but a man filled with shame and self-hate. Ultimately, the outcome was effective: I know I am now a healthier *me*!

~~~~~~~~~~

Life changed for the better after that transfer. No longer in a barred cell, I lived in a one-story cottage that housed one hundred twenty inmates in small rooms. My window was a welcome conduit for fresh air and sunshine, and though at first I had a roommate, I eventually received my own room. Everyone shared a central kitchen where we prepared our own meals and gourmet treats. Holidays lost their bleakness and became joyful again. The basement contained a laundry, a recreation area, offices, and meeting rooms.

Each man in the treatment program was paid a small wage, and additional monies could be earned by working for thirty cents to one dollar and twenty cents an hour, depending on seniority. I started as the unit janitor and in the end became an assistant to the unit's lieutenant. Half my earnings automatically paid restitution to my victims and the rest went for my daily needs, especially food and hygiene.

Both Erin and I appreciated the longer visiting hours; for two hours we would sit next to each other and hold hands while we talked and prayed. I was increasingly able to empathically listen and validate her pain. Her warmth and wisdom meant so much to me.

After parting with a kiss, I was strip-searched before I could return to my room. I usually didn't mind the procedure, except with one guard who patted me down with inappropriate touches. I felt violated but said nothing. As an inmate I knew that to file a complaint with a superior would mark me for greater abuse. After the incident, I prayed for God's protection and was never again shamefully debased.

~~~~~~~~~~

Six months before my release in May 1998, to ease my reentry into our home, Erin and I chose to receive marriage counseling from two professional therapists who had also led my Phase III Group. We discussed such issues as making necessary personal adjustments, learning how to forsake unhealthy life patterns, growing together with honest communication and intimacy, understanding the emotional impact of my newfound freedom, finding gainful employment, facing possible shaming judgments, and other difficulties that might arise.

In our third session, Erin expressed concern that I still had an unhealthy emotional dependency with her and suggested that all visitations (including hers) be discontinued for whatever time was necessary for this to be broken. The only contact with those on the outside would be when she and I participated in counseling sessions.

I felt angry at her proposal for breaking my codependent neediness, but the therapists thought it was a great idea that would strengthen our relationship. Visits from my pastor, family, and friends had helped me to deal with prison life, and I wondered if I could manage without this lifeline, without phone and mail privileges. However, I came up with a way to calm my mind: *Oh well*, I thought—*I have my TV and my own room, no big deal.*

But God had other plans. Three days later, my almost-new TV blew up—white smoke came out the back! I was totally frustrated. There wasn't time or money to get it fixed before my release. In desperation, I glanced out my single window, and again, my eyes noticed a bleak, barren tree that looked like I felt. I was comforted with the thought: the season of winter was almost over, and spring would burst forth with new life for both the tree and for me.

Feeling better, I sat down on the side of my bed. Soon I was surrounded by unexplainable warmth that had to be God; waves of overwhelming love were touching my heart! *Before,* I knew that God loved me because Erin loved me; *now* I glowed with the breakthrough revelation that *God really loves me,* as I am, no strings attached, "warts and all." I could also see that I had developed an idolatrous relationship with Erin. I had made her my rock of security and source of well-being, putting her into a spot similar to where I had placed my mother. She aggravated me when she didn't perform to my egotistic expectations, becoming to me like an enemy rather than an ally. I had loved and resented her at the same time!

The therapists had expected me to go into a depression in response to isolation from family and friends. As they observed me, though, they were amazed that I was flourishing. At the next counseling session with Erin, I shared about being consoled by God's love. Because idolatrous love with unhealthy emotional dependencies was exposed and confessed, a significant benchmark in my spiritual journey had been reached.

Just before my release, I learned that, based on a point system, I would be placed in the category considered "least likely to re-offend" after being discharged. Because I was not considered a community threat, there would be no sex-offender notification meeting. I was relieved; Erin did not need the grief this would have entailed.

I truly found freedom in prison and courage to face the future. I will be forever grateful to the director, therapists, and educators of the program provided for inmates like me. *A faithful God brought light into my dark Babylon!* I am blessed.

> Blessed are they whose transgressions are forgiven,
> whose sins are covered. Blessed is the man whose sin
> the Lord will never count against him. (Romans 4:7–8)

Chapter 5

God, the Caring Gardener

The LORD will guide you always;
he will satisfy your needs in a sun-scorched land
and will strengthen your frame.
You will be like a well-watered garden,
like a spring whose waters never fail. (Isaiah 58:11)

"Therefore I tell you, do not worry about your life....
Consider how the lilies grow." (Luke 12:22, 27)

In the spring of 1998, Tom was able to till the earth in our backyard garden once again. As he turned over the soil, all the decayed clippings and weeds from the past season were cultivated into the black dirt. Discarded debris enriched and fertilized our garden.

Similarly, nothing is wasted in God's garden; *no wasted tears, no wasted years.* He turned our broken beginnings into a fruitful future by blending our cries of pain with His showers of gain.

The Living Word not only prepares our hearts, He also plants, enriches, and clears the weeds. After we have rested in God's secret place, He will reproduce His life in us (see Matthew 13:23, 38). The sprouting believer is protected, supported, and lifted up; the mature Christian needs pruning to yield ever-increasing love.

As I consider how my lilies and other plantings became a garden, I think about my heavenly Father and His winning ways. God, the Gardener, carefully prepares hearts for His Son to be their vital Light, Water, and Seed for increase. Paul emphasized to Timothy, "Remember that Jesus Christ, of the Seed of David, was raised from the dead according to my gospel" (2 Timothy 2:8). God's Spirit of Truth continues the care by revealing heart areas that have hard places of unbelief, hidden rocks of idolatry, or choking thorns of sin (see Luke 8:4–15). In Christ's love, revelation leads to repentance; poor soil is transformed into good ground. In God's garden of grace, I become reconciled to Him and reconnected to His other blooms doing His will and reflecting His image. "The LORD is close to the brokenhearted, and saves those who are crushed in spirit" (Psalm 34:18).

The book of Psalms is like a beautifully tended garden with flowering words that will bloom as heart blossoms. During difficult days, I often pick a poetic prayer to be my bouquet of hope. Psalm 86 deposits an especially rich aroma that overflows toward others like a fragrant rose. Many times I have been encouraged through this cry of King David:

> Hear, O LORD, and answer me,
>> for I am poor and needy.
> Guard my life, for I am devoted to you.
>> You are my God; save your servant
>> who trusts in you.
> Have mercy on me, O Lord,
>> for I call to you all day long.
> Bring joy to your servant,
>> for to you, O Lord,
>> I lift up my soul.
> You are forgiving and good, O Lord,
>> abounding in love to all who call to you.
> In the day of my trouble I will call to you,
>> for you will answer me.
> For you are great and do marvelous deeds;
>> you alone are God.
> Teach me your way, O LORD,
>> and I will walk in your truth;
>> give me an undivided heart,
>> that I may fear your name.
> I will praise you, O Lord my God, with all my heart;
>> I will glorify your name forever.
> For great is your love toward me;
>> you have delivered me from the depths of the grave.
> The arrogant are attacking me, O God;
>> a band of ruthless men seeks my life—
>> men without regard for you.
> But you, O Lord, are a compassionate and gracious God,
>> slow to anger, abounding in love and faithfulness.
> Turn to me and have mercy on me;
>> grant your strength to your servant....
> Give me a sign of your goodness,
>> that my enemies may see it and be put to shame,
>> for you, O LORD, have helped me and comforted me.
>> (vv. 1-5, 7, 10-17)

This earth *abounds* with evidence of His care! As I revel in the astounding array of colors in my garden, I feel the touch of heaven. God also basks in and rejoices over His beloved, who are *His* garden of beauty. Delightfully, He calls us His shoots whom He has planted to display His splendor—the work of His hands (Isaiah 60:21).

Through the daily practice of dialoging with and listening to God, He renews and restores my soul by scriptural wisdom and inspirational insights. When He inspires me during such meditative prayer, I record the word pictures I envision. One day, when I was feeling as thirsty as an arid desert, God blessed me with these healing thoughts:

Restorative Showers

God plants His splendid seeds of love into my heart,
but the soil of my soul sometimes is parched with pain.
I feel like a trampled, tender shoot with fragile roots,
struggling, contending to soak up His gentle, gracious rain.

The Lord's shower of precious words and caring ways
faithfully descends upon this child, His little one.
In God's amazing light, I will burst into His bloom of blessing
in the comforting, healing arms of Jesus, His Son.

Through listening prayer, I become like His sparrow
who discovers a special haven, His abiding place of rest.
There I will be renewed, energized by the warm wind of His Spirit;
I will tarry, enjoying the intimacy of the Lord in His heavenly nest.

Another time, when a special friend was getting married, I gave the couple a wedding gift of a poem I had composed that exemplified their lives and honored their celebration. Additionally, I have discovered that for many its words are an appropriate witness of restoration by God's wondrous ways. By revising it and inserting our names, I was pleased to find that it is also a fitting testimony of God's love for Tom and me.

God, the Gardener, Loves and Cares

As tiny seeds of His Spirit, His bulbs of blessing,
the Lord planted Thomas Worthley and Erin Towne
into the homes of their parents, His chosen, blessed ground.
And He watered Tom and Erin with His words,
"I love you and I care."

Both sprang forth as the Gardener's
bright sprouts of splendor, tender green blooms of being,
into the sunshine of His beaming delight.
And He watered Tom and Erin with His words,
"I love you and I care."

Then God, the Gardener, whispered in the wind
for His angels to fly forth as their daily protectors,
to be at their side to guard and guide.
And He watered Tom and Erin with His words,
"I love you and I care."

And as with all tender shoots planted in the rich earth,
threatening storm clouds blew overhead,
But God's invisible hand of support strengthened them with His might.
And He watered Tom and Erin with His words,
"I love you and I care."

Cares of responsibility and weeds of sin and stress
grew menacingly close like thistles among the lilies,
but the fingers from God's heart carefully rooted them up.
And He watered Tom and Erin with His words,
"I love you and I care."

And they grew and blossomed forth into flowers of beauty
because they acknowledged Jesus Christ and His garden of grace
and delightfully drank each dancing droplet of His rain.
And He watered Tom and Erin with His words,
"I love you and I care."

God smiles on them like a radiant rainbow
that promises peace after a morning mist.
God clothes them like royal purple tulips in His glorious garden.
And He wondrously waters them with His words,
"I love you and I care."

Though Tom and I had previously been like an overrun and locked-up garden, God blew His warm winds upon us. *Now* we are a part of His beautiful bounty, sprouts of splendor, and testimonies to His redemption. We are commissioned to grow and glow!

Israel was once described like God's weed, and pest infested garden enclosed by Egypt. In the next section (Part 2), we will discover how Israel's Bridegroom reached out for her, intimately wooing His beloved by covering her defilement with the lamb's shed blood. He adorned His bride with the jewels of Egypt and carried her over His threshold of love into a fragrant future with Him.

In the Song of Songs, God illustrates His quality of love for His people, His glorious garden:

Like a lily among thorns
is my darling among the maidens....
You are a garden locked up, my sister, my bride;
you are a spring enclosed, a sealed fountain....
Awake, north wind, and come, south wind!
Blow on my garden, that its fragrance may
spread abroad. (2:2; 4:12, 16)

Part 2

EXODUS: MODEL FOR RESTORATION

Chapter 6

A Story Never to be Forgotten!

O my people, hear my teaching, listen to the words of my mouth....
I will utter hidden things, things from of old—
what we have heard and known, what our fathers have told us.
We will not hide them from their children;
we will tell the next generation the praiseworthy deeds of the LORD,
his power, and the wonders he has done. (Psalm 78:1–4)

Remember well what the LORD your God did to Pharaoh and to all Egypt.
You saw with your own eyes the great trials, the miraculous signs and wonders,
the mighty hand and outstretched arm, with which the LORD your God brought
you out. The LORD your God will do the same to all the peoples you now fear.
(Deuteronomy 7:18–19)

Amazingly, just before my storm of the century would rage upon me in full fury, I had taught a seminar called "Broken Beginnings and Wounded Warriors." At the time, of course, I had no idea of the devastation that would suddenly strike, leaving me a deeply wounded woman. Less than a month after presenting the material, destructive disclosures engulfed my heart. Looking back, I see that God also primed for me the teaching I prepared from Exodus for others. Freshly discovered truths were like a protective hedge around my heart and a pathway for my own recovery.

Despite their very human struggles with faith, Joseph (starting in Genesis), Moses, Aaron, and Miriam chose to trust in their Lord's promises. In my days of darkness, God's faithfulness to His people in bringing them out of Egypt was an inspiration to me. I could identify with their struggles and oppression. God wanted to free Tom and me from our chains of fear and yokes of bondage. The Good Gardener knew I would desperately need to lean on His strengthening trellis of truth.

The Exodus narrative, which reveals a pattern to follow for deliverance from malice, is a testimony of hope for all who are in pain. When we thumb or breeze through all the pages of the Egypt-based era of Hebrew history, we can easily miss the bounty of blessings. As I contemplated the precepts behind the facts, I was overcome with countless healing insights from the account of Moses confronting, God delivering, and the Israelites receiving.

Seekers of truth who have struggled with a tainted history will find this triumphal story like renewing rain upon a desert. Exodus contains master keys that open doors to the path of life for brokenhearted souls who feel like smoldering wicks or trampled plants.

Just before he died, Moses recited a song of life from the Lord to His people. It begins as a call to listen to God's voice: *"Let my teaching fall like rain and my words descend like dew, like showers on new grass, like abundant rain on tender plants"* (Deuteronomy 32:2). He instructed them to tell their children about their deliverance. He said to take to heart all the words he had solemnly declared—not idle words but words of life (vv. 46–47). He forewarned them to remember always God's wonders and ways. This is a story never to be forgotten! Stories of God's miraculous wonders and praiseworthy deeds must be told to each generation. *All generations must know the truth to be set free.*

> When you take it all in and settle down, pleased and content, make sure you don't forget how you got there—God brought you out of slavery in Egypt (Deuteronomy 6:11-12 MSG).

Impossible Obstacles

How does God restore those with a shattered identity who are striving for significance? When pain is overwhelming and cannot be comforted, how does God break through? How is trust restored for those whose formative years were filled with abuse? How can bruised reeds believe that the Master Gardener tenderly loves every one of His kingdom plants?

Because of their heavy burdens of prolonged discouragement and cruel servitude, the Israelites did not listen to Moses when he announced their freedom from slavery. He proclaimed that God was going to loose them from the Egyptians, but they were unable to believe because of their broken hearts.

While our tales of hardship vary, the general effects of abuse devastate a person's ability to trust. Victims tend to either hide in a cave or erupt like a volcano. How does the heart reopen to others when it was robbed of significance by abusive touches, words, behaviors, environments? Being mired in bitter circumstances makes it difficult for anyone to remember encouraging words from a caring God or to hear good news from someone who actually cares.

Additionally, abuse (physical, sexual, emotional, or spiritual) distorts a person's pictures of God, others, and self. Frank Lake, in *Personal Identity: Its Development*, states that "the earliest experiences which can lead to disturbed feelings of identity ... have their origins in the distress of babyhood."[2] The wounded one might come to perceive that he or she is like a seed that never sprouts, or a withered plant that fails to bloom—even an unwanted dandelion rather than a chosen rose. In families where words are like arrows of death rather than touches of life, there is no heart-song, only lament. The emotionally scarred heart shuts down in order to find a way to survive.

~~~~~~~~~~

The Exodus story of Israel's redemption from bondage truly foreshadows the story of Jesus Christ, the Lamb of God Whose shed blood delivered mankind from slavery to sin. The Hebrew deliverance is a revelation of God's heart for His little lambs, a symbolic foretelling of how Jesus sets the captive free from depravity—a testimony of God's care even for those who appear broken beyond healing. It answers perplexing questions about how we can minister to those with wounded spirits, for it reveals God's tenderheartedness toward all who have lost their capacity to hope.

In spite of what seemed to be impossible obstacles, Protector God triumphed over tyranny. Take note of this: how He dealt with the Israelites in Egypt is different from how He dealt with them when they were in the desert or in the Promised Land. In their brokenness, they needed a Papa God to love them as a devoted father would care for his ailing child. He heard their cries, soothed their pain, healed their wounds, and protected them from further injury by patiently cleaning up their messes. *He loved them unconditionally,* and in His arms He carried them out of Egypt into the wilderness. The desert became the place where God's people could embrace His ways and, through repentance, release the waywardness that had lodged in their hearts.

~~~~~~~~~~

The believer's life is a walk of faith on a narrow road with obstacles to overcome. A mature Christian who knows and lives in God's love is not immune to the storms of life, but he is *"like a person who builds a house on a strong foundation laid upon the underlying rock. When the floodwaters rise and break against the house, it stands firm because it is well built"* (Luke 6:48 NLT).

Even if they have been healthy and well, warriors in God's army can suddenly be wounded or gradually come under heaviness. Jesus, the Mighty Warrior, told His disciples in the Garden of Gethsemane that He was overwhelmed with sorrow and needed their support.

In my spiral of darkness in 1994, I felt like a fragile "Big Girl tomato plant" battered by ill winds continuously threatening my sense of well-being. I looked like a big person on the outside, but on the inside I felt like a forsaken child. As a seasoned believer who knew the love of God, I still struggled to remember His care in my dark place. The disclosure of Tom's immorality, in addition to Dad's illness and death, brought me to a place of dismal despondency. No one could extinguish my burning pain or entirely comfort me in my grief. I clung somberly to the truth written to me on a bookmark by a friend: "If the law had not been my delight, I would have perished in my affliction" (Psalm 119:92).

In my days of anguish, God's Word surrounded me as a protective trellis that kept me from toppling like an uprooted vine. However, it was His impartation of love through His personal word to me that lifted my inconsolable heartache. Now, my heart, like a mature "Big Girl tomato," is bursting to share redemptive insights that have not only encouraged me but also have given me keys to gates of restoration.

Digging for Treasure

As a child I loved being told of the Hebrews' dramatic deliverance. At that time, it was simply a wonderfully action-packed tale with a fabulous supernatural ending. Once I became an adult, however, questions begin to rumble through my mind, questions that wandered outside the obvious. What was God's specific purpose for *ten* plagues—why ten, and not just one woe of affliction? What is the significance of each judgment? What are the individual revelations for healing and deliverance today? What are the precepts that will impact my life and ministry? Are there insights into God's heart that will impart hope to others?

In this journey of discovery, it is meaningful to first consider the narrative's background. In examining how the descendants of Abraham, Isaac, and Jacob found freedom from enslavement and terror, we can see an even clearer picture. We gain greater understanding by viewing the lives of the primary characters as prophetic symbols. Consider the following *analogies:*

- **Joseph:** As the believer who dies in Christ, knowing that someday his body will be caught up into heaven (1 Thessalonians 4:16).
- **Moses:** As Christ, the Redeeming King and Tender Shepherd Who brings deliverance to His people (Hebrews 3:1–6).
- **Aaron:** As prophet and high priest, an ambassador of Christ who declares the Word of the living God (Ephesians 6:19–20).
- **Miriam:** As a sister in the Lord with a servant heart (Luke 1:38).
- **Israel:** As believers, in covenant relationship with Christ (Romans 8:14–17).
- **Pharaoh:** As a destroying power exalting self against God (Ephesians 6:12; 2 Thessalonians 2:3–4).
- **Egyptian magicians** (with staffs): As religious leaders, like the Pharisees, who practice deception (Matthew 3:7).

- **Slave drivers** and their underlings: As collaborators and infiltrators—the enemy within the camp (Jude 1:4, 11–19).
- **Egypt**: As the world system, under satanic influence (Revelation 18:1–8).
- **Locusts:** As demons whose mission is to destroy life just as locusts would devour a plant (Joel 2:25; 1 Timothy 4:1).
- **Slavery:** As bondage and abuse that rob a person of basic identity (e.g., dignity) and the meeting of crucial needs (Romans 8:15–17).

Whom, When, Where, and *Why?*

In addition to considering the prophetic significance of the characters, the era, and the setting, we need to answer the question of why God's people were in slavery. The story of restoration begins with the life of Joseph (see Genesis 37–50). His father, Jacob, was the patriarch whom God renamed "Israel" ("because you have struggled with God and with men and have overcome," 32:28). He unwisely favored Joseph who was the eleventh of Jacob's twelve sons and the first child from his beloved Rachel. Joseph's envious brothers, outraged by the preferential treatment and status he was granted, threw him into a pit and then (before telling Jacob he'd been killed by a wild animal) sold him to a caravan of Ishmaelite traders, who eventually took him from Canaan to Egypt.

For Joseph, facing life in Egypt would be a formidable place of pagan gods and foreign customs. Ancient Egyptian religion was characterized by a complex polytheism with many deities and nature gods. Protection over virtually every aspect of life was ascribed to some deity, and human rulers were an integral part of the belief system. Upon ascending the throne, the king would enter a temple so his priests could perform a ritual believed to transform him into an all-powerful god. Since Pharaoh was supposedly an incarnation of the sun god (*Re/Ra*), his very word was accepted as law. Early Egyptians believed that Ra created the world; the sun disc was their symbol of creation and renewal. Egyptian ritual included sexual immorality with temple prostitutes.

Jacob and his family worshiped only one God, the LORD God (*Yahweh*), the all-powerful Creator who had entered into a caring covenant relationship with them (Genesis 2:15; 9:9). God commanded Jacob's household to get rid of all foreign idol-gods, which would defile His glory and fracture their well-being or wholeness (35:2). Idolatry is an abomination to Him (see Exodus 20:3–4); an idol is a manmade image that is useless as a source of life and help. Behind all such worthless resources and pagan gods are demons, spiritual beings controlled by satan (Deuteronomy 32:17). The psalmist warns God's people not to worship them (106:28, 34–39).

~~~~~~~~~~

In spite of almost inconceivable and unjust personal hardships, Joseph, a faithful and obedient man of God, found favor with Pharaoh, ruler of Egypt. Years later, after Joseph had risen to the highest position any Hebrew would hold in that land, God providentially preserved his family when they were driven by famine in Canaan to seek provisions in Egypt. God's love, which restored Joseph to his now-repentant brothers, eventually paved the way for the entire family to migrate.

Nevertheless, Joseph knew that the settling of the Lord's people in Egypt was not to be permanent, for he believed God's covenant promise that Canaan, the Promised Land, was their inheritance. On his deathbed, he made the sons of Israel swear an oath that at God's appointed time his embalmed body would be taken back to the land of promise: "God will surely come to your aid, and then you must carry my bones up from this place" (Genesis 50:25). For two subsequent centuries his descendants prospered in Egypt with favor from its rulers. The covenant promises and the oath sworn to Joseph were remembered, passed down from fathers to children.

~~~~~~~~~~

Over time, as the Israelites were thriving and multiplying in Egypt, a new pharaoh, who the Bible says did not know about Joseph (Exodus 1:8), grew afraid of their strength; he worried that inevitably they would join forces with his enemies and then depart. Therefore, he dealt craftily with them and formulated a horrific solution: Pharaoh took away their freedom, putting slave masters over them to oppress them with forced labor.

However, his plan did not halt their expansion:

> The more they [the Israelites] were oppressed, the more they multiplied and spread; so the Egyptians came to dread the Israelites and worked them heartlessly for over two hundred years. They made their lives bitter with hard labor in brick and mortar and with all kinds of work in the fields; in all their hard labor the Egyptians used them ruthlessly. (vv. 12–14)

When *nothing* seemed to stop the Hebrew increase, this pharaoh shockingly decreed that all male Hebrew newborns were to be thrown into the Nile River to drown, though every female baby could live (v. 22). Imagine the terror and agony and discouragement of simply trying to survive under those crushing weights of tyranny, oppression, and injustice!

~~~~~~~~~~

Israel's troubles in Egypt, thousands of years ago, mirror the worldwide anguish in our times; much of what happened then sounds like today's headlines. Terrorism and anti-Semitism from many fronts are on the rise around the world. Whether a Hitler, a Stalin, a Mao, or a Saddam—all oppressors are fueled and empowered by satan's furious hatred. Debilitating forces and negative energy will create an atmosphere of paranoia and chaos in a totalitarian state or in a reprobate family.

In an article titled "Tyranny of Mind," Robert Okin, a psychiatrist who has worked with victims in Peru, Kosovo, and South Africa, reports the vicious effects of Saddam Hussein's evil through hands-on torturers and eager informants: "Tyrannical regimes do many things, but they always intimidate ... and in so doing create a chronic type of trauma."[3]

When basic needs are denied, a person is robbed of dignity, security, provision, and love. People under tyranny become terrorized, believing that they have no significance. Unfortunately, this can distort a victim's view of God, others, and self. How can these twisted perceptions ever change? *How does God restore? How does He turn injustice into justice?*

Marvelously, God hands us keys to the gates of freedom through the story of the Israelite release from enslavement in Egypt. The heavenly Father masterfully prepared and then partnered with Moses and his family. Yahweh chose Moses, soft-spoken son of a slave and son of royalty, to thunder in Pharaoh's face, *"Let my people go!"* This was God's battle cry for His people's freedom, their deliverance from bondage. This was a foreshadowing of things to come, the fulfillment of these types in the person and work of His Son.

On the cross, Jesus, Son of Man and Son of God, defeated evil; by faith in His finished work, *anyone* is able to be redeemed from the curse of slavery to sin. Wickedness has a continuing presence on earth because satan and his iniquitous followers will carry on with their beguiling, destructive ways until the fulfillment of all things. However, there will come that day when *"no longer will anything be cursed. For the throne of God and of the Lamb will be there, and his servants will worship him ... the Lord God will shine on them. And they will reign forever and ever"* (Revelation 22:3, 5 NLT). Filled with this expectancy, His redeemed implore, *"Come Lord Jesus"* (v. 20).

Now, Jesus Christ, Whose Spirit moves through the priesthood of believers, is our Trumpet of Redemption. All over the world, God's ambassadors, serving as His trumpets, are blaring, *"Let my people go!"* His saints believe:

Everything that was written in the past was written to teach us,
so that through endurance and the encouragement of the Scriptures
we might have hope. (Romans 15:4)

Chapter 7

Preparation for Victory

Then we cried out to the LORD, the God of our fathers,
and the LORD heard our voice and saw our misery, toil and oppression.
So the LORD brought us out of Egypt with a mighty hand...
with great terror and with miraculous signs and wonders. (Deuteronomy 26:7–8)

Speak to him and say: This is what the Sovereign LORD says:
"I am against you, Pharaoh King of Egypt,
you great monster lying among your streams." (Ezekiel 29:3)

Who can endure the day of his coming?
Who can stand when he appears?
For he will be like a refiner's fire or a launderer's soap.
He will sit as a refiner and purifier of silver;
He will purify the Levites and refine them like gold and silver.
(Malachi 3:2–3)

Dark-hearted king! Loss of freedom! Hard labor! Ruthless treatment! Murder of innocents! Tyranny! Terror! Impossible circumstances! The cruel butcher of babies ruling Egypt!

Why would Father God ordain a beautiful baby like Moses to be born into oppression and affliction? Didn't his godly parents from the priestly line of Levi deserve better divine care than misery under a monster? How can a mother keep her milk flowing while under constant life-and-death stress?

Hiding a healthy, squealing newborn from state-sponsored killers would send most mothers into total panic. Logic would not choose any of the alternatives open to Jochebed, mother of Moses; her options looked dismally hopeless. When he was only three months old, and she couldn't continue to conceal him, she placed her child in a waterproof basket in the reeds along the bank of the Nile and told his young sister, Miriam, to watch and see what happened (Exodus 2:1–10).

Placing her already helpless son into another realm of such risk was a faith-filled, prophetic act. Surely Jochebed had discerned God's will and had steeled herself to obey, even though it went directly against her instincts. I don't know if I could have done it! I think my imagination would have pictured and focused on river rats, currents, criminals, waves, and crocodiles. No thank you—not my son!

But there isn't a word in the biblical account about Jochebed's anxiety. I don't think she was superwoman, so *how* did she do it? Perhaps she remembered miracles of deliverance Yahweh had performed for her ancestors, especially Joseph. I imagine she knew the story of Noah, and possibly of Enoch. Though the narrative doesn't speak of help for her from angels, perhaps like with Mary, mother of Jesus (see Luke 1:35–37), an angel communicated to Jochebed that nothing is impossible with God.

Most Israelites would have known the promises given to Abraham, including the prophecy that his descendants would be strangers in a foreign country where they would be mistreated and enslaved for four hundred years (Genesis 15:13). It's conceivable that God's still small voice quieted Jochebed's heart by revealing that her child would be the future deliverer of his people, for Hebrews 11:23 states, "By faith Moses' parents hid him for three months after he was born, because they saw he was no ordinary child, and they were not afraid of the king's edict."

Somehow, Jochebed knew that her little babe was extraordinary, that God's glory was upon him. Her abundant faith is evidence to me that the Lord had revealed Himself to her as the living God. Only by knowing His love intimately could the parents of Moses have had the peace and bravery to walk through this crisis.

Mercy Under a Marvelous God

No impossible circumstances for Yahweh! No wickedness could stop the promise-keeping God! The evidence of His faithfulness to Israel shows how meticulous and precise He was in positioning all the players into the right place at the right time.

How did He come through for Jochebed and her family? Pharaoh did not intimidate God, the King of kings, and neither were Moses' parents terrified by the decree. The testimony of divine loyalty for the children of Israel is *awesome.*

Here is a summary of subsequent events (Exodus 2–4; Hebrews 11:23–28):

- Baby Moses survived infanticide and flourished.
- While bathing in the river, Pharaoh's daughter found Moses and had compassion.
- On Miriam's recommendation, the king's daughter hired Moses' own mother to nurse and care for him!
- Eventually, Moses was adopted and became the grandson of Pharaoh.
- Inflamed by faith, an adult Moses refused to be known as the son of Pharaoh's daughter.

- Moses regarded disgrace for God's sake as more valuable than the riches of Egypt.
- Moses fled for his life but persevered in the desert because he met the holy God.
- Moses found his wife in a wilderness, by a well.
- Moses flourished for nearly forty years as a shepherd and a father of two sons.
- God heard the groaning of His people in Egypt and "remembered" His covenant with Abraham.
- The Angel of the Lord appeared to Moses in a flame of fire in the midst of a bush.
- The Lord had seen the affliction of His people and was ready to rescue them.
- God was going to perform wonders and restore them to the Promised Land.
- God revealed another facet of Himself to Moses: "I AM," Yahweh, the Living God.
- God called Moses to be His leader who would bring the Israelites out of Egypt.
- God instructed Moses and imparted His authority to him.
- God confronted Moses' fears.
- God's wonders strengthened Moses' faith, and God's assurances blessed his wounded heart.
- God warned Moses that the new pharaoh's hardheartedness would delay—but not stop—the deliverance.
- God declared that the Israelites would leave Egypt with an increase of riches.
- God called Aaron to comfort his brother Moses and serve as his spokesman.
- Moses and Aaron first reported to the elders, then to the rest of the people.
- After Moses performed signs before the people, they believed.
- When the people knew their God cared, they bowed down and worshiped Him.

~~~~~~~~~~

God spent *eighty years and nine months* preparing Moses for this momentous moment in history—the time when He chose two Israelite brothers to confront a foreboding Egyptian monarch. However, before God could thunder in Egypt, He needed to impart healing love into Moses' fragile heart.

The fearless leader had been a fearful young man: his first big moment of valor had deteriorated into infamous disaster (Exodus 2:11–15). While watching his own people suffer injustice under hard labor, one day Moses spotted an Egyptian beating a Hebrew; he reacted by killing the abuser and hiding him in the sand.

The next day Moses was disturbed when he saw two Hebrews fighting, so he asked the one in the wrong, "Why are you hitting your fellow Hebrew?"

The man arrogantly replied, "Who made you ruler and judge over us? Are you thinking of killing me as you killed the Egyptian?" Then Moses was afraid and thought, *What I did must have become known!*

When Pharaoh heard about the incident, he wanted Moses arrested and executed, so Moses fled to the land of Midian and became a fugitive.

Fiery Transformation

Forty years after fleeing Egypt, Moses continued to be terrified of its powerful king. However, when a faithful God called and dialogued with Moses through flames of fire from within a bush, an important phase of Moses' transformation took place. *Redemption out of Egypt could not have happened without first the blaze of refinement.*

What was the result of being in the Refiner's fire? When impurities in Moses' heart were burned away, God's beauty beamed forth like precious gold. The hardships that tested Moses became blessings of transformation. The desert flame is a place of intimacy where the Lord shares revelations from His tender heart (Zechariah 13:9). *Revelation always precedes transformation.*

From a blazing bush, God revealed His blueprint for Israel's victory. Moses responded in fear, certain that no one would believe or listen to him. Nevertheless, God didn't point a finger of judgment. He knew His timid one needed courage and purpose. *In the fire, God imparted hope,* using what was at hand to encourage His servant. He told Moses to throw his probably worn and nondescript staff to the ground, and it became a frightening serpent. When Moses obediently picked up the snake, it became a staff again. And look at what the Bible says it became when Moses left his home to follow God's path to triumph: "So Moses took his wife and sons, put them on a donkey and started back to Egypt. And he took *the staff of God* in his hand" (Exodus 4:20).

Amazing—a dead piece of common wood became vitalized and holy when Moses obeyed the Lord's voice! There would have been no triumph over tyranny without God's plan and man's obedience. The Hebrew slaves probably felt like lifeless, discarded pieces of wood for kindling, nobodies, without significance. When Moses embraced the staff of God, he was transformed into a type of redeemer for the deliverance of his people. Moses, formerly the forsaken one, was called to sacrificially love the dead-men-walking Israelites. He was changed into a wounded healer, a shepherd for the sheep.

~~~~~~~~~~

In like manner, Jesus, the forsaken Son of Man, embraced the cross and redeemed humanity from slavery to sin: "He was pierced for our transgressions, he was crushed for our iniquities; the punishment that brought us peace was upon him, and by his wounds we are healed" (Isaiah 53:5). *God chose two insignificant pieces of wood—staff and cross—to become significant symbols of His glory.*

When Jesus was illustrating His Father's plan of salvation to Nicodemus, a seeker of truth, He metaphorically compared His death on the cross to Moses twice lifting up a snake in the desert. The first time Moses lifted a living serpent was for Israel's deliverance from *slavery to Pharaoh.* Years later, during their wilderness journey, a bronze serpent on a pole was for Israel's deliverance from *slavery to sin.* The living Christ needed to die a fiery painful death only once for the sins of mankind. His work of redemption for fallen humanity was completed at the cross, as He said, "It is finished!" (John 19:30).

The story of salvation from sin through the blood of Christ is prefigured throughout the Old Testament; it was God's foreknown plan before the creation of this world (Ephesians 1:4–5). Jesus, the Truth, told Nicodemus the truth:

> Just as Moses lifted up the snake in the desert, so the Son of Man must be lifted up, that everyone who believes in him may have eternal life. For God so loved the world that he gave his one and only Son, that whoever believes in him shall not perish but have eternal life. For God did not send his Son into the world to condemn the world, but to save the world through him. (John 3:14–17)

Later He proclaimed that "I, when I am lifted up from the earth, will draw all men to myself" (12:32). The cross of Christ is a symbol of hope for Christians, a sign of restoration to all who believe. However, note that while the cross is lifted up as a symbol of redemptive love to God's people, it is an image of terror to those who love darkness and to those who have been spiritually abused by evil.

~~~~~~~~~~

The cross was a crucible of fire for Jesus. When He swallowed the shame of sin, He became as a despised serpent and a forsaken leper: "He himself bore our sins in his body on the tree, so that we might die to sins and live for righteousness; by his wounds you have been healed" (1 Peter 2:24). Like the hand of Moses, which had become leprous when he placed it inside his cloak, but was restored when he brought it back into the light (Exodus 4:6–7), Jesus went into the darkness (the grave) but was resurrected and restored victoriously as the Light of the World. *The Wounded One became the Healer of Wounds!*

Today, a person turning to the Lord will find his veil of deception is removed:

> Now the Lord is the Spirit, and where the Spirit of the Lord is, there is freedom. And we, who with unveiled faces all reflect the Lord's glory, are being transformed into his likeness with ever increasing glory, which comes from the Lord, who is the Spirit. (2 Corinthians 3:17–18)

God desires all who behold His glory to love others, just as the Good Shepherd cares for His sheep. True hope, true freedom, and true glory belong to all who embrace the cross by following the example of Jesus. He did the will of His Father even though He suffered, choosing death so others could have life. The Lord transforms dead-men-walking into saints of glory. The redeemed will be like Moses—transformed into God-likeness!

The Husband of Hope: The Bridegroom of Blood

Another phase of Moses' transformation as God's leader took place through the shedding of his son's blood in the desert on the way back to Egypt from Midian. A short time into the journey, this man of God faced the wrath of God—and sure death. Moses had another crucial lesson to learn! In distress, his wife, Zipporah, would call him a "bridegroom of blood." Even so, without the shedding of blood, Moses would never have become the husband of hope, the symbolic deliverer of the Israelites.

This desert testing of Moses is a mysterious encounter with the holy God. En route to Egypt, he and his family were stopped at an overnight lodging place when the Lord suddenly showed up, threatening to kill Moses. How was this *possible?* Moses, God's enemy? *What had happened?* Had he suddenly become leprous—an outcast about to die? None of us knows the details of what Zipporah witnessed, but the important fact is this: she knew their son had to be circumcised on the spot, or Moses would die under God's hand (Exodus 4:24–26).

Zipporah must have known that in the covenant God had given to Abraham, He had conveyed that all who were either born into a covenant household or bought with money must be circumcised:

> My covenant in your flesh is to be an everlasting covenant. Any uncircumcised male, who has not been circumcised in the flesh, will be cut off from his people; he has broken my covenant. (Genesis 17:13–14)

The male's cut foreskin was the symbol that signified acceptance of the covenant, and of God Himself, by His people. Moses could not have represented God in Egypt if he had neglected this covenantal mark.

Good works! Miracles! An impressive man! Bearer of the Staff of God! Remarkable character! Best of families! All commendable qualities ... but for Moses and everyone else, male circumcision was the only acceptable sign of faith in the Abrahamic covenant.

> You will be the father of many nations. No longer will you be called Abram; your name will be Abraham, for I have made you a father of many nations. I will make you very fruitful; I will make nations of you, and kings will come from you. I will establish my covenant as an everlasting covenant between me and you and your descendants after you for the generations to come, to be your God and the God of your descendants after you. The whole land of Canaan, where you are now an alien, I will give as an everlasting possession to you and your descendants after you; and I will be their God. (Genesis 17: 4–8)

As the Lord had made known, *there could be no covenant relationship without bloodshed!* Circumcision was a nonnegotiable declaration that sin could be cut away only through the shedding of blood; only then could God's promises be activated in a believer's life. Until Jesus came and fulfilled His work in replacing the signs of the covenant with His perfect life, death, and resurrection, there was no other figurative way for human sin to be symbolically (rather than actually) removed.

To save her husband's life, Zipporah cut off their son's foreskin and placed the evidence at Moses' feet, uttering, "Surely you are a bridegroom of blood to me" (Exodus 4:25). Moses was spared, and his fellowship with God restored, through covenant obedience.

Today through the obedient shedding of His Son's blood, we have available to us a covenant relationship with Father God. The temple in Jerusalem had a heavy veil (curtain) around the sacred sanctuary known as the Holy of Holies; no one was ever permitted there, on pain of death, except for the Jewish high priest—*once a year,* on the Day of Atonement. The Holy of Holies was the seat of God's presence in the tabernacle. When the high priest went inside annually on their behalf to present the atoning sacrifice (which symbolized Christ's future mission), his fellow priests tied a rope to him. If inside the veil he was slain for impurity, they could retrieve him without going in and also facing death.

Christ's sacrifice eliminated this barrier. At the completion of His atoning death, the temple veil was torn in two, and the opportunity for intimacy with God was restored for mankind! Through His death, Jesus became the "Bridegroom of Blood," the Husband of Hope to the bride of Christ. Those who by faith accept His work are welcomed to approach the Father's throne of grace ... *with confidence!* (Hebrews 4:16).

~~~~~~~~~~

Curiously, the Exodus 4 account states that only one son was circumcised at that time, and it doesn't say why. Both of Moses' and Zipporah's sons were present. Since they had been married almost forty years earlier, their sons were probably adults, and perhaps one had already been circumcised. Zipporah was a Midianite (a descendant of Abraham through his second wife, Keturah) and the Midianite custom was to circumcise the male just before his marriage instead of at infancy. Perhaps in the case of his other son, Moses, originally wanting to please his wife, had accommodated Midianite practice instead of God's way for the Israelites.

This partially obscured truth may foreshadow Christ's restoration of Gentiles. Moses was Zipporah's bridegroom of blood—a Hebrew united with a non-Hebrew. Jesus is the "Bridegroom of Blood," the heavenly Groom to His bride. Christ's death for man's sin initiated the new covenant for God's people, opening the way for Gentiles as well as Jews to become sons of Abraham through faith (Galatians 3).

The believer's heart is *circumcised by faith* when surrendered to Jesus Christ. A new covenant, a marriage, with God is confirmed and sealed when the heart trusts that the blood of Jesus covers sin. Now, because of Christ's shed blood, both Jew and Gentile can be made one in Him by *"the mark of God on your heart, not of a knife upon your skin"* (Romans 2:29 MSG).

~~~~~~~~~~

Moses' family then stayed in Midian while he and Aaron journeyed on to Egypt. Possibly the travel would have been too difficult for the son after surgery. Circumcision on an adult male can be excruciating; recovery time is a necessity.

Not until Moses and the Israelites were delivered out of Egypt and had been living for a while in the desert did the family reunite. Zipporah, with their sons and her father, Jethro, left the homestead so that they could again live with Moses, and they had a delightful reunion! For the first time the family of Moses got to know his "family" (God's people).

Might this be a foreshadowing of glorious future events—a prophetic picture of the restoration that awaits us at the end of the ages? The Bible says that Jews and Gentiles united in Christ—made one through the Bridegroom of Blood—will be His redeemed people, living in the fullness of God's everlasting promises.

He himself is our peace [Jesus], who has made the two one and has destroyed the barrier, the dividing wall of hostility, by abolishing in his flesh the law with its commandments and regulations. His purpose was to create in himself one new man out of the two [Jew and Gentile], thus making peace, and in this one body to reconcile both of them to God through the cross, by which he put to death their hostility. (Ephesians 2:14–16)

Someday all of God's people *together* will praise Him; from the wellspring of life, countless tongues will rejoice. In the all-encompassing warmth of absolute love, the redeemed will proclaim, "We know the One Who loves us; we know we belong!" I imagine us singing (Psalm 68:4–6 AMP):

> Sing to God, sing praises to His name,
> cast up a highway for Him
> Who rides through the deserts—
> His name is the Lord—
> be in high spirits and glory before Him!
> A father of the fatherless and a judge and protector
> of the widows is God in His holy habitation.
> God places the solitary in families
> and gives the desolate a home in which to dwell;
> He leads the prisoners out to prosperity...

Chapter 8

The Dawning of Hope

The LORD did not set his affection on you and choose you
because you were more numerous than other people....
But it was because the LORD loved you and kept the oath
He swore to your forefathers that he brought you out with a mighty hand
and redeemed you from the land of slavery,
from the power of Pharaoh king of Egypt.
Know therefore that the LORD your God is God;
he is the faithful God, keeping his covenant of love
to a thousand generations of those who love him. (Deuteronomy 7:7–9)

He [Moses] also performed the signs before the people,
and they believed. And when they heard
that the LORD was concerned about them and had seen their misery,
they bowed down and worshiped. (Exodus 4:30–31)

"For I know the plans I have for you" declares the LORD,
"plans to prosper you and not to harm you,
plans to give you hope and a future." (Jeremiah 29:11)

God moved with signs and wonders! Moses and Aaron were trusted leaders! People believed and worshiped the Lord!

End of despair? End of story? No—just the beginning of dashed expectations.

God yearned for a festival in the desert, a private place where He could lovingly commune with His covenant people (Exodus 5:1). The enraged Pharaoh wasn't about to let up on his enslaved workers. Instead of heeding the words of Aaron and Moses, his heart hardened, and he arrogantly chose to assert his power. So Moses wanted a three-day journey into the desert sun for the Hebrews to worship their God? Pharaoh and the Egyptians considered Pharaoh to be the sun god. Why should he concede? *"Who is the LORD that I should obey him and let Israel go? I do not know the LORD and I will not let Israel go"* (v. 2). Even after being warned about plagues or death, his answer remained a fixed *No!*

~~~~~~~~~~

Rather than dashing hope, God is the One Who restores hope. He says in Hosea,

> I am now going to allure her [Israel]; I will lead her into the desert and speak tenderly to her. There I will give her back her vineyards, and I will make the Valley of Achor ["valley of trouble"] a door of hope. There she will sing as in the days of her youth, as in the day she came up out of Egypt. (2:14–15).

God, the sure defender, would carry His vulnerable ones out of Egypt like a mother eagle "that stirs up her nest, that flutters over her young, He spread abroad His wings and He took them, He bore them on His pinions" (Deuteronomy 32:11 AMP). When Israel was young, He loved him and called him out of Egypt as a father beckoning his son (Hosea 11:1). He comforted His children with soothing words and gentle ways, like a mother holding and rocking her distressed child. *The Lord desired to change their discouragement into delight, their sadness into song, their groaning into gladness.* Before God imparted clemency to His chained people—before He redeemed them from Pharaoh's cruel hand—He demonstrated His incredible power. He gloriously conveyed His light and love to hurting hearts.

A Prophetic Gift of Hope

God manifested himself to Israel as a caring, protective eagle. However, to Pharaoh He exposed himself as the dread warrior Who would make this potent king a powerless prey. The phenomenal encounters that ensued were necessary for both the Egyptians and the Israelites. God purposed to leave a testimony in Egypt, evidence to both the downtrodden and the arrogant that He is the only God, the great *I AM*. This was His season to love the Egyptians through the rod of correction and the Israelites through a staff of mercy.

Like all threatened tyrants, Pharaoh quickly moved to break spirits. The same day Moses warned of impending doom from the Lord, Pharaoh gave an order to the overseers that they were no longer to supply the slaves with straw for brick-making. The Hebrews would have to forage for it themselves *while meeting the same quotas as before.* When the unrealistic expectations weren't fulfilled, the Israelite foremen were beaten and ridiculed. Realizing their hopeless situation, they found Moses and Aaron, and, fearing for their own lives, angrily called God's judgment upon the brothers, blaming them for Pharaoh's hateful ways (Exodus 5:19–21).

A dubious and perplexed Moses questioned why God was allowing troubles to increase instead of bringing rescue (v. 22): "Is it for *this* that You have sent me?" God patiently responded that *now* Moses would see the fireworks of judgment explode over Pharaoh. Yahweh's mighty hand would force the king to loose the Israelites. He reminded Moses of His covenant promises. He assured Moses that He had heard the enslaved people's groaning. He would restore!

Moses was then directed to deliver a message of redemption, a declaration that the God of Israel would turn tyranny into triumph:

> Say to the Israelites:
> "I am the LORD, and I will bring you out from the yoke of the Egyptians. I will free you from being slaves to them, and I will redeem you with an outstretched arm and with mighty acts of judgment. I will take you as my own people, and I will be your God. Then you will know that I am the LORD your God, who brought you out from under the yoke of the Egyptians. And I will bring you to the land I swore with uplifted hand to give to Abraham, to Isaac and to Jacob. I will give it to you as a possession. I am the LORD" (Exodus 6:6–8).

This was a good-news announcement of great joy; the best news slaves could ever hope to hear—a wonderful word of hope from God's heart to the bound and wounded hearts of His people. He would:

(1) Be their Living God ("I am the LORD").
(2) Break the Egyptian yoke.
(3) Free them from slavery.
(4) Redeem them by His outstretched arm.
(5) Bring mighty acts of judgment on the oppressors.
(6) Embrace His people in an intimate relationship.
(7) Keep His covenant promises of inheritance.

Nevertheless, instead of delighted cheers—"We're free, finally free!"—*there was only silent disbelief.* The brokenhearted people were *too discouraged* to be able to trust Moses; previous good news from him had only seemed to result in making matters worse. Lack of faith shrouded all hope. Pharaoh had roared like a lion, and they had responded with paralyzing terror. *People perish when they lack vision, blinded to God's redemptive revelation* (Proverbs 29:18).

Why would God give a prophetic message to people unable to assimilate what they were hearing? A loving mother wouldn't force-feed a daughter too ill to digest food; a tender father wouldn't make his broken-legged son go jogging.

I believe God's declaration was a trumpet blast of deliverance *to the unseen world.* He knew that the primary battle was not with Pharaoh but against the spiritual forces *behind* Pharaoh: "Our struggle is not against flesh and blood, but against the rulers, against the authorities, against the powers of this dark world and against the spiritual forces of evil in the heavenly realms" (Ephesians 6:12). Words are powerful in warfare; *God's prophetic word is essential.* Intercession by declaration is absolutely necessary for breaking the will of wicked spirits. (I'll share more on this in chapters 11–14.)

~~~~~~~~~~

Furthermore, Moses didn't seem to comprehend the significance of his obedience, for he responded with shame to God's next command: "Go tell Pharaoh, king of Egypt, to let the Israelites go out of his country" (Exodus 6:11). Moses envisioned himself as a man of faltering lips, a zero in the arena of speech. Who would pay him any regard? If his own people couldn't even receive what he was declaring, why would Pharaoh?

Moses still tended to focus on his own perceived inadequacies. Perhaps his memories were flashing back to when he had tried and failed to deliver his people through aggression, forty years earlier. Perhaps recollections of childhood pain were overwhelming him in a flood of fear. From infancy, separated from his mother after being weaned, Moses had been raised in a stress-filled environment.

I sometimes wonder if the unique pressures of Moses' upbringing caused him to stutter. His brother, Aaron, without impediment of speech, had enjoyed the security of being nurtured and taught by godly parents. Certainly the Egyptian royal palace, with all its showy, decadent luxury, did not prevent depravity from marking Moses with shame.

The Lord was undaunted by Moses' protestation of incapability, and again He commanded both Moses and Aaron to bring the Israelites out of Egypt. God explained a plan in which the people would be assigned to divisions under the headship of their clans. *Everyone* would find a place of belonging when Israel was gathered into family tribes; this structure would impart to each freed slave, "*You* belong, *you* have identity, *you* are part of the covenant—you and your family are not forgotten or forsaken!"

Pivotal Encounter of Power

Now the Lord would say to Moses, the man who believed he was the wrong man for the task and would not be heeded:

> I have made you like God to Pharaoh, and your brother Aaron will be your prophet. You are to say everything I command you.... The Egyptians will know that I am the LORD when I stretch out my hand against Egypt and bring the Israelites out of it. (Exodus 7:1–2, 5)

In these repeated, progressive revelations, what Moses needed to see and accept was that God would manifest His presence in him. It wasn't about Moses' power or cleverness or ability to articulate—Moses needed only to believe and obey. The power of faith would enliven the prophetic truth spoken into his heart and begin to set him free from looking to his own resources and abilities. Moses was being sent to Pharaoh as God's ambassador! Who needs an oratory gift when the God of heaven and earth is speaking?

We can more and more grasp and affirm the refinement of Moses; a man of shame was becoming a man of splendor. His God, the only God, believed in him, had chosen him, and promised to work through him. Beyond words, Yahweh imparted divine authority that would manifest in miraculous signs. After previously failing to free his people and being exiled from his home, Moses had believed he was powerless and unwanted. Being God's cherished and chosen son made him a changed man!

~~~~~~~~~~

Again the Lord assured Moses that he would be given the words to speak and that Aaron would be the confrontational mouthpiece to address Pharaoh. He told Moses that even though there would be a power encounter, Pharaoh would not listen, would harden his heart, and would acknowledge God's supremacy the hard way.

Forewarned, Moses and Aaron went before Pharaoh and were immediately opposed. The Lord had commanded that when Pharaoh challenged them to perform a miracle, Aaron was to throw his staff down, and it would become a snake. When the king saw that Aaron's rod became a serpent, he demanded his sorcerers to respond in kind. As each magician threw down his staff, it became a snake; *then* the rod of Aaron devoured each serpent, signifying to the Egyptians that nothing, including their magic, would stand against the God of gods.

Significantly, a rearing cobra god (usually named Wadjet) was symbolically depicted on the headdress of Pharaoh. Wadjet was a serpent goddess, ready to strike and kill his enemies,[4] but this false protector of Pharaoh became a defeated foe.

The ruler's response was prideful unbelief, and he refused to let the people go. Like all who prefer wickedness, he had "exchanged the glory of the immortal God for images made to look like mortal man and birds and animals and reptiles" (Romans 1:23). Even though the Lord's supernatural act *and* its superiority had unfolded right before his eyes, he rejected the true God.

While freedom from Pharaoh's cruel hand would be a process, this was the decisive turning point in the conflict between the king of Egypt and the Lord of all. Moses had believed God and he became a mighty man of God, a faithful leader to God's people. Now living obediently as "one like God," he was able to fully trust his Lord to have the absolute upper hand over wickedness. *The gods of Egypt were no match for God Almighty,* even though behind Pharaoh's gods were demons, spiritual beings controlled by the devil. Pharaoh, having chosen darkness, remained deceived and doomed. Two men: one, the most powerful king on earth, became a vanquished foe; the other, a lowly shepherd, became a man who was like God.

Staffs and Rods ... and the Cross

To better understand the meaning and significance of staffs and rods during biblical times, I read from Vine's Expository Dictionary of Biblical Words.[5] The Hebrew word is matteh, often translated "staff" when used for shepherding, but translated "rod" when used for authority. Whether Moses was caring for sheep or for people, he used his staff to comfort and to guide. When he needed to confront wild beasts or reprobate men, the staff became a rod of authority, a weapon to protect against predators.

As I ponder the importance of the miracle of the staff, I see a revelation of the miracle of the cross! The swallowing of the serpents before Pharaoh illustrates the crucifixion of Jesus Christ. Colossians 2:15 says that Jesus disarmed the powers and authorities by making a public spectacle of them when He triumphed over them by laying down His life. As we've seen, the shepherd's staff, like the outcast's cross, was an ordinary piece of wood until God chose it as an instrument to manifest His glory and demonstrate His majesty. Father God's mighty hand, through the impartation of His glory, first powerfully redeemed Israel, then miraculously redeemed mankind.

Nevertheless, the greatest act of love in human history at times has seemed to remain a curse. The cross brought painful memories to the early church, sorrow sometimes overshadowing the meaning of the events. That the cross had been the instrument of Christ's torture and death presented the challenge of people seeing the glory represented by it.

The brokenhearted Israelites initially failed to see the staff of Moses as a blessing. Their lives didn't immediately change for the better, and Pharaoh, through harsh taskmasters, had dashed their hopes. Like Pharaoh, satan has veiled the truth of God's love by using deceived or vile people to spiritually abuse others. Monstrous damage is done when the cross of Christ is misrepresented. For example, misguided or corrupt individuals and organizations have misused the cross as a rod against Jews throughout history. Tragically, the symbol of Christ's passion for them became an anathema to them.

In satanic cruelty, the symbol of Christ's death is desecrated to curse innocent victims. The devil, the deceiver, desires that every person hate the cross of Christ and miss the actual message of Calvary's love: everlasting salvation from unending darkness.

Pharaoh foolishly mocked the rod and warnings of Moses, just as the foolish today mock the cross and warnings of Christ. Paul says that the ignorant stumble over the message of the cross, to their ruin, but the wise embrace the message as God's powerful plan for their salvation (1 Corinthians 1:18, 23–24). "When justice is done, it brings joy to the righteous but terror to evildoers" (Proverbs 21:15). The staff and the cross are symbols of comfort to the redeemed; the rod and the cross are symbols of discomfort to the rebellious.

Many miss the truth that Christ's crucifixion was fulfillment of Scripture. After His death, most of His followers were discouraged and confused. For instance, two men walking to a village called Emmaus had lost hope—they didn't get it. However, the resurrected Jesus thought their enlightenment was so important that He came beside them to explain what

Moses and the prophets had said about Him; He wanted them to know that nothing about His death had been in vain (Luke 24:17, 26–27). He may even have pointed out to these disciples His story of redemption from the Exodus account, with all the parallels of Moses' staff to His cross!

Consider the comparisons of how the rod Moses used was a foreshadowing of Christ's cross, remarkably substantiating Israelite deliverance through the shed blood of Jesus:

GOD'S STAFF/ROD (USED BY MOSES) COMPARED WITH CHRIST'S CROSS
(See Appendix if you desire to read the Scriptures listed on this chart.)

(1) Moses, "like God," with Aaron the prophet, embraced the Lord's rod and faced evil for the joy of redeeming Israel from slavery.	**(1)** Jesus Christ, God and Prophet embraced the cross and faced death for the joy of redeeming sinful man from slavery. (Hebrews 12:2)
(2) In obedience, Aaron threw down his rod before Pharaoh for Israel's redemption.	**(2)** In obedience, Jesus laid down His life for man's redemption. (John 15:13)
(3) Moses made a public spectacle of Pharaoh when the rod swallowed all the sorcerer's staffs /snakes, disarming their power and authority for evil.	**(3)** Jesus made a public spectacle of evil at the cross, by victoriously swallowing death and by disarming the authorities of evil. (Colossians 2:15; 1 Corinthians 15:54)
(4) Moses, one like God, defeated Pharaoh's sting of death by the rod.	**(4)** Jesus, as God, defeated death's sting through death on the cross. (15:55)
(5) Moses triumphed over Pharaoh when the rod swallowed the snakes of sorcery and manmade religion.	**(5)** Christ triumphed over satan by nailing legalistic, soul-diminishing religion to the cross. (Colossians 2:14)
(6) The rod was used by Moses as the way of peace for reconciling the Israelites to Yahweh God.	**(6)** The cross of Christ is used by God as the way of peace for reconciling mankind to Him. (1:20)
(7) The rod was the power and wisdom of God to the Israelites, but a stumbling block to Pharaoh and foolishness to the Egyptians.	**(7)** The cross is the power and wisdom of God to those who believe, but a stumbling block and foolishness to the world. (1 Corinthians 1:23)
(8) Through the rod, the Israelites were redeemed from slavery and lavished with blessings and grace.	**(8)** Through Christ's blood, the believer is redeemed from slavery to sin and lavished with grace. (Ephesians 1:7–8)
(9) The rod was peace for the Israelites but terror for Pharaoh and the uncircumcised Egyptians.	**(9)** Through the cross, Jesus became peace for the Gentiles—no longer aliens to the covenant. (2:11–13)
(10) The rod led the Israelites out of Egypt so they would no longer die in slavery but would live in righteousness with the Lord as their Healer.	**(10)** The cross is God's way to bring mankind out of slavery to sin, transformed to righteousness; the Lord Jesus is the Healer. (1 Peter 2:24–25)
(11) The rod freed the Israelites from the bondage of Egypt.	**(11)** The cross frees believers from the bondage of the world. (Galatians 6:14)
(12) The rod broke the yokes of injustice, the yokes of slavery for the Israelites.	**(12)** The Crucifixion breaks the yoke of injustice, the yoke of slavery to sin. (5:1)

Every book in the Bible, from Genesis to Revelation, declares the message of the cross. There is no other way to be delivered from corruption and death! Hebrews 9:22 says, "The law requires that nearly everything be cleansed with blood, and without the shedding of blood there is no forgiveness." The sinless Jesus Christ fulfilled the requirements of the law; His blood was shed to take away the sin of the world (John 1:29). Because Father God loves every human being and does not want anyone to perish; He patiently waits, desiring all to come to repentance (2 Peter 3:9). He gave His One and only Son, so that anyone who trusts in Him will not be condemned but have eternal life (John 3:16).

Eternity with God is a *gift* that delivers man out of darkness and into God's kingdom of light: "It is by *grace* you have been saved, *through faith*—and this not from yourselves, it is the gift of God—*not by works*, so that no one can boast" (Ephesians 2:8–9). Man needs to trust God's unmerited favor to receive God's bountiful salvation:

> *Because if you acknowledge and confess*
> with your lips that Jesus is Lord
> and in your heart believe (*adhere to, trust in, and rely on the truth*)
> that God raised Him from the dead,
> *you will be saved* (Romans 10:9 AMP).

Chapter 9

Deliverance from Despair

My heart began to despair over all my toilsome labor
under the sun. (Ecclesiastes 2:20)

The vineyard of the LORD Almighty is the house of Israel,
and the men of Judah are the garden of his delight
And he looked for justice, but saw bloodshed;
for righteousness, but heard cries of distress. (Isaiah 5:7)

Evil men will be cut off,
but those who hope in the LORD will inherit the land. (Psalm 37:9)

The LORD is my rock, my fortress and my deliverer;
my God is my rock, in whom I take refuge,
my shield and the horn of my salvation.
He is my stronghold, my refuge and my savior—
from violent men you save me. (2 Samuel 22:1–3)

The descendants of Joseph, struggling for their basic needs, had become a picture of despair. The season for the Lord's triumph over tyranny had begun; darkness was descending on the Egyptian empire. God had declared that He would break the vile arm of Egypt, ending her defiant strength. He was grieved that His covenant people were subject to an unjust leader; He saw their plight, and with compassion He was preparing to lift their bitter yoke of heaviness.

The Hebrews were like oxen yoked with a wooden harness, unable to bend their necks to feed themselves. They were exhausted from toiling under the desert sun, slaves bound to aching activity in hopeless captivity. In the absence of freedom, discouragement overshadowed their lives; they hated Pharaoh's oppressive control and felt helpless. Harsh words had pierced their hearts like brambles trapping a small animal. They could not liberate themselves from their pressure-packed prison. God's broken people needed a divine messenger to voice *"Restore!"* and enact their release.

Not all cases of injustice are so venomous and vicious, but almost every-one has suffered from unfairness, mistreatment, disservice, and wrongful injury. Sometimes friends cause pain by rejecting, criticizing, shaming, or manipulating; hunger for control creates slanted relationships that keep others in captivity. David lamented:

> If an enemy were insulting me, I could endure it; if a foe were raising himself against me, I could hide from him. But it is you, a man like myself, my companion, my close friend, with whom I once enjoyed sweet fellowship. (Psalm 55:12–14)

Any time someone demands his own stubborn way, refusing the Lord's instruction, others will be wounded.

Many (like David) have had a rebellious, envious, blaming, obsessive, explosive, insecure "Saul" in their life. The arrogant assert their rights and then insist on unswerving loyalty to their purposes. Cruel figures of authority—in a family, a school, a church, a city, a state, a nation—can have mouths like dragons. Their sharp words gouge like barbs that grow into thorns of destruction.

The Breaker Anointing

God Almighty imparted the vision, courage, and resolution to His chosen vessels, Moses and Aaron. He prepared them for the battle against Pharaoh and Egyptian strongholds with His breaker anointing, ordaining them to be like a battering machine that would crush Pharaoh's gates and breach his demonically fortified walls.

Moses and Aaron were forerunners to Jesus Christ, the resurrected Savior Who broke through for mankind by rending the temple veil. As *the Breaker,* He opened the kingdom of heaven to all believers. God promised in Micah 2:13 (AMP):

> *The Breaker [the Messiah] goes up before them.*
> *They will break through,*
> *pass through the gate*
> *and go out through it,*
> *And their King will pass on before them,*
> *The Lord at their head.*

Jesus Christ leads, protects, and guides His servant warriors so that through spiritual warfare they will break down opposition and release the captives of these turbulent times. Someday satanic kings "will make war on the Lamb, and the Lamb will conquer them, for He is Lord of lords and King of kings, and those with him are called and chosen and faithful" (Revelation 17:14 RSV).

Moses was eighty and Aaron was eighty-three when they confronted Pharaoh. Some might conclude that they were over-the-hill commanders, but God had prepared them for this time in history. This revelation of God's name, *"I AM WHO I AM,"* was written on their hearts (Exodus 3:14; 6:2). Knowing Yahweh was with them, they stepped forward as confident and obedient warriors, ready to follow the Lord's battle plans. They knew their present, eternal, living God was ready to act on their behalf.

Great People of the Bible and How They Lived describes the scene:

> For a moment the two men gazed in wonder at the figure before them. Less than 10 feet away sat the world's most powerful monarch, a tall handsome man clothed in sheer white linen and wearing the high red and white crown of Egypt. A heavy jeweled collar hung around his neck, and his arms and fingers were wrapped in brilliant bracelets and rings. Golden slippers adorned his feet. In his right hand he held an inlaid gold shepherd's crook, symbol of his great authority. Sardinian bodyguards, Arabian handmaidens with long, feathered fans, priest and court officials clustered around his gilded throne. At his feet lay a royal pet, a male lion."[6]

Imagine facing this!

Without God as their Battering Ram and Gate Crasher, the mission would have been preposterous (Ezekiel 21:22). The task was formidable: Moses and Aaron were demanding of Pharaoh the release of hundreds of thousands of Israelites from captivity. They were a king's valuable property, but they were *the King's* valuable people. God Almighty was going to do the impossible for His people, and they would do the possible for Him. With God, nothing is unachievable (Luke 1:37).

> I assure you, even if you had faith as small as a mustard seed you could say to this mountain, "Move from here to there," and it would move. (Matthew 17:20 NLT)

The time to raise the rod of God and thunder *"Let my people go"* had arrived! Fierce battles followed. Ten catastrophic plagues ensued over at least twenty days before Pharaoh was finally (though temporarily) willing to let the Israelites go. Not until grief-stricken wailing covered Egypt did the king relent.

Remarkably, God's people were delivered from Pharaoh's hand and land after exactly 430 years, in fulfillment of Scripture. Exodus 12:40–41 says, "The length of time the Israelite people lived in Egypt was 430 years. At the end of the 430 years, to the very day, all the LORD's divisions left Egypt." The Lord had said to Abraham, when he was still called Abram,

> Know for certain that your descendants will be strangers in a country not their own, and they will be enslaved and mistreated four hundred years. But I will punish the nation they serve as slaves, and afterward they will come out with great possessions. (Genesis 15:13–14)

God was in total control; Pharaoh, his magicians, and all the gods of Egypt were powerless to reverse the birth pangs, the plagues. Sometimes they could counterfeit the judgments, but their worthless sorcery accomplished nothing.

The Lord's Distinction

Thinking about the frightened slaves, I've wondered what they experienced when God struck with the first judgment on their oppressors. In Goshen, the settlement where they lived, they probably were on their normal treadmill of drudgery, quivering as they waited for Pharaoh to retaliate. After centuries of bondage they had become an irresolute people who would need time to assimilate and acknowledge what was being done on their behalf.

The Lord, however, was resolute, and His purposes were clear: Yahweh made a distinction so as to protect and provide for the Israelites while pouring out wrath on their tyrannical masters (Exodus 11:7). During the first plague, His people in Goshen had fresh water to drink, while the Egyptians had no water. (The entire Nile changed to blood.) In the plagues that followed, frogs didn't overrun the Israelite homes. No nasty gnats came out of their ground. No filthy flies ruined their land. No judgment touched their livestock and harvest. No curse of boils infected their skin.

Until this point, very little beyond mere survival had been expected of the captives. Primarily they were clinging to a bare existence; mainly they were too discouraged to hope or trust God's promises. Moses didn't rebuke them with an angry "Get over it!" Their picture of God was being enlarged; this was not the time for their training in spiritual disciplines. They were not commanded to repent of besetting sins. They were not reprimanded for being poor listeners. They were not reproached for having fear. They were not ordered to keep praising God. They were not told to die to self. They were not denounced for their faith struggles. They were not expected to address Pharaoh. They were not directed to pray. *This was the season for God to transform their valley of trouble into a door of hope* (Hosea 2:15).

Before the seventh plague, the Hebrews at last *were* given something to do: stay home and rest! After finding a place that would protect them and all they owned, including their animals, they could relax. To their credit, they believed the accuracy of God's weather forecast. In obedience they sought shelter when warned of the coming storm. Faith in God was again springing up in them. They said yes to Yahweh by staying right where they were; their seed of faith was growing into a sprout of hope.

What the captives acted upon, in spite of everything, is extremely important—an example of faith to all who are oppressed. While Moses and Aaron were confronting Pharaoh and proclaiming liberty, Israel rested in the safety of "Goshen," which in Hebrew means "drawing near."[7] While judgments were upon the Egyptians, their captives were drawing nearer to God! Their tears were beautiful prayers to their caring "I AM" (Psalm 56:8). *God's people chose life—they didn't give up.*

Some of Pharaoh's officials also believed the announcement. Wisely opting not to ignore the alert, they saved their non-Israelite slaves, their livestock, and themselves by taking shelter. Those who rejected the warning of the "mother of all storms" were beaten down by hail upon their livestock and fields. God displayed His power through the worst thunderstorm ever to fall on Egypt (Exodus 9:16), and the Israelites were saved by His immeasurable mercy.

~~~~~~~~~~

Following the seventh plague, the Lord said to Moses,

> Go to Pharaoh, for I have hardened his heart and the hearts of his officials so that I may perform these miraculous signs of mine among them that you may tell your children and grandchildren how I dealt harshly with the Egyptians and how I performed my signs among them, and that you may know that I am the LORD. (10:1–2)

God did not create human beings to live apart from Him by worshiping themselves or anything else. *No one else and nothing else is God.* The only acceptable attitude in response to Him is humility. He desires fellowship with those He has created, and we can receive this as we recognize the importance of humbling ourselves before Him.

It would be a grand-scale understatement to say that by now, nothing was going well for Pharaoh. The Lord had finally abandoned him to his hardheartedness. Already destruction had fallen upon the Egyptians. In the eighth plague, they were stripped of everything green that remained by devouring locusts, but the land in Goshen was saved. In the ninth plague, hellish darkness engulfed Pharaoh and all his people (though the Israelites had light—vv. 21–23). Totally separated from God's light, the Egyptians would all have died if the days of the curse had not been limited.

~~~~~~~~~~

Throughout the edicts, the Good Shepherd spared His covenant people because they were His beloved bruised lambs. He had come to rescue them. He wanted them to remember: during the first judgment, their water was sweet, not bloody like the Nile. During the second, their homes stayed free of frogs. During the third, their air was clean, no pesky gnats disturbing their well-being. During the fourth, their land was undefiled, unpolluted by swarms of flies. During the fifth, their livestock were protected from death. During the sixth, their skin remained healthy, free of boils. During the seventh, their families and harvest were protected during the hail storm. During the eighth, their fields remained green, without locusts. During the ninth, their homes basked in sunshine, spared the overwhelming darkness. *The Light of the World was blessing the Israelites by shining His face upon them so they would have His peace.*

"Get Out of Here!"

After the eighth judgment, Pharaoh's heart seemed to be softening: He said, "I have sinned against the LORD your God and against you. Now forgive my sin once more and pray to the LORD your God to take this deadly plague away from me" (Exodus 10:16–17). But now *the Lord* had hardened the cynical king's heart; he was reaping what he had sown (Exodus 9:12). After the ninth plague, double-minded Pharaoh continued to change his mind about permitting the Israelites to leave Egypt and worship the Lord. He said: "Go, worship the LORD. Even your women and children may go with you" (Exodus 10:24). But after Moses insisted on the livestock being brought along as well, Pharaoh raged, *"Get out of my sight! Make sure you do not appear before me again! The day you see my face you will die!"* (v. 28). The intimidation had no power over Moses, for God had sealed him as His witness in Egypt—a testimony that there is only one living God, the "I AM." God's word would soon be a sword of death piercing the heart of Pharaoh and a sword of life protecting the heart of Moses.

Now, for the last time, Moses ominously forewarned the stubborn monarch of the next woe that was coming (11:4–7). With conviction, he prophesied:

> This is what the LORD says: "About midnight I will go throughout Egypt. Every firstborn son in Egypt will die, from the firstborn son of Pharaoh, who sits on the throne, to the firstborn son of the slave girl, who is at her hand mill, and all the firstborn of the cattle as well. There will be loud wailing throughout Egypt—worse than there has ever been or ever will be again. But among the Israelites not a dog will bark at any man or animal."

He added that Pharaoh's officials would turn against him by bowing at Moses' feet.

Pharaoh did not heed. God's justice would make his rock-hard heart again reap what it had sown when he'd ordered the deaths of all male Israelite newborns: the death of his own firstborn son.

Before the tenth plague, prosperity was restored to God's people—those redeemed by His grace would inherit a bounty. They were not to leave Egypt as stripped slaves but as His bride, adorned with jewels. God told them to ask their Egyptian neighbors for articles of silver and gold. This blessing was in fulfillment of prophecy (3:21–22):

> I will make the Egyptians favorably disposed toward this people, so that when you leave you will not go empty-handed. Every woman is to ask her neighbor and any woman living in her house for articles of silver and gold and for clothing, which you will put on your sons and daughters. And so you will plunder the Egyptians.

We learn later that God also planned for the gold and other blessings to be adornment for the tabernacle of His presence, but never for pagan purposes (vv. 20:23; 25:1–9).

It's All About the Lamb of God

No longer would the Israelites feel exposed and bare; the Bridegroom of Blood would wash away their defilement and cover their wounds. The sign implemented to spare them from the angel of death was a slain lamb's sprinkled blood upon their doorposts (a foreshadowing of Christ's redemptive blood). The Lord's Angel would observe the blood and pass by their dwellings, but strike a death blow to the uncovered Egyptian households. The Hebrew people were healed by the wounds of the One pierced for their transgressions (Isaiah 53:5). *It's all about Jesus, the Lamb of God.*

Again, I'm comforted to realize that there were numerous blessings but few demands upon God's brokenhearted people. Their vision of Him needed to become clearer and more vivid as the end drew near; and with their expanding view of Him, their fears were growing smaller while their faith increased. Soon they would not merely rest and receive, but would also stand, eat, and walk as He guided. For now, God's wounded ones had become spiritually healthy enough to listen and then obey.

Moses enlightened them with the news that the final plague would usher in their departure. God wanted them to know that He would continue to make a distinction between Egypt and Israel. Their cords to Pharaoh would be broken by the obedience of the father in each family. If they would cover their doorposts with the non-defective lamb's symbolically redemptive blood, destruction would pass over their dedicated homes (Exodus 12:21–23). After the elders followed all the instructions, the covenant people bowed down and worshiped their Lord with faith and joy (v. 27), the song of the redeemed filling their hearts. Possibly they sang "the song of the Lamb" that will be sung in heaven (Revelation 15:3–4):

> *Great and marvelous are your deeds, Lord God Almighty.*
> *Just and true are your ways, King of the Ages.*
> *Who will not fear you, O Lord, and bring glory to your name?*
> *For you alone are holy. All nations will come and worship*
> *before you, for your righteous acts have been revealed.*

In Egypt, instead of a song, there was lament. Pharaoh and his people would never forget their night of sorrows; grief would be in their memories and in their bones.

> At midnight the Lord struck down all the firstborn in Egypt, from the firstborn of Pharaoh, who sat on the throne, to the firstborn of the prisoner, who was in the dungeon, and the firstborn of all the livestock as well. Pharaoh and all his officials and all the Egyptians got up during the night, and there was loud wailing in Egypt, for there was not a house without someone dead. (Exodus 12:29–30)

A devastated Pharaoh, who had never wanted to see Moses again, once more changed his mind. He demanded that all the Israelites, with their flocks, leave the country at once, curiously adding, *"and also bless me"* (v. 32). Still turned against the Lord and mired in darkness, the king must have been seeing Israel's departure as his blessing. His misappropriated and insincere parting words fit his profile of twisted evil.

The king, who thought he could disregard God and His prophets, was now ignored. Moses and Aaron knew God Almighty was watching over His people.

> And like a huge eagle hovering in the sky,
> GOD-of-the-Angel-Armies protects Jerusalem.
> I'll protect and rescue it.
> Yes, I'll hover and deliver (Isaiah 31:5 MSG).

Chapter 10

Roadmap to Freedom

There will be a highway for the remnant of his people...
as there was for Israel when they came up from Egypt. (Isaiah 11:16)

Your road led through the sea, your pathway through the mighty waters—
a pathway no one knew was there!
You led your people along that road like a flock of sheep,
with Moses and Aaron as their shepherds. (Psalm 77:19–20 NLT)

He guided them safely, so they were unafraid;
but the sea engulfed their enemies. (Psalm 78:53)

The Word of God is the map that will guide His followers along a prosperous road, His path of righteousness. The story of Moses, drawn from the waters of death as a vulnerable child, was like a life preserver to me when I felt like a little one cast into the open sea. As the stark reality of my husband's infidelity flooded my soul, God's truth calmed my spirit when I clung to His living words.

But what happens to those too fatigued to hang onto a lifeboat? Sometimes people are so battered and weary that their Bible, their guide to hope, is almost too heavy to open. *They need our understanding, not our judgment.* Perhaps they're in the condition of being like spiritual infants. If I put a guidebook in a baby's crib, the child, too young and undeveloped to appreciate it, wouldn't have the slightest idea what to do with it.

As in life, many have difficulties in following a map, and some don't see its significance. Some are too sick to leave their beds. Some are unable to comprehend its directions. Some are so oppressed that their vision is blocked by a mental fog. Some are too exhausted to read. Some are trapped in urgency and are overwhelmed. Some are broken from discouragement. And some don't understand the language.

None of these difficulties is a problem for God!

The Lord knows the captives, those whose hope is fading without direction or purpose. Because people will perish without redemptive vision, He desires to guide the weary ones, caught in briars of passivity and thorns of pain, to His freedom trail. God proclaims, "Rebuild the road! Clear away the rocks and stones. Prepare a glorious highway for my people's return from captivity.... I will refresh the humble and give new courage to those with repentant hearts" (Isaiah 57:14–15 TLB).

People do not need to remain bound by strongholds, whether of Egypt or of a family. Jesus, the Lifter of our heads, is able to call upon a stronger fellow believer to help carry burdens until suffering ones are able to carry their own loads (Galatians 6:2–5). I will always be grateful for all the "oaks of righteousness" (Isaiah 61:3) who covered my family and me from scorching heat. They were embodiments of God's heart, ministers of loving grace.

God *will* make a highway out of Egypt—*Holiness Way*. "A highway will be there; it will be called the Way of Holiness. The unclean will not journey on it; it will be for those who walk in that Way; wicked fools will not go about on it" (35:8). This is the path of liberation from tyranny, leading to abundance and the Promised Land.

King David wrote that people are to be envied in whose hearts are the highways to Zion. When they pass through the valley of weeping, they make it a place of springs by God's strength. Dwelling in His presence, they tell of His glory (Psalm 84:4–6). Following the Lord's roadmap to freedom, ruin becomes restoration, contempt becomes contentment, and sadness becomes song! As an overseer, the apostle John expressed the blessing of being led along in fullness—the Greek word is *eudoō*, meaning "all will go well" or, literally, "to have a good journey, to be led along a prosperous road" (3 John 1:2).[8]

From Trap of Terror to Testimony of Triumph

After leaving Egypt, the Israelites expected that *finally* their way would be free of troubles. Because God would be with them, they envisioned their journey without obstacles. Though they marched out boldly, their confidence blew away like a field of flowers lifted by a tornado. They were dumbfounded and dismayed when they were led to an apparently impassable "Sea of Reeds" (or Red Sea). Their confusion and terror rapidly escalated when they looked back and saw Pharaoh and his entire army rushing upon them. They felt *trapped!*

In dread, they accused Moses of bringing them out to die. What they saw and felt right then was more real to them than any words from God; their doubt and anxiety kept them from remembering Who was protecting them. But Moses didn't panic: "Do not be afraid. Stand firm and you will see the deliverance the LORD will bring you today. The Egyptians you see today you will never see again. The LORD will fight for you; you need only to be still" (Exodus 14:13–14).

The experience of terror became an experience of triumph. What threatened to destroy the Israelites became the very means to save them. Moses knew the God Who had saved him from Pharaoh in his younger years. By faith he raised his staff over the sea, the waters parted, and the people were able to move through on dry ground. The Angel of the Lord, in front of them, moved between them and the Egyptians. Envision the miracle: The protective covering of light over the Hebrews became a terrorizing cloud of darkness to Pharaoh's army! (The Lord's Angel was a pre-incarnate appearance [theophany] of Jesus, the Covering Light for all believers.)

Egypt's mighty men could do nothing. When they were able to resume their pursuit, God's people were safely on the other side. The villainous horde recklessly rushed ahead like a lion descending on its prey. The Lord threw them into confusion, and the monstrous force became like a cornered mouse. After Moses obediently raised the rod of God, the sea closed over Pharaoh's chariots and men. No one survived. Pharaoh's army, like satan's, was blinded by pride, unaware that they were already defeated foes.

~~~~~~~~~~

So *why* another brush with Pharaoh? Hadn't God's people gone through enough already? Moses had told them about Pharaoh's defeat—assured it, promised it. Why did they need to face him again? Why weren't the testimony of Moses and the works of God enough to dispel their fears?

The lingering effects of abuse may be one reason that the Hebrews struggled with faith in God. It seems their unhealed hurts would trigger their emotions, and then panic would engulf them. Even though they knew that in the tenth plague death had passed over their homes, trusting God seemed to be a challenge beyond their reach. The previous miraculous encounters perpetrated upon Egypt were not so observable right in Goshen. *The Israelites needed a personal experience with God,* an experience that would impact their lives with purpose. They needed to see the imminent reality of God's almighty power, a revelation that He is the One Who defends. Only the direct touch of His love would heal their core of pain.

Their senses and emotions, damaged through bondage, had swung from high alert to lethargic stupor. Their defiled imaginations had envisioned a big Pharaoh and a small God. Their wounds from slavery left in them an aftermath of lies, fear, and passivity. They saw themselves as frail insects instead of God's chosen people. Since the experiences of oppressive captivity had blinded them to truth, experiences of God's glory were needed to open the eyes of their hearts. He would heal their inner turmoil by making Himself known to them.

This supernatural deliverance is a story of hope for any disheartened people whose minds have become as "a dark Pharaoh" to their souls. When we come to the end of our own resources and look beyond ourselves, we will discover the Healer Who still destroys the chariots of shame and the army of deceit. Once false strongholds are identified, truth can be received by visualizing the attackers drowning in the Lord's restorative waters of deliverance. In His light, the lies of darkness about God, others, and self will disappear. This transformation of the inner man continues in us until we are finally home in heaven.

The journey out of Egypt led Israel to pass over a narrow road through a great body of water, metaphorically depicting a broken person leaving a tangled web of bondage and finding freedom by being immersed and cleansed in God's sea of love. Jesus taught that we *must* enter through the narrow gate to find deliverance from the shackles of sin and yokes of slavery.

> Wide is the gate and broad is the road that leads to destruction, and many enter through it. But small is the gate and narrow the road that leads to life, and only a few find it.... *I am the gate; whoever enters through me will be saved.* (Matthew 7:13–14; John 10:9)

A Snapshot of Redemption

By reflecting on the Israelites' journey out of Egypt, I discovered a road-map to freedom for the weary and wounded. Even if some are not interested in unfolding a map, usually all will enjoy the inviting scenery depicted on its cover. In like manner, God's roadmap imparts an awesome picture right up front—the Prince of Peace. This is a snapshot of redemption.

After leaving Egypt, the Israelites encountered what appeared to be certain death. Obeying Moses, they faced their sea of terror. But God parted the waters, and a pathway of salvation was revealed: A freedom trail! The Lord's people walked between the protective walls of water; the unrighteous men of Egypt were destroyed when they tried to pass through. This is a photo of God's benevolence upon all who choose His path to liberty and life. Figuratively, this event represents the way of the cross.

Yahweh declared three separate times that He would gain glory through this event (Exodus 14:4, 17–18). Many centuries later the apostle Paul quoted, "The Scripture says to Pharaoh, 'I raised you up for this very purpose, that I might display my power in you and that my name might be proclaimed in all the earth'" (Romans 9:17).

As the covenant people followed Moses, a way was made through the sea; similarly, Christians must follow Jesus, the Way of salvation. This shows the believer who affirms God's covenant of grace by being baptized into Christ. This is a vision of glory!

The Lord invites everyone who desires healing: "Come and see what God has done, how awesome his works in man's behalf! He turned the sea into dry land, they passed through the waters on foot—come, let us rejoice in him" (Psalm 66:5–6).

Especially you who are weary and brokenhearted: give God the opportunity to show you His redemption. The natural picture is also a spiritual picture for all to behold! Pause and reflect; linger. Savor each truth. See His wondrous ways.

Picture: As the Israelites were set free from captivity, envision the Lord Almighty fighting for you.

> *The cowering prisoners will soon be set free; they will not die in their dungeon, nor will they lack bread. For I am the LORD your God, who churns up the sea so that its waves roar—the LORD Almighty is his name. (Isaiah 51:14–15)*

Picture: As Father God carried the Israelites through the mighty waters, envision that He will carry you through your pain.

> *The waters saw you, O God, the waters saw you and writhed; the very depths were convulsed....Your path led through the sea, your way through the mighty waters, though your footprints were not seen. You led your people like a flock by the hand of Moses and Aaron. (Psalm 77:16, 19–20)*

Picture: As the parting waters made Israel glad, envision God's stream of water that makes your heart glad.

> *There is a river whose streams make glad the city of God, the holy place where the Most High dwells. (46:4)*

Picture: As the waters gave Israel new life, envision the Lamb of God as your living water Whose springs replace your tears.

> *The Lamb at the center of the throne will be their shepherd; he will lead them to springs of living water. And God will wipe away every tear from their eyes. (Revelation 7:17)*

Picture: As the Israelites left slavery behind them by going through the sea, envision your burial with Christ through baptism as leaving your place of death, your "Egypt," your slavery to sin.

> *[You have] been buried with him in baptism and raised with him through your faith in the power of God, who raised him from the dead. (Colossians 2:12)*

Picture: As the water stood firm like a wall, envision Jesus standing unmovable, resolute, and steadfast for you.

He divided the sea and led them through; he made the water stand firm like a wall. (Psalm 78:13)

Picture: As God crushed the monster's head in the waters, envision Jesus destroying satan's power over you.

It was you who split open the sea by your power; you broke the heads of the monster in the waters. (74:13)

Picture: As the Israelites were baptized into Moses, envision yourself being baptized through Jesus' cross of glory.

I do not want you to be ignorant of the fact, brothers, that our forefathers were all under the cloud and that they all passed through the sea. They were all baptized into Moses in the cloud and in the sea. (1 Corinthians 10:1–2)

Picture: As the Israelites moved out of Egypt by faith, envision yourself going through the waters of baptism as your testimony of faith.

In the days of Noah while the ark was being built ... only a few people, eight in all, were saved through water, and this water symbolizes baptism that now saves you also—not the removal of dirt from the body but the pledge of a good conscience toward God. It saves you by the resurrection of Jesus Christ, who has gone into heaven and is at God's right hand—with angels, authorities and powers in submission to him. (1 Peter 3:20–22)

Picture: As the Israelites descended into the sea of death, then ascended to new life, envision your sinful man as now dead, and you are raised with Christ to a new life of glory.

We were therefore buried with him through baptism into death in order that, just as Christ was raised from the dead through the glory of the Father, we too may live a new life. (Romans 6:4)

Picture: As the Israelites walked the path to life because of the lamb's blood covering, envision that now the living way is opened to all who walk by faith through the blood and body of Jesus.

Since we have confidence to enter the Most Holy Place by the blood of Jesus, by a new and living way opened for us through the curtain, that is, his body, and since we have a great priest over the house of God, let us draw near to God with a sincere heart in full assurance of faith, having our hearts sprinkled to cleanse us from a guilty conscience and having our bodies washed with pure water. Let us hold unswervingly to the hope we profess, for he who promised is faithful. (Hebrews 10:19–23)

God will raise His staff over the flock's anxious waters and make a pathway to peace. This is good news for *all* who have struggled under burdens of sin and slavery. Like the Israelites, who found liberation from captivity and whose hearts envisioned the Promised Land, we will come to sing the song of the redeemed (Exodus 15:2 AMP).

> *The Lord is my Strength and my Song,*
> *and He has become my Salvation.*
> *He is my God, and I will praise Him,*
> *my father's God, and I will exalt Him.*

Who Are Called to War?

In all heroic hostilities, there are those who stay at home while others fight the battles. The Hebrews needed Moses, a deliverer who could understand and follow God's map and, with Aaron, confront wickedness. They were God's appointed messengers to carry His blessings to Israel.

In a family, there usually aren't many who have the maturity and preparation to be the trustees of their father's will. The family's elders normally are the ones who have oversight of the inheritance. It takes time for small sprouts to grow into fruitful trees. Consider Deborah, a prophetess and mother who took on the role of warrior and led the army of Israel to victory over Sisera, a barbaric Canaanite commander, who by cruel oppression had destroyed normal village life (Judges 4:6–9; 5:7, 24–27). The apostle to the Gentiles was a smug seedling called Saul before he became Paul, an "oak of righteousness" (Isaiah 61:3).

The devil's schemes are revealed to anointed leaders whom God has placed in authority. The degree of jurisdiction varies—not all are called to be in a position of identificational intercession like Esther or Paul. Many are summoned as parents, called to pray for their children. Others are spiritual parents who intercede for those whom they have spiritually birthed.

In the spiritual arena, all are invited to stand under the shelter of God's strength, but not all are commissioned to battle the forces of darkness. Remember: God told the Israelites to seek shelter during the seventh plague, while Moses and Aaron alone declared destruction upon Pharaoh and his followers. *Their proclamations released God's thunder against Egypt while His people rested in safety.*

~~~~~~~~~~

Children from abusive families are often robbed of rest because of a malicious influence that permeates their surroundings. In Revelation 2:18–29, Christ speaks about a satanic stronghold that had a grip on a church in the city of Thyatira. Even though this body of believers demonstrated loving works and an uncomplaining faith, they tolerated wickedness from Jezebel, a woman who spoke from an idolatrous, immoral heart.

This is an ominous parallel to the evil wife of King Ahab, who wanted to destroy God's prophet Elijah. She also was behind the murder of Naboth, in which she used two dishonest men to falsely accuse him. (See 1 Kings 21:1–16.)

The Christians in Thyatira may not have had in their midst a person with this literal name, but Jezebel clearly represented a prophetess styled after the pattern of nasty Queen Jezebel. By her teaching, she misled Christ's servants into sexual sins and idolatry. When confronted by a true prophet, she was unwilling to repent of her vile ways and viciously attacked the messenger. Like the abusive queen, this woman hid behind a smokescreen of significance while creating a powerful stronghold of control that arrogantly opposed truth and deceptively spoke what was untrue.

In *The Three Battlegrounds*, Francis Frangipane addresses this spiritual battle:

> Jezebel is fiercely independent and intensely ambitious for pre-eminence and control. It is noteworthy that the name *Jezebel*, literally translated, means "without cohabitation." This simple means she refuses "to live together" or "co-habit" with anyone. Jezebel will not dwell with anyone unless she can control and dominate the relationship. When she seems submissive or "servant-like," it is only for the sake of gaining some strategic advantage. From her heart, she yields to no one.[9]

He also explains that even if Jezebel is addressed as "she," the spirit behind her is genderless. This principality, seeking to enslave, covertly manipulates leaders through words and sexual perversity rather than overtly using physical force.

Perhaps the message of Jesus to the redeemed in Thyatira is the relevant word you need for today (Revelation 2:24–25):

> Now I say to the rest of you in Thyatira, to you who do not hold to her [Jezebel's] teaching and have not learned [the devil's] so-called deep secrets (I will not impose any other burden on you): Only hold on to what you have until I come.

This is a word of hope to all who have suffered under the control of another. The Lord doesn't burden those under oppression; He desires to lift the captive's heavy load! He assures those with fearful hearts, "Be strong, do not fear; your God will come, He will come with vengeance; with divine retribution He will come to save you" (Isaiah 35:4).

John's letter to a number of churches had messages for three distinct groups:

I write to you, dear *children*, because your sins have been forgiven on account of his name; because you have known the Father. I write to you, *fathers*, because you have known him who is from the beginning. I write to you, *young men*, because you have overcome the evil one; because you are strong, and the word of God lives in you. (1 John 2:12–14, rearranged)

Spiritually mature believers enlist in God's army because they know their Sure Defender and remember to utilize His Word. His immature lambs or bruised children need to know that Papa God *remembers, finds, adopts, restores, loves, heals, nourishes, perfects,* and *carries* them out of darkness into His light. He confirms His tender care in Isaiah 40:11: "He tends his flock like a shepherd: He gathers the lambs in his arm and carries them close to his heart; he gently leads those that have young."

Christ invites all bruised and weary lambs to come and let Him carry them on His shoulders. He'll knead their knots of agony and anxiety, and, in gentleness, He will teach His ways of restoration and bring inner peace.

A Message for the Weary

To the weary: Enjoy resting in the shelter of the Most High, under the shadow of the Almighty. Rest with this thought: Abba cares for you, and He will never forsake you (Joshua 1:5). Don't be ashamed because deep truths may be overwhelming when you're in depression. Even warriors need time to be refreshed. When battle-weary, take time out to rest, relax, recharge, and be restored. In the midst of conflict, a cup of cold water is sometimes better than a wealth of words (2 Samuel 23:15; Matthew 10:42).

If you know you struggle with following a map, consider skipping over the next chapter about warfare for now. If tears and groans are what you can muster, know that they are significant to the Lord, and He will fight for you as your Advocate. People in despair need another to contend for them; not everyone is in a place to receive or understand lessons of war. If this isn't the season for you to learn about battle strategies and principles for breakthrough, it may be the time to sit on the receiving end of the ministry. God will provide for you through someone else. God has His timetable (Ecclesiastes 3:1–4, 7–8):

> There is a time for everything,
>   and a season for every activity under heaven:
>
> a time to be born and a time to die,
>   a time to plant and a time to uproot,
>
> a time to kill and a time to heal,
>   a time to tear down and a time to build,

a time to weep and a time to laugh,
  a time to mourn and a time to dance ...

a time to tear and a time to mend,
  a time to be silent and a time to speak,

a time to love and a time to hate,
  a time for war and a time for peace.

Chapter 11

Precepts from History

I will walk about in freedom, for I have sought out your precepts.
(Psalm 119:45)

The precepts of the LORD are right, giving joy to the heart.
The commands of the LORD are radiant, giving light to the eyes. (19:8)

When you hear of wars and rumors of wars, do not be alarmed.
Such things must happen, but the end is still to come. (Mark 13:7)

For those struggling with a cruel oppressor and for those who minister care to them, the story of the Exodus provides a picture of hope, love, salvation, deliverance, and heaven! God's triumph over tyranny against seemingly impossible obstacles demonstrates His wondrous restoration. By looking back at His marvelous ways, our vision for the future can become brighter and clearer.

Even when biblical characters provide tragic examples of disobedience, their struggles can serve as reminders and warnings. We receive comfort from the emphasis on God's faithfulness to His covenant community in spite of our faithlessness. Christ *will* provide the power to endure until the way out is clear (1 Corinthians 10:13).

~~~~~~~~~~

Our focus up to this point has been mainly from the perspective of the captives—their conditions, emotions, and activities before, during, and after the plagues. Now we will change direction, focusing on strategies useful in spiritual conflict, the Lord's wartime objectives for overcoming dark forces. The tactics employed against Egyptian corruption have counterparts in combating the schemes of darkness we face today!

Because the characters and events of the Exodus account figuratively represent life issues, it's helpful to recall their typological *analogies*. Again, envision Moses as Jesus Christ, the Deliverer; Aaron as Christ's ambassador; Pharaoh as satan; Egypt as sin and the world system; and Egyptian slavery as worldly bondage.

Keeping those in mind, I'll compare the historical factors of warfare Moses employed in liberating Israel to factors of warfare Jesus demonstrated in liberating His redeemed. The following study will not be an atlas on spiritual warfare; the scope will be limited to strategies that concern (1) shattering bitter imprisonment and (2) possessing Christ's rich legacy. Simply put: *breaking the leash of hopelessness and imparting the Lord's garland as a necklace of hope.*

The following points provide significant background information to consider before examining the keys to breakthrough.

The Battle Against Evil

Any battle initiated by God is just, and delivers peace:
His heart is to protect and to restore freedom.

God's plan from the beginning was serenity and beauty. He placed man in a beautiful garden with His Tree of Life. Every need was met, for Adam and Eve had it all—provision, dignity, intimacy, freedom, unconditional love. They lost it when they chose to defy God and eat forbidden fruit from the tree of knowledge of good and evil.

An internal war in man began. Blame, shame, and pain became a part of everyday life. Man was cursed: Death lurked at Adam and Eve's front door because they'd chosen to entertain and embrace deception. They lost the garden blessings and inherited murder and enmity. Wars of greed followed.

It was impossible for man to break free from captivity; God alone had power to dismantle the stranglehold of evil. His heart for restoration was remarkably portrayed from the beginning, providing sacrifices as burnt offerings to cover their sins and save them from death. But during the time of the Exodus, the Israelites, God's chosen people, were bound to Pharaoh and slavery. Because of their besetting sins and family iniquities, they had been robbed of what man was originally given.

My own back yard provided a graphic example of this principle. Several years ago, after an extremely dry summer, my Minnesota garden was invaded by grasshoppers and other insects. I felt angry and sad when I noticed that so many plants had been voraciously devoured, leaving bedraggled leaves or nothing at all. When my acorn squash plants were destroyed at the roots, Tom and I were robbed of their fruit. I felt overwhelmed by the invasion, so I let winter take its course. By spring, heavy rains had renewed my garden, and green life emerged in full bounty. Beauty had been restored.

In the Apocalypse, locusts are presented as venomous hordes given the power to inflict pain and malice (Revelation 9:1–11). This is something similar to what the Israelites had experienced, for instead of being like a garden of provision and prosperity, Egypt had become like a field of thorns and suffering for them. After generations and centuries of bondage and destruction, they were like my hopeless, locust-infested plants. The people needed the Lord to come as their Restorer and Warrior.

> The LORD will march out like a mighty man, like a warrior he will stir up his zeal; with a shout he will raise the battle cry and will triumph over his enemies. (Isaiah 42:13)

Almighty God initiated the confrontation against Pharaoh; Moses repeatedly was given His exact course to follow. When he and Aaron obeyed, the Lord broke through the gates of hell. Every judgment on Pharaoh was a turn in the right direction; the tenth plague would result in the critical collapse of his will.

When the Israelites were prepared to follow Moses out of Egypt, not one was left out, not one was sick! God was like an unstoppable train: His power started the engine, the people stepped aboard. Moses and Aaron commandeered the locomotive, and the cars of deliverance moved everyone forward on the tracks of abundance.

> The threshing floors shall be full of wheat, and the vats shall overflow with new wine and oil. So I will restore to you the years that the swarming locust has eaten. (Joel 2:24–25 NKJV)

God's triumphal march in Israel's history foreshadows the day when Jesus will lead all who have been redeemed from slavery to sin into heaven. "This is why [God] says: 'When he ascended on high, he led captives in his train and gave gifts to men'" (Ephesians 4:8, from Psalm 68:18).

When we, like Paul, experience the internal war between our old sinful nature and our new nature in Christ (see Romans 7), we realize that without Him we are wretched, that the only hope for anyone is the Lord Jesus. Sometimes I see my mind as a "controlling Pharaoh" that contends against the peace in my heart. I feel confused when fearful thoughts bounce around in my head and feel like devouring locusts. I know I need to stay rooted and grounded with Jesus, my Tree of Life. Remember:

> Since we have a great high priest who has gone through the heavens, Jesus the Son of God, let us hold firmly to the faith we profess. For we do not have a high priest who is unable to sympathize with our weaknesses, but we have one who has been tempted in every way, just as we are—yet was without sin. Let us then approach the throne of grace with confidence, so that we may receive mercy and find grace to help us in our time of need. (Hebrews 4:14–16)

The Engagement Mission

Every engagement has a mission or purpose.
God is a righteous judge Who seeks peace
and liberty for His vulnerable ones.

The Lord's mission statement is, "Defend the cause of the weak and fatherless; maintain the rights of the poor and oppressed. Rescue the weak and needy; deliver them from the hand of the wicked" (Psalm 82:3–4). He had heard the groaning of His covenant people. Isaiah 5:7 later says, "He looked for justice, but saw bloodshed; for righteousness, but heard cries of distress." Because He hates tyranny, He resolved to deliver them from slavery—to break their connections to Pharaoh and to bring them out from beneath domination. His target: To restore them to the Promised Land. Isaiah (58:6, 9–12) reveals God's method for the rebuilding of lives:

> Is not this the kind of fasting I have chosen: to loose the chains of injustice and untie the cords of the yoke, to set the oppressed free and break every yoke? ... If you do away with the yoke of oppression, with the pointing finger and malicious talk, and if you spend yourselves in behalf of the hungry and satisfy the needs of the oppressed, then your light will rise in the darkness, and your night will become like the noonday.... You will be like a well-watered garden, like a spring whose waters never fail. Your people will rebuild the ancient ruins and will raise up the age-old foundations; you will be called Repairer of Broken Walls, Restorer of Streets with Dwellings.

These are the biblical words for *"restore"*: *chayah,* "to make alive"; *shub,* "to return what was stolen"; *shalam,* "to make whole or complete"; and *katartizō* (Greek), "to make thoroughly right."[10] When I put the meanings together, I read this:

> Everyone who puts their trust in Jesus Christ, the Redeemer, will be made alive, complete, and thoroughly in right standing. All that has been stolen from the redeemed will be restored. Father God's mission will be accomplished!

The Lord promises to restore by His mercy: "The God of all grace, who called you to his eternal glory in Christ, after you have suffered a little while, will himself restore you and make you strong, firm and steadfast" (1 Peter 5:10). God's mission for the church: To loose burdensome chains, to break every binding shackle, to rebuild the ancient ruins, to raise up the age-old foundations, to repair broken walls, and to restore dwellings. The bride of Christ will be presented to Him without spot or wrinkle. He will rebuild the past wreckage inside His church and the devastations within individual souls. He freely shares His immeasurable riches with His beloved bride, caring for His church like a loving husband for his cherished wife:

Christ loved the church and gave himself up for her to make her holy, cleansing her by the washing with water through the word, and to present her to himself as a radiant church without stain or wrinkle or any other blemish, but holy and blameless. (Ephesians 5:25–27)

The Lord *continues* to hear our brokenhearted moans, but He also desires intimacy. The Bridegroom wonders if He will find a faithful response from His bride! "Will not God bring about justice for his chosen ones, who cry out to him day and night? Will he keep putting them off? I tell you, he will see that they get justice, and quickly. However, when the Son of Man comes, will he find faith on the earth? (Luke 18:7–8).

During dark days of oppression and pain, *we obtain victory by trusting that the God Who loves us will vindicate and bring relief.* These are comforting words of truth for all who need encouragement:

- He will make your righteousness shine like the dawn, the justice of your cause like the noonday sun. Be still before the LORD and wait patiently for him; do not fret when men succeed in their ways, when they carry out their wicked schemes. (Psalm 37:6–7)

- The LORD works righteousness and justice for all the oppressed. He made known his ways to Moses, his deeds to the people of Israel. (103:6–7)

- He will be a spirit of justice to him who sits in judgment, a source of strength to those who turn back the battle at the gate. (Isaiah 28:6)

- I [the Lord] will betroth you to me forever; I will betroth you in righteousness and justice, in love and compassion. (Hosea 2:19)

Cries of pain *do* reach His heart, and He *will* fight for justice and peace:

The LORD Almighty is with us; the God of Jacob is our fortress. Come and see the works of the LORD....He makes wars cease to the ends of the earth; he breaks the bow and shatters the spear, he burns the shields with fire. (Psalm 46:7–9)

Jesus Christ told the early believers that He must wait in heaven "until the time for the complete restoration of all that God spoke by the mouth of all His holy prophets for ages past [from the most ancient time in the memory of man]. Thus Moses said to the forefathers, 'The Lord God will raise up for you a Prophet from among your brethren as [He raised up] me; Him you shall listen to and understand by hearing and *heed in all things whatever He tells you'*" (Acts 3:21–22 AMP).

The Commander in Chief

A man does not become commissioned into an army
unless he knows the name of his commander in chief.

Moses needed to know God's name before the conflict that would soon be engaging him. When Moses was being commissioned to return to Egypt, he asked God for His name to proclaim for encountering Pharaoh and for assuring his dispirited people. God replied, *"I am who I am. This is what you are to say … I AM has sent me to you"* (Exodus 3:14). Israel needed *"I AM WHO I AM,"* the unchanging, ever-present God of all eternity, to break their shackles and to destroy the powers keeping them in slavery.

Like Moses, John was assured by God when he was a prisoner of the Romans on the Isle of Patmos. Jesus Christ said to him, "I am the Alpha and the Omega, the Beginning and the End, He Who is and Who was and Who is to come, the Almighty" (Revelation 1:8 AMP).

King David was a warrior, but he knew he was not commander in chief over the troops. First he asked, *"Who is this King of glory?"* Then he declared, *"The LORD strong and mighty, the LORD mighty in battle"* (Psalm 24:8). David knew that when he cried out to God for help, his Deliverer would shoot His arrows and scatter the enemy with powerful bolts of spiritual lightning (18:14). David knew by maintaining focus on his Commander that together they could advance against a troop and scale the wall of any fortress or stronghold (v. 29).

> The Commander of the armies of heaven is here among us. He, the God of Jacob, has come to rescue us. Come, see the glorious things that our God does. (46:7–8 TLB)

When the Pharisees incited the Jews to stone Jesus, He had proclaimed His lordship: "I tell you the truth … before Abraham was born, *I am!"* (John 8:58). There is only one Living God—past, present, future. Jesus, though He lived on earth almost two thousand years after Abraham, was, as the second person of the Trinity, the "Lord of the Hosts" Who led the Israelites out of Egypt. Jesus, the Bondage Breaker, warred against the bondage maker! He is the Prince of Peace Who destroyed the power of Pharaoh and Pharisee.

Jesus consoled His disciples: "Peace I leave with you; my peace I give you" (14:27). He comforted and released the woman at the well from slavery to sin when He revealed to her that He is the Living Water: "Everyone who drinks this [well] water will be thirsty again, but whoever drinks the water I give him will never thirst. Indeed, the water I give him will become in him a spring of water welling up to eternal life" (4:13–14).

Throughout His ministry Jesus announced His eternal identity (names from AMP):

- I am the God of Abraham. (Matthew 22:32)
- I am the Christ. (24:5)
- I am the Son of God. (27:43)
- I am the Bread of Life. (John 6:35)
- I am the Light of the World. (8:12)
- I am the Door for the Sheep. (10:7)
- I am the Good Shepherd. (10:11)
- I am God's Son (10:36)
- I am the Resurrection and the Life. (11:25)
- I am the Way and the Truth and the Life. (14:6)
- I am the True Vine, and My Father is the Vinedresser. (15:1)
- I am a King. (18:37)
- I am the Alpha and the Omega. (Revelation 1:8)
- I am the Ever-Living One. (1:18)
- I am the Root and Offspring of David; the Brilliant Morning Star. (22:16)

Those who knew Jesus testified to His lordship. John the Baptist saw Him and proclaimed, "Look, the Lamb of God who takes away the sin of the world!" (John 1:29, 36). Paul cited the prophet Isaiah when he proclaimed, "The deliverer will come from Zion; he will turn godlessness away from Jacob. And this is my covenant with them when I take away their sins" (Romans 11:26–27). John declared, "The Word became flesh and made his dwelling among us. We have seen his glory, the glory of the One and Only, who came from the Father, full of grace and truth" (John 1:14). Peter proclaimed, "Jesus Christ heals you" to the paralytic (Acts 9:34). After the Crucifixion, Mary Magdalene and other women told the disciples that they had found His tomb empty and that the risen Christ had appeared to them (Luke 24:9). Matthew reported, "When Jesus ... saw a large crowd, he had compassion on them and healed their sick" (Matthew 14:14). The author of Hebrews recounted that Jesus, a priest forever after the order of Melchizedek, is "king of righteousness" and "king of peace" (7:1–2).

Obviously man has a choice: believe truth or believe deception. Either Jesus was a liar, or He spoke the truth.

One day, Jesus Christ, as Commander in Chief of His army, will return to earth to bring ultimate justice to His people. At that time, satan's power to deceive will be crushed. Jesus will declare a reign of peace and rule over the earth with impartial love.

> I saw heaven standing open and there before me was a white horse,
>> whose rider is called Faithful and True.
> With justice he judges and makes war ...
> He is dressed in a robe dipped in blood, and his name is the Word of God.

The armies of heaven were following him, riding on white horses
  and dressed in fine linen, white and clean.
Out of his mouth comes a sharp sword
  with which to strike down the nations.
He will rule them with an iron scepter.
He treads the winepress of the fury of the wrath of God Almighty.
On his robe and on his thigh he has this name written:
  KING OF KINGS AND LORD OF LORDS. (Revelation 19:11, 13–16)

The Victory Declarations

Most wars begin with a declaration of intent.
All of God's battles begin with triumphal proclamations!

As we have seen, the Lord marches out in might. Like a warrior He will stir up His zeal in us to proclaim *His will* here on Earth. With a triumphal shout, God's warriors will raise the battle cry that will defeat His enemies. When the cries for liberation reach the heavens, God blasts His shophar, and declarations for victory are proclaimed on earth. Moses, God's ambassador to Pharaoh, sounded God's victory cry to free His covenant people from slavery.

Throughout the Bible many declarations of victory are made by God's people.

Shouts of joy and victory
resound in the tents of the righteous:
"The LORD's right hand has done mighty things!
The LORD's right hand is lifted high; the LORD's right
hand has done mighty things!" (Psalm 118:15–16)

As for me, I will declare this forever;
I will sing praise to the God of Jacob.
I will cut off the horns of all the wicked,
but the horns of the righteous will be lifted up. (75:9–10)

Raise the war cry, you nations, and be shattered!
Listen, all you distant lands.
Prepare for battle, and be shattered!
Prepare for battle, and be shattered! (Isaiah 8:9)

Devise your strategy, but it will be thwarted;
propose your plan, but it will not stand,
for God is with us. (8:10)

We noted earlier that *the Son of God is God's Trumpet of War!* Like the elders of Israel, Christ's announcement of freedom to captives in the synagogues was a war cry against religious leaders stripping God's blessings from the people (Matthew 23:13, 15, 27 RSV).

> Woe to you, scribes and Pharisees, hypocrites! because you shut the kingdom of heaven against men; for you neither enter yourselves, nor allow those who would enter to go in.

> Woe to you, scribes and Pharisees, hypocrites! for you traverse sea and land to make a single proselyte, and when he becomes a proselyte, you make him twice as much a child of hell as yourselves.

> Woe to you, scribes and Pharisees, hypocrites! for you are like whitewashed tombs, which outwardly appear beautiful, but within they are full of dead men's bones and all uncleanness.

This was the time for the Lord to deliver His people from slavery caused by legalism and hypocrisy. Early in His ministry, Jesus entered the temple and read from the scroll of Isaiah that the Spirit of the Lord was upon Him. He announced restoration to the poor, the prisoner, the blind, and the oppressed. A declaration of freedom to people bound in shackles of death—then *and* now!

The Freedom Fighters

God's warriors contend for the freedom of others
who are enslaved by tyranny and heavy burdens.

God empowers and trains His soldiers. David said, "Praise be to the LORD my Rock, who trains my hands for war, my fingers for battle" (Psalm 144:1). While still a shepherd, David was called to be a freedom fighter. It was spoken of him: "I have seen a son of Jesse of Bethlehem who knows how to play the harp. He is a brave man and a warrior. He speaks well and is a fine-looking man. And the LORD is with him" (1 Samuel 16:18).

Moses also had the attributes of a warrior; God commissioned him as His freedom fighter! The Lord found a man of faith whose life was surrendered to Him. Moses believed that God would execute victory by His Word, by His Spirit, and by signs and wonders.

There would be a day when Israel would no longer feel like worms under Egyptian feet—their Redeemer would help them. Fearful worms transformed into fearless warriors! "See, I will make you into a threshing sledge, new and sharp, with many teeth. You will thresh the mountains and crush them, and reduce the hills to chaff" (Isaiah 41:15). Scripture declares:

In that coming day, no weapon turned against you will succeed. And everyone who tells lies in court will be brought to justice. *These benefits are enjoyed by the servants of the LORD; their vindication will come from me.* I, the LORD, have spoken! You also will command the nations, and they will come running to obey, because I, the LORD your God, the Holy One of Israel, have made you glorious. (Isaiah 54:17; 55:5 NLT)

~~~~~~~~~

Today, who are the soldiers, no longer like fragile seedlings but like strong oaks, called to take back the ground that a "Pharaoh" has claimed?

We, the priests of God, will learn and mature when Jesus is on our throne. Christians can grow in the Lord by resting beside their wonderful High Priest, soaking up the Word, filled with the presence of His Spirit. With Paul, we "press on toward the goal to win the prize for which God has called me heavenward in Christ Jesus" (Philippians 3:14). Note: this doesn't always mean striving! The Lamb of God is the Redeemer Who lifts heavy shackles. When He chooses, the Deliverer sends His messengers to address roadblocks—the priests of God co-labor with Christ so that others will no longer remain under a burdensome load. Mature believers are able to walk alongside the younger ones.

Paul saw the importance of faith, love, and hope as the necessary attributes of maturity: "We continually remember before our God and Father your work produced by faith, your labor prompted by love, and your endurance inspired by hope in our Lord Jesus Christ" (1 Thessalonians 1:3).

To all warriors the Lord implores, "Be strong and courageous. Do not be terrified; do not be discouraged, for the LORD your God will be with you wherever you go" (Joshua 1:9). Jesus Christ is the armor for God's army—their Belt of Truth, their Breastplate of Righteousness, their Covering of Peace, their Shield of Faith, their Helmet of Salvation, and their Sword of the Spirit (Ephesians 6:13–17). He promised His disciples, "I have given you authority to trample on snakes and scorpions and to overcome all the power of the enemy" (Luke 10:19).

God's troops, living the crucified life and filled with His Spirit, are able to break unjust chains by declaring His word of truth, by speaking in His name, and by knowing that their power is through His shed blood: "They overcame him (satan) by the blood of the Lamb and by the word of their testimony; they did not love their lives so much as to shrink from death" (Revelation 12:11). Spirit-led intercession *does* lead to breakthroughs! "Pray in the Spirit on all occasions with all kinds of prayers and requests. With this in mind, be alert and always keep on praying for all the saints" (Ephesians 6:18).

The Ancient Adversary

Wars of woe originate with satan, the ancient serpent,
who desires to conquer what doesn't belong to him.

The devil, satan, ancient serpent, great dragon, strongman, slanderer, accuser, tempter, destroyer, deceiver, the lawless one, prince of demons—different names for the same wicked entity, the same fallen archangel. *Each* name is the epitome of evil. God's enemy uses demons as his troops of terror, the seductive, magical powers behind sorcery. Other unexplainable means that are also demonically empowered are divination, enchantment, incantation, necromancy, occult magic, spells, voodoo, and witchcraft.

The original cosmic conflict began when God threw a rebellious, mighty angel out of His dwelling place:

> There was war in heaven.... The great dragon was hurled down—that ancient serpent called the devil, or satan, who leads the whole world astray. He was hurled to the earth, and his angels with him. (Revelation 12:7, 9)

> Through your widespread trade you were filled with violence, and you sinned. So I [the Lord] drove you in disgrace from the mount of God, and I expelled you, O guardian cherub, from among the fiery stones. (Ezekiel 28:16)

The former guardian archangel called Lucifer rebelled against God and became a destroyer who incited depraved humans to be like him. When the deceiver enticed Adam and Eve to reject God's truth, he took the form of a serpent. The emblem of a coiled cobra on the front of Pharaoh's headdress was indicative of where that man received his power; "that ancient serpent called the devil" was the force behind the Egyptian warrior-ruler. Satan provoked him to oppose Moses through sorcery, and his wizards were practitioners of dark magic and professors of the arts of witchcraft.[11]

Jannes and Jambres, court magicians, withstood Moses and Aaron by demonically reproducing God's first two works. Paul wrote to Timothy about these two men as an example of those with depraved minds who oppose truth (2 Timothy 3:8–9). Exodus 8:6–7 says Egyptian sorcerers were able to bring up frogs from the Nile, just as Moses and Aaron had, but they could not create life out of dust. Only God, the Creator, could execute this third woe when Moses struck the ground with the rod and dust became gnats.

When Moses experienced oppressive opposition, when everything seemed to get worse rather than better, he brought his doubts to God. Sometimes I've felt like Moses and wondered why my life seemed to become more painful *after* asking my Redeemer for help!

The prophet Amos wrote about troubles that "will be as though a man fled from a lion only to meet a bear, as though he entered his house and rested his hand on the wall only to have a snake bite him" (Amos 5:19).

Isaiah said that terror becomes a pit and the pit becomes a snare (Isaiah 24:17). Mockers taunt, *"Where is your God?"* (Psalm 42:3).

Now I have a clearer realization of this truth: even though the serpent's power was destroyed through the cross of Christ, satan retains the power to deceive and destroy until Jesus returns. He works like the decapitated head of a deadly viper, which flails around furiously though no longer attached to its body, its jaws flying open and snapping shut, still able to inject venom into its victim with lethal fangs. The devil is the master of lies and duplicity (John 8:44). His vile device of terror is oppression by deceit and violence. He fires words intended to be like blades of death at the brokenhearted, whispering, *Give up—there's absolutely no hope for you. You are forsaken, alone forever.*

As the serpent symbolizes deception, it is helpful to expose the ways of darkness by considering serpentine ways. Snakes have forked tongues; some are capable of injecting neuro-toxic poison that immobilizes their prey, which may break down its tissues and causes its organs to fail. Since there is no simple guideline by which to identify every poisonous snake, wisdom says that when in any doubt, leave snakes alone. Know this as well: reflex bites are as dangerous as bites from live snakes. An apparently dead serpent may be only injured, stunned, or playing dead.[12]

The devil, "that ancient serpent," is a forked-tongued fabricator who desires to paralyze his victims with venom of terror. Christ destroyed his head at the cross, but the liar is still capable of opening his mouth to speak poisonous words and frighten his targets like a hissing snake. Remember reflex bites? He's still biting, lividly and blindly seeking to overthrow God's kingdom before Jesus comes back to consummate His victory.

Regarding those who call truth falsehood and falsehood truth, the Bible warns,

> Even from birth the wicked go astray; from the womb they are wayward and speak lies. Their venom is like the venom of a snake, like that of a cobra that has stopped its ears, that will not heed the tune of the charmer, however skillful the enchanter may be. (Psalm 58:3–5)

Jesus called the Pharisees "a brood of vipers" after they claimed He cast out demons by the power of Beelzebub, prince of demons. At the same time He said of satan: "How can anyone enter a strong man's house and carry off his possessions unless he first ties up the strong man? Then he can rob his house" (Matthew 12:29). The devil, bound by Christ's death and resurrection, flees when he is resisted by truth:

> Be self-controlled and alert. Your enemy the devil prowls around like a roaring lion looking for someone to devour. Resist him, standing firm in the faith, because you know that your brothers throughout the world are undergoing the same kind of sufferings. (1 Peter 5:8–9)

Remember to guard your heart. There are many "Pharisees" today who bully another through intimidation, coercion, pressure, or manipulation. This is rebellion. This is witchcraft (see 1 Samuel 15:23).

The Lethal Weapon

The dream of every warrior is to possess a weapon
that instantly strikes a fatal blow to the enemy.

Right after the fall of man, God provided His people with the ultimate weapon, the Deliverer Who would destroy the serpent. It is written: "I will put enmity between you [the devil] and the woman, and between your offspring and her Offspring; He will bruise and tread your head underfoot, and you will lie in wait and bruise His heel" (Genesis 3:15 AMP). Even though the deceiver was allowed to hinder the walk of God's people as he struck Jesus' heel, his head was crushed at Calvary. One clearly stated purpose for Jesus coming to earth was to bind satan, the strong man, and set free all enslaved by this fallen angel.

The Lord knew His vulnerable lambs in Egypt had been oppressed and deceived; they needed the yokes of darkness and deceit removed from their necks. As their protector, He struck out against those who had sought to destroy them, just as He does today when the body of Christ cries out to Him for deliverance:

> The LORD Almighty will lash them [your tyrants] with a whip, as when he struck down Midian.... He will raise his staff over the waters [and make a highway], as he did in Egypt. The burden [of tyranny] will be lifted from your shoulders, their yoke from your neck; the yoke [of injustice] will be broken. (Isaiah 10:26–27)

However, at least one question remains: if Israel's deliverance was accomplished when the serpents of sorcery were swallowed, why couldn't they have simply walked out of Egypt? Again, part of the answer is that while God had won the war, He used the plagues to destroy the enemy's armor, armaments, yokes, gates, structures, and supply lines. According to His plan and foreknowledge, Israel's redemption unfolded through the judgments fired like missiles of woe upon the gods of Egypt. Through this chain of events, a powerful statement of vindication was declared to God's seen and unseen enemies.

~~~~~~~~~~

In warfare, the mind of man becomes a battlefield. Painful and traumatic experiences open gates for deception, coming as thoughts that will form strongholds. *Abuse does not have the power to destroy a person, but the lies associated with the events do.* If thoughts are not surrendered to Jesus, they can become mind destroyers.

> Though we live in the world, we do not wage war as the world does. The weapons we fight with are not the weapons of the world. On the contrary, they have divine power to demolish strongholds. We demolish arguments and every pretension that sets itself up against the knowledge of God, and we take captive every thought to make it obedient to Christ. (2 Corinthians 10:3–5)

When Jesus was led by the Spirit into the wilderness to be tempted by satan, He used Scripture as His weapon against the words of the deceiver, and every time the devil fired a salvo of deception, Jesus shot back an arrow. *"Wisdom* is better than weapons of war" (Ecclesiastes 9:18). When the devil tempted a famished Jesus to turn stones into bread, He answered, *"It is written:* 'Man does not live on bread alone'" (Luke 4:4). Why did He repeatedly say "It is written"? Because there is no difference between God's character and God's Word! *If He says it, we can believe it.*

> The word of God is living and active. Sharper than any double-edged sword, it penetrates even to dividing soul and spirit, joints and marrow; it judges the thoughts and attitudes of the heart. Nothing in all creation is hidden from God's sight. Everything is uncovered and laid bare before the eyes of Him to whom we must give account. (Hebrews 4:12–13)

We can agree with the devil's lies and speak his words of death, or we can agree with God's truth and speak His words of life. The tongue has the power of life and death, and those who love it will eat its fruit (Proverbs 18:21).

> Resist the devil, and he will flee from you. Come near to God and he will come near to you. Wash your hands, you sinners, and purify your hearts, you double-minded. Grieve, mourn and wail. Change your laughter to mourning and your joy to gloom. Humble yourselves before the Lord, and he will lift you up. (James 4:7–10)

In God's appointed time, the power of satan to deceive will come to an end, as John's vision of the future reveals: "The devil, who deceived them [Gods people], was thrown into the lake of burning sulfur, where the beast and the false prophet had been thrown. They will be tormented day and night for ever and ever" (Revelation 20:10). After the Lord's kingdom is fully established on earth, never again will satan, working through deceived sinners and destructive demons, battle against what God has been building through wise saints and ministering spirits. Whether internal or external, *war will be no more!*

And he will be called Wonderful Counselor,
Mighty God, Everlasting Father, Prince of Peace.
Of the increase of his government and peace there will be no end.
He will reign on David's throne and over his kingdom,
establishing and upholding it with justice and righteousness
from that time on and forever.
The zeal of the LORD Almighty will accomplish this. (Isaiah 9:6–7)

Chapter 12

Keys to Breakthrough

They blessed Rebekah and said to her,
"Our sister, may you increase to thousands upon thousands;
may your offspring possess the gates of their enemies." (Genesis 24:60)

Enter into His gates with thanksgiving... and into His courts with praise!
Be thankful and say so to Him, bless and affectionately praise His name!
(Psalm 100:4 AMP)

One who breaks open the way will go up before them;
they will break through the gate and go out. Their king will pass
through before them, the LORD at their head. (Micah 2:13)

"I tell you the truth, I am the gate for the sheep....
Whoever enters through me will be saved.
He will come in and go out, and find pasture" (John 10:7, 9).

When I was walking through my stormy season, the Lord imparted hope to me through His Word:

I will go before you and will level the mountains; I will break down gates of bronze and cut through bars of iron. I will give you the treasures of darkness, riches stored in secret places, so that you may know that I am the LORD, the God of Israel, who summons you by name. (Isaiah 45:2–3)

I didn't understand exactly what the treasures of darkness were for me, but I thanked God for all the blessings coming from His heart. His promises were like a fresh wind blowing upon my soul. Clouds of oppression lifted as I would sense the Lord leveling my overwhelming mountains and rough places.

Looking back, the most precious treasure was my sweet fellowship with Him while in the crucible of affliction. I now have a deeper love for God, clearer understanding of Him and His precepts, and insights that have been helpful as I pray for others.

One day as I was giving pastoral care to a woman struggling with sexual addictions, I envisioned her drowning in a wild river. She would try to keep her head above water, but undercurrents would pull her down. The picture I saw was similar to what David said in one of his psalms: "The cords of death entangled me; the torrents of destruction overwhelmed me" (18:4). I felt helpless as a helper and asked God for further direction.

Then I remembered spiritual warfare tools that had brought break-throughs for my family and me, especially from Exodus. By the end of our prayer time, she was able to see herself floating with Jesus, enjoying peaceful waters and warm sunshine. The Wonderful Counselor had imparted a realization into her heart that God had not forgotten her. She was receiving from *Yahweh-Shammah*, "The LORD [Who] is There" (Ezekiel 48:35).

By His mighty hand, the heavy burden was lifted from the shoulders of Israel, and He still lifts anchors of affliction today: *"My enemies will turn back when I call for help. By this I will know that God is for me"* (Psalm 56:9). Long ago the Spirit of God gave a redemptive vision and pertinent prophecy for those who feel chained to pain.

> O my people who live in Zion, do not be afraid of the Assyrians, who beat you with a rod and lift up a club against you, as Egypt did. Very soon my anger against you will end and my wrath will be directed to their destruction. (Isaiah 10:24–25)

Who Values Keys?

While an adult usually appreciates his keys for what they open or start, a child is intrigued with their shapes and colors and the noise they make when they are rattled. God has given His church priceless keys to kingdom blessings, but many in the body of Christ childishly overlook the significance of His keys to breakthrough.

In the natural world, a key is usually not appreciated until it has been lost or broken and the person is prevented from unlocking a door or reaching a desired destination. Many times a misplaced key has been a source of great distress for me. So quickly I could change into a frantic, out-of-control woman over a tiny piece of missing metal.

During a vacation in Hawaii, we had a lost-key incident with the potential for serious consequences. Tom and I had joined my parents on Maui to celebrate their fiftieth wedding anniversary, and one sunny morning we took off in a rented car for a drive across the island to see a remote area with seven waterfalls. The trip was somewhat harrowing in that only one narrow road wound into the park, wide enough in most spots for just one vehicle. After exploring miles of exquisite scenery and tropical beauty, we discovered another road onto a peninsula called Key Point.

To our delight, we found a park where we could stop to eat lunch and stretch our legs. A path down to the ocean enabled us to dip our toes in the refreshing water and find sea treasures. The crashing waves against the rocks were spellbinding! We didn't want to leave until a sudden storm began to rain on our picnic. We scrambled like deer as we hiked back to the car.

The three of us, slower than Tom, expected that he'd have the car running and ready to go. Instead of being inside, though, he stood looking dumbfounded. In one desperate moment, we all realized that somewhere along the path or in the Pacific the key had accidentally fallen out of Tom's bathing suit pocket. He felt terrible. I was feeling *dread.*

In the soaking rain, we retraced our steps to no avail. Because the area was so remote, there were no public phones and no other people nearby to give us assistance. Desperate, we asked God to *please* find the key for us. I remember asking Him for mercy, for I was deeply concerned about my parents becoming ill from the chilly downpour. Already feeling sick inside, I labored to wear a mask of courage.

When I returned to the heavy foliage along the trail to search for the key, amazingly, I felt the Lord's unseen hand guiding me to look under a small leaf beside the pathway. I found it! Hootin' and hollerin', I shouted the good news like a cheerleader whose underdog team had just won a state title. Back at the car, we all took a moment to thank God for His faithfulness.

Priceless Keys to God's Bounty

I also erupted with delight when the Lord revealed to me spiritual keys, which open doors to His kingdom blessings! Once again, the Exodus narrative of Moses' encounters with Pharaoh and the ten plagues contains priceless keys to that treasure chest. Its pertinent wisdom about unjust yokes and strongholds is essential for passing through God's gate of favor.

The way God delivered the Israelites from pain is a pathway to freedom for anyone struggling under oppression. He could have whisked His people out of Egypt on the wings of angels, but He had a more perfect way: *He desired them to be transformed by intimacy.* He wants His lambs to know Him, to fellowship with Him, and to be trained in His ways.

Before the Israelites walked through God's gate to freedom, He sent Moses and Aaron to co-labor in lifting yokes of slavery, breaking strongholds of darkness, shutting gates to Egypt, and destroying obstacles and armaments of deception. Pharaoh's fortifications had kept Israel enslaved to evil.

Moses, as one like God with the breaker anointing upon him, destroyed depravity's vice-grip over his people. The rod of God destroyed the staffs of the magicians and broke the power of the sorcerers. The account doesn't record how many staffs were broken when the curse was reversed, but there might have been ten. Since *every plague was against all the gods of Egypt,* each would represent a cluster of demonic strongmen—the invisible, ruling spirits over Egyptian life and property (Exodus 12:12).

Moses and the covenant people were set free *positionally* when the rod consumed all the staffs like a bolder crushing every serpent's head. No contest: the Lord was the victor. Note, though, that the people did not immediately experience their *actual* or *situational* freedom. Because of the Lord's specific purposes, they had to choose patience and trust, believing He would be faithful to finish what He had begun on their behalf.

Paul wrote, "I want to know Christ and the power of his resurrection and the fellowship of sharing in his sufferings, becoming like him in his death" (Philippians 3:10). God is delighted when leaders realize by revelation the full impact of Christ's victory over satan and all demonic underlings through His death on the cross. Like Moses, pastors are transformed from fearful shepherds to faithful guides when they embrace the Cross. The devil's head *was* destroyed, and hell's hold over death *was* defeated. However, we must remember that the Lord still has purposes to carry out, and we must endure evil's continuing presence until Jesus returns to enact its ultimate vanquishing.

The Way Out of Captivity

After God triumphed over Pharaoh, who represented the serpent's head, He directed Moses to use His rod to destroy the disengaged serpent's tail, an assignment to be handled over a period of time, since the deceiver always spins numerous tall tales. Israel's deliverance was a multi-step process against evil's tails of pretense. The sorcerers, with their web of lies, were determined to keep the Hebrews bound to slavery.

Again, though the people were at first set positionally free, there was still a salvation that had to be worked out experientially. This is usually true in warfare. For example, envision a nation engaged in a war in which the enemy plants minefields, randomly spacing and hiding devices for explosion on contact. When the conflict ends and peace is *positionally* declared, the explosives in the minefield don't just disappear. That field must be regained by carefully going over every bit of ground before *actually* removing the lethal devices. Then, after debris is cleared, the land can be rejuvenated into healthy growth.

God's warriors can safely traverse any mined field if Jesus Christ is allowed to be their minesweeper. He will not only detonate and destroy each deceptive stronghold as it's uncovered, He will also restore the disturbed and damaged soil with life-giving truth. The Lord transforms the mind and heals the heart through the planting of His Word.

~~~~~~~~~~

After the breakthrough in Pharaoh's court, the Israelites continued to follow God's guidance for their complete deliverance out of Egypt. While miracles rescued them from slavery, the transformation of their inner man took a lifetime. Eventually, in the wilderness, God would confront the strongholds lodged in their souls. They needed time to assimilate His goodness and to trust in His care. Because abuse had filled their memories with painful thoughts, God provided a transitional period for heart healing.

Restoration of the believer's soul progresses through love, faith, and obedience. By shining His light into us through His word, the innermost thoughts and motives of our heart are revealed for conviction and repentance of wrongdoing (Hebrews 4:12). In order for God to rebuild us into a sound structure, transformation unfolds in layers and stages like the peeling of an onion. God's heart absorbs our tears of anguish *and* the odorous decay of our sinful flesh so that we become like Christ from our very core! Paul advised new-covenant believers:

> My dear friends, as you have always obeyed—not only in my presence, but now much more in my absence—continue to work out your salvation with fear and trembling, for it is God who works in you to will and to act according to his good purpose. (Philippians 2:12–13)

Truth About Yokes

It is difficult to comprehend what God was accomplishing in lifting Israel's yoke without knowing how yokes were used in biblical days. The spiritual picture becomes clearer when we examine the natural picture.

> [Scripture's references to yokes] is an agricultural simile, and refers to the custom of raising the yoke from the neck and cheeks of the oxen so that they can more readily eat their food. The yokes used in the East were very heavy, and pressed so much upon the animals that they were unable to bend their necks to eat.[13]

Most dictionaries describe the yoke as a wooden frame around the neck by which the animals were fastened to a pole or bar, including a connected harness about the head. A yoke couples two things together—metaphorically, a servant to a master, for example. The Old Testament gives beautiful word pictures of God's tenderness in loosening and removing the muzzle so His chosen people could eat.

> When Israel was only a child, I loved him. I called out, "My son!"—called him out of Egypt....I lifted him like a baby, to my cheek.... I bent down to feed him. (Hosea 11:1, 4 MSG)

I am the LORD your God, who brought you out of Egypt so that you would no longer be slaves to the Egyptians; I broke the bars of your yoke and enabled you to walk with heads held high. (Leviticus 26:13)

You have shattered the yoke that burdens them, the bar across their shoulders, the rod of their oppressor. (Isaiah 9:4)

They will know that I am the LORD, when I break the bars of their yoke and rescue them from the hands of those who enslaved them. (Ezekiel 34:27)

I will break their yoke from your neck and tear your shackles away. (Nahum 1:13)

When I read these verses, I see a lovely spiritual exchange. A gentle God comforts His precious ones with kindness after He unties their cords of death. God not only lifts the heavy bonds of oppression, He also then invites the needy to be bonded with Him. God, "Whose name is Strength" (Psalm 22:19), continues to give rest to the soul by carrying the burdens too demanding to carry alone.

After being set free from the hand of Saul, David sang, "I love you, O LORD, my strength" (18:1). David frequently felt overwhelmed by circumstances. Sometimes he grieved the Lord with sinful choices, but he continued to be a man after God's own heart because he humbled himself and turned to his Deliverer for help (e.g., 1 Samuel 13:14; Acts 13:22). He was grateful because God had delivered him from the grasp of death!

Truth About Strongholds

As we've discovered, the enemy's curses and strongholds were actually swallowed up in the first encounter with the rod/cross; nevertheless, there followed fierce battles to remove the residue and debris that remained in the path to freedom. Once more: the glorious gift gained positionally needed to be actualized in experience.

In ancient Egypt, anything that people couldn't control became a deity to worship and placate. Though today many assume they can harness dark spiritual powers and utilize them as they wish, the Egyptians knew that what they believed were gods (and what are really demonic forces) are *not* interested in serving humans. They hoped they would be protected from harm by fearing and deferring to countless entities.[14] Egypt was oppressed by magicians who practiced secret arts. Their false signs and wonders were empowered by demons called "fallen angels," spirits against God that are now the energy behind wickedness (see Matthew 25:41; Revelation 12:7–9).

What happened in the natural realm (through Pharaoh and his people) against Israel provides insight into the spiritual realm for Christians today. Ruling territorial spirits come as deceptive lights that desire to destroy

God's children by undermining truth (2 Corinthians 11:13–15). The Bible describes the unseen but real hierarchy of evil as composed of malicious rulers, insidious authorities, powers of this dark world, spiritual forces of evil in the heavenly realms.

Strongholds usually arise *in the mind* as deceptive thoughts and attitudes, *in the will* as divisive argumentation, and *in the emotions* as useless, frightening imaginations. Like a fortress that camouflages deception and attacks truth, some form of these lies is embedded in the souls of many:

(1) God has forgotten me;
(2) God does not love me;
(3) I am not loveable;
(4) Nobody cares about me;
(5) There is no help for me in my pit of darkness.

Relationships are destroyed when foul forces make pathways into a person's psyche. Their goal: to destroy love, because God is love (1 John 4:8). *Bondage is often evidenced when a person struggles with giving and receiving acceptance through healthy intimacy.*

The Israelites' deliverance from Egypt contains a process that powerfully destroys deception, opens windows to the heart, and brings rest to the soul. This is a basic prayer-ministry model for those struggling with an unfruitful life because they've never been rooted and established in love.

~~~~~~~~~~

Even prophets admitted to hearing whispering threats. The devil attacked Jeremiah with terrorizing words.

Terror is on every side! "Denounce him! Let us denounce him!" say all my familiar friends, watching for my fall. "Perhaps he will be deceived, then we can overcome him, and take our revenge on him" (Jeremiah 20:10 RSV).

God honored Jeremiah's heart of faith and understood his cries of desperation in the midst of battle. He knows the frailty of even the faithful, and He did not rebuke Jeremiah for vocalizing his wounded emotions. The hurting one often needs a caregiver who is like God, allowing another's pain to be released like steam vented from a boiling pot.

To prevail, Jeremiah spoke truth:

The LORD is with me like a mighty warrior; so my persecutors will stumble and not prevail. They will fail and be thoroughly disgraced; their dishonor will never be forgotten. Sing to the LORD! Give praise to the LORD! He rescues the life of the needy from the hands of the wicked. (Jeremiah 20:11, 13)

The battle strategies for the restoration of Israel are the same for the church. God's shepherds are able to reclaim the inheritance for their flock by taking back the ground damaged by darkness. Paul warned,

> Keep watch over yourselves and all the flock of which the Holy Spirit has made you overseers. Be shepherds of the church of God, which he bought with his own blood. I know that after I leave, savage wolves will come in among you and will not spare the flock. Even from your own number men will arise and distort the truth in order to draw away disciples after them. (Acts 20:28–30)

Redemption of God's parched people is still through His shed blood and by the power of His Spirit. Wise shepherds walk by faith and lead their broken lambs to Jesus Christ, the Shepherd of their souls. The Word of truth says, "In *him* we have redemption through his blood, the forgiveness of sins, in accordance with the riches of God's grace that he lavished on us with all wisdom and understanding" (Ephesians 1:7–8).

When God's people are bound, the Almighty Deliverer is the answer for their liberation. No one can be delivered by the strength of his own endeavors; the breaker anointing frees the redeemed from the binding of strongman. The Lord promises to all who cry out to Him to be their Sure Defender, their Strong Fortress: "The LORD is a refuge for the oppressed, a stronghold in times of trouble" (Psalm 9:9).

Truth about Gates

> Lift up your heads, O you gates; be lifted up, you ancient doors,
> that the King of glory may come in. (Psalm 24:7)

> Open for me the gates of righteousness;
> I will enter and give thanks to the LORD. (118:19)

Contemporary gates protect valuable properties and wealthy dwellings; the flimsy ones are usually mere decor. In biblical days, gates were extremely important: according to *Unger's Bible Dictionary*,[15] the city gate was a place for the gathering of people, for making public announcements, for the reading of Scripture, for holding court, for hearing news and gossip, and for honoring visiting dignitaries. Priests and prophets delivered their warnings, teachings, and blessings at the city gate. Criminals were punished outside the gate; beggars asked for alms by the gate. In heathen cities, the open area outside the gate was used for sacrifice. City gates were carefully guarded and closed at nightfall.

The Hebrew word *petah* is used interchangeably to mean gate, doorway, entrance or opening.[16] "In the first biblical occurrence, *petah* is used figuratively. The heart of Cain is depicted as a house or building with the devil crouching at the 'entrance', ready to subdue it utterly and destroy its occupant" (Genesis 4:7).[17] Symbolically, "gates" sometimes scripturally represent a city itself or openings to a person's soul. The Bible references gates of righteousness, gates of heaven, gates of death, and gates of hell.

Through Moses, Yahweh implored,

Hear, O Israel: The LORD our God, the LORD is one. Love the LORD your God with all your heart and with all your soul and with all your strength. These commandments that I give you today are to be upon your hearts. Impress them on your children. Talk about them when you sit at home and when you walk along the road, when you lie down and when you get up. Tie them as symbols on your hands and bind them on your foreheads. Write them on the doorframes of your houses and on your gates. (Deuteronomy 6:4–9)

Today, the Holy Spirit imparts truth to a believer's conscience, writing the Word on the heart of those who love God (Romans 2:15).

Jesus spoke about knocking at the gate of one's heart, saying, "Here I am! I stand at the door and knock. If anyone hears my voice and opens the door, I will come in and eat with him, and he with me" (Revelation 3:20). Think about this: the King of kings desires to be your friend. Jesus yearns for intimacy with His bride!

~~~~~~~~~~

Jesus declared he is the Gate for His sheep. Only those who are made righteous, whose sins are covered by the blood of the Lamb, may pass through. Consider and choose to make Jesus Christ the King of your life by praying:

Lord Jesus Christ, Open Your Floodgates of Heaven:

> Lock my gates to evil rulers and vile gods,
>   Shut all my doors to chaos.
> But unlock my gates to You, my Almighty God—
>   Open Your *Door of Glory!*
>
> Lock my gates to destruction,
>   Shut all my doors to disease.
> But unlock my gates to You, my Redeemer—
>   Open Your *Door of Life!*
>
> Lock my gates to sin and shame,
>   Shut all my doors to bondage.
> But unlock my gates to You, my Liberator—
>   Open Your *Door of Deliverance!*

> Lock my gates to curses,
>> Shut all my doors to poverty.
> But unlock my gates to You, my Blessing—
>> Open Your *Door of Grace!*
>
> Lock my gates to prideful strongholds,
>> Shut all my doors to injustice.
> But unlock my gates to You, my Stronghold—
>> Open Your *Door of Justice!*
>
> Lock my gates to violence,
>> Shut all my doors to failure.
> But unlock my gates to You, my Protector—
>> Open Your *Door of Favor!*
>
> Lock my gates to darkness,
>> Shut all my doors to deception.
> But unlock my gates to You, my Light—
>> Open Your *Door of Truth!*
>
> Lock my gates to terror,
>> Shut all my doors to fear.
> But unlock my gates to You, my Peace—
>> Open Your *Door of Love!*
>
> Lock my gates to hopelessness,
>> Shut all my doors to despair.
> But unlock my gates to You, my Hope—
>> Open Your *Door of care!*
>
> Lock my gates to grumbling,
>> Shut all my doors to unrighteousness.
> But unlock my gates to You, my Joy—
>> Open Your *Door of Righteousness!*

When God's people desire to make Christ the Lord of their life, He promises to *"throw open the floodgates of heaven and pour out so much blessing"* (Malachi 3:10). The Bible says that every spiritual blessing in the heavenly realms is the inheritance for the redeemed! Glory, redemption, life, liberty, deliverance, health, grace, strength, justice, protection, favor, light, truth, peace, love, hope, care, joy, and righteousness ... these are just *some* that God pours out upon those who love Him.

Occasionally, a family expecting a small inheritance is surprised when a larger legacy is discovered. The recipients are delighted when a legal representative makes known to them the expanded portfolio of their wealth.

The Holy Spirit is the One Who reveals our astonishing spiritual birthright and connects us, God's family, to it.

The mature in Christ will take hold of all He has for them (Philippians 3:12). Desiring to know the Lord intimately, they press in for a fuller view and clearer picture of Him as revealed in His Word. There are spoils of war in God's kingdom, but only those who seek, ask, and knock on the door of His heart receive full bounty: "Everyone who asks receives; he who seeks finds; and to him who knocks, the door will be opened" (Matthew 7:8).

These are the words of the Holy One, the True One ...
"See! I [Jesus] have set before you a door wide open
which no one is able to shut ....
Because you have guarded and kept My word of patient endurance ...
I also will keep you [safe] from the hour of trial (testing)
which is coming on the whole world ....
He who overcomes (is victorious), I will make him
a pillar in the sanctuary of My God" (Revelation 3:7–8, 10, 12 AMP).

Chapter 13

Battle Strategies

They swarmed around me like bees,
but they died out as quickly as burning thorns;
in the name of the LORD I cut them off.
I will not die but live,
and will proclaim what the LORD has done! (Psalm 118:12, 17)

When Jesus had called the Twelve together,
He gave them power and authority
to drive out all demons and to cure diseases. (Luke 9:1)

Before embarking on a military campaign, the commander of the troops presents the strategies to his field generals. This important briefing includes objectives, updates, and the detail plans for reaching the desired goals.

Our Commander in Chief's main desire is for all men to be set free from injustice so they will know Him intimately, "This is good, and pleases God our Savior, who wants all men to be saved and to come to a knowledge of the truth" (1 Timothy 2:3–4). God's servants are empowered to fulfill His mission.

God will never permit an evil ruler to annihilate Abraham's descendants because His blood covenant with them is eternal. He dispatched His trusted emissaries, Moses and Aaron, commissioning them to lead the Israelites to a place where they would be able to freely show their passion for and devotion to Him. As His ambassadors, they spoke to the people and to Pharaoh on the authority of "I AM." The brothers learned the importance of making declarations in the *Lord's* name and power.

Through the work of Jesus Christ, God's people are now under the new covenant, given His authority to do mighty deeds that honor Him (see Luke 22:20; 1 Timothy 6:18). Paul, within Christ's covenant, delivered a slave girl from a spirit of divination that had possessed her to predict the future. She was instantly set free from fortune-telling when he spoke in God's authority to the spirit: "In the name of Jesus Christ I command you to come out of her!" (Acts 16:18). Jesus said,

I tell you the truth, anyone who has faith in me will do what I have been doing. He will do even greater things than these, because I am going to the Father. And I will do whatever you ask in my name, so that the Son may bring glory to the Father. You may ask me for anything in my name, and I will do it. (John 14:12–14)

Prophetic Prayers

It is the *Elijah ministry* that prepares the way for receiving God's love and hearing His truth. John the Baptist walked in this ministry of restoration: "He will go on before the Lord, in the spirit and power of Elijah, to turn the hearts of the fathers to their children and the disobedient to the wisdom of the righteous—to make ready a people prepared for the Lord" (Luke 1:17). Moses, Elijah, and John were prophets anointed to impart life and speak truth to imprisoned people bound in chains of darkness. The earnest prayers of the righteous still move mountains! (James 5:17; Mark 11:23).

I proclaim righteousness in the great assembly; I do not seal my lips.... I speak of your faithfulness and salvation. I do not conceal your love and your truth from the great assembly. (Psalm 40:9–10)

Declaring truth while ministering will destroy lying arrows, break chains, unbind cords, and lift yokes for heart healing. *Proclamations of emancipation led by God's Spirit initiate a powerful beginning* for setting free imprisoned ones unable to loose themselves. "Scorn has broken my heart and has left me helpless; I looked for sympathy, but there was none, for comforters, but I found none" (Psalm 69:20).

In the parable of the sower, Jesus revealed that some people have hearts like a hard path. An evil one comes like a devouring bird to snatch the seed that was sown but didn't settle in (Matthew 13:3–4, 19). Vile spirits take advantage of the wounded. Frequently, abusers have trampled upon hearts, causing the Word to fall by the wayside and satan to be empowered by the vacuum.

A man's spirit sustains him in sickness, but a crushed spirit who can bear? (Proverbs 18:14)

Sighing comes to me instead of food; my groans pour out like water. What I feared has come upon me; what I dreaded has happened to me. (Job 3:24–25)

The way is prepared for breakthroughs by first forbidding the devourer to have access to the person, and then inviting Jesus to come and sow seeds of truth. God's words of life discharge hope into scarred souls. His rebuke to oppressors dispatches terror to satan's kingdom but gives comfort to the wounded. They see that, *finally*, someone is praying and warring on their behalf!

Also, *a prophetic word from a gentle caregiver opens the way for repentance and renewal.* Even though the abused soul has been victimized, he or she has areas of sinfulness, too. Being set free from the weights of others can help the wounded to recognize and address individual shortcomings, as encouragement soothes their hurting hearts. God's kindness is indispensable for healing emotional wounds, and His goodness leads to repentance (Romans 2:4). Through spiritual warfare, those overcome by sorrow and trouble will be spiritually released to experience Christ's love and to begin their journey of restoration. Prophetic prayers are the words of life that destroy old foundations of shame and fear and build new foundations of compassion and faith.

The Elements of Change

What process transformed Israel from feeling like a parched desert of despair to a well-watered garden of hope? Moses and Aaron were God's anointed representatives who followed His will for imparting the spiritual exchange. The Spirit will stir up the hearts of His faithful, and then He will make a way when they respond to the call. Jesus promises to give His authority to heaven-sent ambassadors to proclaim truth here on earth.

The Lord calls His "oaks of righteousness" to be as sheltering mothers who love the oppressed, the brokenhearted, the poor, the hungry, the homeless, and the naked. God's warriors are empowered to be as protective fathers who break the chains, untie the binding cords, lift the heavy burdens, and set the oppressed free. Jesus calls the church to rebuild the ancient ruins, to be repairers of the breach, restorers of devastated generations (Isaiah 61:4).

> On this rock I will build my church, and the gates of Hades will not overcome it. I will give you the keys of the kingdom of heaven; *whatever you bind on earth will be bound in heaven, and whatever you loose on earth will be loosed in heaven.* (Matthew 16:18–19)

Jesus commanded His redeemed to *bind* (Greek *deō*), which means "to tie or fasten," and to loose (Greek *leō*), which means "to untie."[18] Rabbinical authorities considered that "to bind is to forbid" and "to loose is to allow."[19] Christ's use of the words for binding and loosing means He invites His followers to declare the truth. We can do this for the captives so their binding connections to deception and darkness are broken, and also to impart new connections to His reality and light.

Prayers of intercession are powerful because Father God promises to empower truth spoken on earth with His heavenly authority. Jesus desires us to declare words of life that close gates to idol gods and open gates to heaven. Doors of opportunity for the building of His church will open wherever God's anointed ones speak on behalf of the King.

Quoting from Isaiah, Jesus proclaimed in fulfillment, "The Spirit of the Lord is on me, because he has anointed me to preach good news to the poor. He has sent me to proclaim freedom for the prisoners and recovery of sight for the blind, to release the oppressed" (Luke 4:18). Following His example in ministering to those in captivity, *anointed shepherds are called to loose them through preaching the good news, through proclaiming liberty, and through bringing recovery of sight to the blind.*

Peter understood what Jesus declared about the kingdom keys because he knew that Jesus Christ was the Rock, the Chief Cornerstone. Later he too cited Isaiah:

> Look! I'm setting a stone in Zion, a cornerstone in the place of honor. Whoever trusts in this stone as a foundation will never have cause to regret it. To you who trust him, he's a Stone to be proud of, but to those who refuse to trust him, the stone the workmen threw out is now the chief foundation stone. For the untrusting it's … a stone to trip over, a boulder blocking the way. (1 Peter 2:6–8 MSG)

Turning the Keys to Victory

On behalf of the Israelites, God dealt with the spiritual rulers of ancient Egypt through Moses. Their strongholds included groupings of deities under a hierarchy of more highly revered powers. The assignment of the principalities was to obstruct God's workings and will (see Daniel 10:13). However, this complex structure would not hinder Yahweh from shattering all ten heads of the serpent. Since God Almighty executed judgment against *all* the gods of Egypt, by the time of the tenth plague He had totally destroyed every demonic stronghold binding Israel to slavery (Exodus 12:12). *If God used ten plagues, almost certainly there were ten main categories of unseen spirits assigned to keep His people yoked to Egypt.*

Jesus was lifted up as God's Living Word against satan and his demons. Foreshadowing Christ as the Deliverer, Moses triumphed over wickedness when he lifted the rod against Pharaoh and the gods of Egypt, standing firmly on God's living words. The ten judgments against Pharaoh and the Egyptian gods reveal the territorial spirits and their specific areas of enslavement. Because *these forces still work universally against mankind,* I have discovered that it is important to declare their defeat. These proclamations create a greater revelation of our inheritance in Christ. We release God's power in proclaiming victory through Jesus Christ before dealing with personal strongholds in another's life.

Remember: Moses used the rod of God to defeat the demonic deities enslaving the Israelites as a foreshadowing of the cross. Jesus Christ made a public spectacle of evil powers by swallowing up death in victory. He came to destroy yokes of injustice and free us from the emotional baggage and bondage of wickedness.

Employing the Prayer Keys

I begin each ministry session with a covering prayer, usually something like this:

Dear Lord Jesus,

I thank You for Your presence. Let Your Spirit of Wisdom and Revelation open up the eyes of our hearts. Please put Your comforting arms around (the individual's name) and hide us in Your shelter. May Your blood, Jesus Christ, protect us, our loved ones, and all that pertains to us so that nothing of evil may retaliate against us now or later. Through Your precious blood, dear Savior, please seal this room and time from all hindrances to Your will. I ask that all who are present will hear Your voice. Please bathe us in Your light and write Your truth upon our hearts. We desire to be led by Your Spirit. May Your Living Word penetrate and divide our soul from our spirit so that the attitudes of the heart are revealed. May grace and peace from Father God and the Lord Jesus Christ continue to bless and to fill us. In the name of the Lord Jesus Christ I pray. Amen.

The Holy Spirit utilizes Scripture to reveal deception. Since truth is the vehicle for conveying and releasing integrity in our inner parts, it's beneficial for us to begin with a moment of listening prayer. Many times the Lord will grant a word of knowledge. Jesus says, "If you hold to my teaching, you are really my disciples. Then you will know the truth and *the truth will set you free*" (John 8:31–32). The impartation of Christ's words is the harbinger of truth.

Paul told the Roman believers, "I long to see you so that I may impart to you some spiritual gift to make you strong—that is, that you and I may be mutually encouraged by each other's faith" (Romans 1:11–12). People need encouraging truth conveyed to their hearts; otherwise they will continue to produce the fruit of unbelief. These are examples of appropriate passages to read and impart for understanding at the beginning of a prayer session:

[God said through Moses,] I am the LORD, and I will bring you out from under the yoke of the Egyptians. I will free you from being slaves to them, and I will redeem you with an outstretched arm and with mighty acts of judgment. I will take you as my own people, and I will be your God. Then you will know that I am the LORD your God. (Exodus 6:6–7)

[The LORD said,] I led them with cords of human kindness, with ties of love; I lifted the yoke from their neck and bent down to feed them. (Hosea 11:4)

[Jesus said,] Come to me, all you who are weary and burdened, and I will give you rest. Take my yoke upon you and learn from me, for I am gentle and humble in heart, and you will find rest for your souls. For my yoke is easy and my burden is light. (Matthew 11:28–30)

[Jesus Christ was sent by His Father] to proclaim freedom for the prisoners and recovery of sight for the blind, to release the oppressed. (Luke 4:18)

[Jesus promised,] I will build my church, and the gates of Hades will not overcome it. (Matthew 16:18)

Following God's strategy for crushing evil, on the authority of Christ's name and by the power of His blood, I will close the gates of the territorial spirits whose mission is to keep God's people yoked to injustice by declaring, *out loud,* that strongholds over the person were destroyed at the cross. For His glory, by His hand, and as His servant on behalf of another, via proclamation, I:

- shut each gate to the powers behind the stronghold.
- break the demonic chain of bondage from the person.
- affirm that Jesus Christ is lifting each particular yoke of wickedness.

God's name and God's love is the antidote for all curses: "The name of the LORD is a strong tower; the righteous run to it and are safe" (Proverbs 18:10). The names I have used are only suggestions; the Holy Spirit may reveal others more suited to specific situations.

In brief, after asking the Lord to affirm the person, via proclamation, I:

- declare the specific name of Jesus Christ.
- release the blessings of "*I am* the Lord."
- impart Christ's yoke, which characterizes His love.

The declarations are made more meaningful by pausing and giving the person time to assimilate the revelations. Manna from heaven is like freshly baked bread, needing to be savored. We can be robbed of the full favor if the fare is hastily gulped. Tarry long enough to allow for him or her adequate time to share, to grieve the unhealed hurts, and to receive God's consolation. *Also, it is important that the recipient affirms the blessing.*

After a declaration, I occasionally give a personal testimony or share an inspiring story about God's faithfulness. The depressed find hope and encouragement in accounts of healing in His care. When I'm in a painful place, recalling His blessings helps me to remain steadfast—sharing about His heart increases the bonds of love and brings intimacy. Testimony of the Lord's goodness restrains darkness and helps to destroy deceptive thoughts (see Revelation 12:11).

Remember: for Israel, *this was the foundational phase in which God revealed His great love and poured out His kindness.* While they were still in Egypt, God did not commission Moses and Aaron to the task of calling the crushed people to repentance; they first needed His miraculous mercy. This was the period for Yahweh to sever their ties to Egypt and strengthen their ties to His heart.

This is normally *not* the time in ministry to deal with individual sin. God later provides a wilderness season to work through life issues and transform His people into His image. When a person, emotionally, is in a despairing place of death, proclamations of liberty will begin to bring the freedom to walk into life and pointedly turn away from the ways of death.

After Lazarus' family removed the stone covering his burial place, Jesus called his friend out of the tomb, by name, for God's glory: "The dead man came out, his hands and feet wrapped with strips of linen, and a cloth around his face. Jesus said to them, 'Take off the grave clothes and let him go'" (John 11:44). This unbinding would have taken some time. I can only imagine the joy Lazarus experienced when he was able to walk free of the binding rags. *The soul's restoration is always a process initiated by God.*

If the Holy Spirit does reveal emotional baggage, sinful habits, attitudes, thoughts, or generational iniquity, *then* work through to absolution. Because we rightfully belong to Him, the Lord is jealous when we share our affection with other gods and pass those tendencies on to our children (Exodus 20:5). Everyone has weaknesses that are inherited and energized by deceptive spirits. The Spirit desires to uncover family skeletons that are sources of shame or embarrassment. Generational iniquities are family landmines that can explode at unexpected times—so much better if they are deactivated by a gentle God. The good news is that Christ was bruised for our iniquities: His shed blood is the only cure for our spiritual black-and-blue marks (see Isaiah 53:5).

With some individuals, Jesus may expose the lies and the emotional roots associated with a stronghold. Give the person time to express feelings, grieve pain, and hear healing truth. After this, deliberately nail the exposed deceptions to the cross of Christ. Following the heart healing, some are ready to ask God for forgiveness for believing a lie rather than truth, or for any other issues that need to be confessed.

~~~~~~~~~~

In addition to hearing that Jesus is the "I am" for every blessing, some find it helpful to visualize a word picture of Christ. This is not guided imagery but, rather, Jesus removing the hurtful images in the imagination and imparting His revelations. *Defiled imaginations need to be re-symbolized.* For example, after the first stronghold is broken by edict, the person could conceivably envision the Lord's heavenly stream of blessing flowing down upon him for cleansing and refreshment. Perhaps, with spiritual eyes, he will see God drying up polluted rivers of shame. The heart's portraits may vary, for God loves to give creative revelations that personally enhance our love for Him. All visions inspired by the Spirit will always be true to the Word. And it's okay if nothing is seen or felt or experienced—God understands.

Sometimes shepherds pray and anoint with oil before they pray for the lambs.

> Is any one of you sick? He should call the elders of the church to pray over him and anoint him with oil in the name of the Lord. And the prayer offered in faith will make the sick person well; the Lord will raise him up. If he has sinned, he will be forgiven. Therefore confess your sins to each other and pray for each other so that you may be healed. The prayer of a righteous man is powerful and effective. (James 5:14–16; see Psalm 23:5)

Above all, *follow the flow of God's Spirit.* Though I've listed one declaration after another, this does not mean every stronghold needs to be broken immediately. Moses and Aaron needed at least three weeks (and some Bible commentators suggest nine months) before the Israelites were delivered out of Egypt.

When people come to Garden of Grace Ministries for care and prayer, our main desire is to facilitate their loving relationship with God. Hearts are prepared and strengthened when they hear this Pauline prayer proclaimed:

I kneel before the Father,
from whom his whole family in heaven and on earth derives its name.
I pray that out of his glorious riches he may strengthen you with power
through his Spirit in your inner being,
so that Christ may dwell in your hearts through faith.
And I pray that you, being rooted and established in love,
may have power, together with all the saints,
to grasp how wide and long and high and deep is the love of Christ,
and to know this love that surpasses knowledge—that you may be filled
to the measure of all the fullness of God. (Ephesians 3:14–19)

Chapter 14

Victory Fulfilled

We will shout for joy when you are victorious
and will lift up our banners in the name of our God.
May the LORD grant all your requests.
Now I know that the LORD saves his anointed;
he answers him from his holy heaven
with the saving power of his right hand.
Some trust in chariots and some in horses,
but we trust in the name of the LORD our God. (Psalm 20:5–7)

He [Jesus] said to them,
"This is what I told you while I was still with you:
Everything must be fulfilled that is written about me
in the Law of Moses, the Prophets and the Psalms."
Then he opened their minds
so they could understand the Scriptures. (Luke 24:44–45)

But thanks be to God, Who gives us the victory [making us conquerors]
through our Lord Jesus Christ. (1 Corinthians 15:57 AMP)

How does God's light break forth for the oppressed under a shadow of death? Satan veils truth, but God's good news initiates freedom from darkness and opens the door to Christ's light.

The god of this age has blinded the minds of unbelievers, so that they cannot see the light of the gospel of the glory of Christ, who is the image of God. For we do not preach ourselves, but Jesus Christ as Lord, and ourselves as your servants for Jesus' sake. For God, who said, *"Let light shine out of darkness,"* made his light shine in our hearts to give us the light of the knowledge of the glory of God in the face of Christ. (2 Corinthians 4:4–6)

The steps to Israel's liberation from the graves of Egypt are a blueprint for providing care to people whose shattered lives have bound them to pain and twisted perceptions through personal and family strongholds of idolatry, iniquity, abuse, hardship, or witchcraft. Remember Pharaoh, Jannes, and Jambres (empowered by sorcery) opposed Moses, but they did not succeed:

Truth brings freedom. To comfort the captives and set them free, we must walk in God's authority, as Moses did. Isaiah 58: 6 records:

> Is not this the kind of fasting I have chosen: to loose the chains of injustice and untie the cords of the yoke, to set the oppressed free and break every yoke?

I find it helpful to view the whole picture of events first, and then apply the details for practical purposes. The following chart presents an overview of God's plan, laying open the course He instructed Moses to follow for bringing His people from tyranny to triumph. The desired goal is for God's beloved to have the revelation that Jesus Christ is their "I Am" Who lives inside of them.

> This mystery has been kept in the dark for a long time, but now it's out in the open. God wanted everyone, not just Jews, to know this rich and glorious secret inside and out, regardless of their background, regardless of their religious standing. The mystery in a nutshell is just this: Christ is in you, therefore you can look forward to sharing in God's glory. It's that simple. That is the substance of our Message. (Colossians 1:26–27 MSG).

The Victorious War Plan (Exodus 7–12)

THE TEN PLAGUES	THE YOKE OF INJUSTICE	THE YOKE OF JUSTICE
God's judgments on all the gods of Egypt and all who worshiped them	DECLARE the shutting of each gate BREAK the demonic chain of bondage LIFT the yoke of burden	DECLARE the name of God RELEASE the blessings of "I am" IMPART the yoke of Jesus Christ
(1) The Plague of Blood	The gods of the Nile and life energy False protectors from drought Yokes of addictions and shame	The RIVER OF LIFE I am your Spring of Water Your Yoke of Grace
(2) The Plague of Frogs	The gods of chaos False protectors from misfortunes Yokes of sexual perversion and chaos	The RIGHTEOUS BRANCH I am your Holy God Your Yoke of Purity
(3) The Plague of Gnats/Lice	The gods of the earth and underworld False protectors from pain Yokes of divination and witchcraft	The LIVING WORD and WISDOM I am your Way, Truth, and Life Your Yoke of Truth and Wisdom
(4) The Plague of Flies	The gods of idolatrous religion False protectors from evil Yokes of idolatry and religious stupor	The SAVIOR OF SHEEP I am your Good Shepherd Your Yoke of Salvation
(5) The Plague on Cattle	The gods of fertility False protectors from barrenness Yokes of passivity	The LORD GOD ALMIGHTY I am your Shield Your Yoke of Strength
(6) The Plague of Boils	The gods of the wind, air, and sky False protectors from curses, disease Yokes of oppression and bitterness	The BRIGHT AND MORNING STAR I am your Healer Your Yoke of Hope and Health
(7) The Plague of Hail	The gods of war and storms False protectors from weather and war Yokes of envy, control, and rage	The GOD OF JUSTICE I am your Shelter Your Yoke of Protection
(8) The Plague of Locusts	The gods of devouring and destruction False protectors from ruin Yokes of terror, fear, and devastation	The RESTORER; the COMFORTER I am your God of Love Your Yoke of Peace
(9) The Plague of Darkness	The gods of the sun and moon False protectors from darkness Yokes of darkness, doubt, and unbelief	The LIGHT OF THE WORLD I am your King of Glory Your Yoke of Light
(10) The Plague on Firstborn	The gods of death and rebellion False protectors over Egypt and Pharaoh Yokes of death, rebellion, and pride	The LAMB OF GOD I am your Living Redeemer Your Yoke of Eternal Life

Though there are no quick fixes or formulas to follow when ministering to others, the Word of God says, "I gain understanding from your precepts.... Your word is a lamp to my feet and a light for my path" (Psalm 119:104–105). The Lord will send forth His light and truth to guide us like He did for the Israelites (43:3). Jesus said:

> The Counselor, the Holy Spirit, whom the Father will send in my name, will teach you all things and will remind you of everything I have said to you. Peace I leave with you; my peace I give you. I do not give to you as the world gives. Do not let your hearts be troubled and do not be afraid. (John 14:26–27)

Remember: It is wise to linger, allowing the Holy Spirit time to reveal and encourage while considering the past and present personal effects of each stronghold. After shutting each gate, please note the Hebrew word *"Selah,"* which the biblical psalmists used when indicating a need for "pause to consider." The Good Shepherd desires time to comfort all His bleating lambs. If there are questions, answer them.

After declaring appropriate truth from the Bible (see the previous chapter), I begin by proclaiming that since all gods and their demonic powers are under the feet of our Lord Jesus Christ, they cannot bind our authority to release God's favor because we are protected through Christ's blood and speak in the authority of His name.

Declarations of Justice

The following proclamations of liberty will activate freedom for the captive of darkness by shutting ten main gates of ruling spirits, breaking chains and lifting yokes. Many will choose to *include their families* for this breakthrough intercession.

Then open Christ's gate of delight and favor through the impartation of His name, truth, and blessings. After the impartation of grace, close each section with the person being set free declaring that Jesus lives and rules his or her heart by affirming one of His distinct names.

> **(1)** *I declare to* (the individual's name) *that you have victory over strongholds rooted in addictions, discontent, disgrace and shame because, at the cross, Jesus triumphed over the gods of foul rivers, false sources of life, so that you can be free from their yokes of injustice.*
>
> In the name of Jesus Christ, I shut your gates to the ruling territorial spirits over polluted rivers of shame and false sources of life; I break their demonic chains of bondage; and I lift their wicked yokes of disgrace. *Selah!*
>
> *Jesus Christ, the River of Life, is your Source for heavenly water:* "There is a river of joy flowing through the City of our God—the sacred home of the

God above all gods" (Psalm 46:4 TLB); "Then the angel showed me the river of the water of life, as clear as crystal, flowing from the throne of God and of the Lamb." (Revelation 22:1)

He says to you, (the individual's name), *I Am your Spring of Water.* (John 4:13–14)

I impart to you Jesus' Yoke of Grace and trust that He is your Cleansing River of Life: "It is by grace you have been saved, through faith." (Ephesians 2:8)

♥ *Now the recipient affirms:* "As the Good Shepherd's lamb, I affirm that Jesus, my River of Life, my Spring of Water, lives inside of me."

~~~~~~~~~~

(2) *I declare to* (the individual's name) *that you have victory over strongholds rooted in sexual perversion, immorality and chaos because, at the cross, Jesus triumphed over the gods of chaotic frogs so that you can be free from their yokes of injustice.*

In the name of Jesus Christ, I shut your gates to the ruling territorial spirits over the chaos of unrighteousness, immorality and misfortune; I break their demonic chains of bondage; and I lift their wicked yokes of chaos. *Selah!*

Jesus Christ, the Righteous Branch, is your Source for holiness: "...I will raise up to David a righteous Branch, a King who will reign wisely and do what is just and right in the land" (Jeremiah 23:5). "It is written: 'Be holy, because I am holy.'" (1 Peter 1:16)

He says to you, (the individual's name), *I Am your Holy God, your Gate of Righteousness.* (Psalm 118:19)

I impart to you Jesus' Yoke of purity and trust that He is your Righteous Branch who will build you up: "So then, just as you received Christ Jesus as Lord, continue to live in him, rooted and built up in him, strengthened in the faith as you were taught and overflowing with thankfulness." (Colossians 2:6–7)

♥ *Now the recipient affirms:* "As the Good Shepherd's lamb, I affirm that Jesus, my Righteous Branch, my Holy God, lives inside of me."

~~~~~~~~~~

(3) *I declare to* (the individual's name) *that you have victory over strongholds rooted in deception, witchcraft, divination and occult because, at the cross, Jesus triumphed over the gods of the underworld so that you can be free from their yokes of injustice.*

In the name of Jesus Christ, I shut your gates to the ruling territorial spirits over the underworld; I break their demonic chains of bondage; and I lift their wicked yokes of deception. *Selah!*

Jesus Christ, the Living Word, is your Source for Truth and the only Way to Father God: "The Word became flesh and made his dwelling among us. We have seen his glory, the glory of the One and Only, who came from the Father, full of grace and truth." (John 1:14)

He says to you, (the individual's name), *I Am your Way, Truth and Life.* (14:6)

I impart to you Jesus' Yoke of Truth and trust that He will teach you Wisdom: "Surely you desire truth in the inner parts; you teach me wisdom in the inmost place." (Psalm 51:6)

♥ *Now the recipient affirms:* "As the Good Shepherd's lamb, I affirm that Jesus, my Living Word, my Wisdom, lives inside of me."

~~~~~~~~~~

(4) *I declare to* (the individual's name) *that you have victory over strongholds rooted in idolatry and counterfeit shepherds because, at the cross, Jesus triumphed over the gods of idolatry, depicted as flies, and honored by false shepherds, so that you can be free from their yokes of injustice.*

In the name of Jesus Christ, I shut your gates to the ruling territorial spirits over fraudulent shepherds and idolatry; I break their demonic chains of bondage; and I lift their wicked yokes of idolatry. *Selah!*

Jesus Christ, the Savior of His sheep, is your Source for deliverance and abundant life: "I am the gate; whoever enters through me will be saved. He will come in and go out, and find pasture." (John 10:9)

He says to you, (the individual's name), *I Am your Good Shepherd.* (10:11)

I impart to you Jesus' Yoke of Salvation and trust Him to give you His full, abundant life: "The thief comes only to steal and kill and destroy; I have come that they may have life, and have it to the full." (10:10)

♥ *Now the recipient affirms:* "As the Good Shepherd's lamb, I affirm that Jesus, my Savior, my Good Shepherd, lives inside of me."

~~~~~~~~~~

(5) *I declare to* (the individual's name) *that you have victory over strongholds rooted in shields of passivity, barrenness and weakness because at the* *cross, Jesus triumphed over the gods of fertility, depicted as cows and bulls, so that you can be free from their yokes of injustice.*

In the name of Jesus Christ, I shut your gates to the ruling territorial spirits over fertility and strength; I break their demonic chains of bondage; and I lift their wicked yokes of *passivity. Selah!*

Jesus Christ, the Lord God Almighty, is your Source for power, protection and fruitfulness: "Great and marvelous are your deeds, Lord God Almighty. Just and true are your ways, King of the ages." (Revelation 15:3)

He says to you, (the individual's name), *I Am your Shield.* (Genesis 15:1)

I impart to you Jesus' Yoke of Strength and trust Him to give you His power and security: "The LORD is my rock, my fortress and my deliverer; my God is my rock, in whom I take refuge. He is my shield and the horn of my salvation, my stronghold." (Psalm 18:2)

♥   *Now the recipient affirms:* "As the Good Shepherd's lamb, I affirm that Jesus, my Lord God Almighty, my Shield, lives inside of me."

<center>~~~~~~~~~~</center>

(6) *I declare to* (the individual's name) *that you have victory over strongholds rooted in oppression, self pity, bitterness and disease because, at the cross, Jesus triumphed over the gods of wind, air, and sky so that you can be free from their yokes of injustice.*

In the name of Jesus Christ, I shut your gates to the ruling territorial spirits over curses of wind, sky and air; I break their demonic chains of bondage; and I lift their wicked yokes of oppression. *Selah!*

Jesus Christ, the Bright and Morning Star, is your Source for heavenly blessings, hope and health: "I, Jesus, have sent my angel to give you this testimony for the churches. I am the Root and the Offspring of David, and the bright Morning Star. The Spirit and the bride say, 'Come!' And let him who hears say, 'Come!' Whoever is thirsty, let him come; and whoever wishes, let him take the free gift of the water of life." (Revelation 22:16)

He says to you, (the individual's name), *I Am your Healer.* (Exodus 15:26; 1 Peter 2:24–25)

I impart Jesus' Yoke of Hope and trust Him to bless you and be the Overseer of your soul: "Evil men will be cut off, but those who hope in the LORD will inherit the land." (Psalm 37:9)

♥   *Now the recipient affirms:* "As the Good Shepherd's lamb, I affirm that Jesus, my Bright and Morning Star, my Healer, lives inside of me."

~~~~~~~~~~~

(7) *I declare to* (the individual's name) *that you have victory over strongholds rooted in rage, domination, jealousy and revenge because, at the cross, Jesus triumphed over the gods of war and storms so that you can be free from their yokes of injustice.*

In the name of Jesus Christ, I shut your gates to the ruling territorial spirits over storms and war; I break their demonic chains; and I lift their wicked yokes of rage. *Selah!*

Jesus Christ, the God of Justice, is your Source for peace and justice: "The LORD longs to be gracious to you; he rises to show you compassion. For the LORD is a God of justice. Blessed are all who wait for him." (Isaiah 30:18)

He says to you, (the individual's name), *I Am your Shelter.* (Psalm 91:1–2; 61:3)

I impart Jesus' Yoke of Protection and trust Him to spread His protection over you: "Let all who take refuge in you be glad; let them ever sing for joy. Spread your protection over them, that those who love your name may rejoice in you." (5:11)

♥   *Now the recipient affirms:* "As the Good Shepherd's lamb, I affirm that Jesus, my God of Justice, my Peace, lives inside of me."

~~~~~~~~~~~

(8) *I declare to* (the individual's name) *that you have victory over strongholds rooted in abuse, devastation, fear and terror because, at the cross, Jesus triumphed over the gods of devastation, known as the "Devourers", so that you can be free from their yokes of injustice.*

In the name of Jesus Christ, I shut your gates to the ruling territorial spirits over ruin and terror depicted as locusts; I break their demonic chains of bondage; and I lift their wicked yokes of terror. *Selah!*

Jesus Christ, the Restorer, the Comforter, is your Source for love: "I have seen his ways, but I will heal him; I will guide him and restore comfort to him." (Isaiah 57:18)

He says to you, (the individual's name), *I Am your God of Love.* (2 Corinthians 13:11)

I impart Jesus' Yoke of Peace and trust that His love never fails you: "I trust in your *unfailing love;* my heart rejoices in your salvation. I will sing to the LORD, for he has been good to me." (Psalm 13:5–6)

♥ *Now the recipient affirms:* "As the Good Shepherd's lamb, I affirm that Jesus, my Comforter, my Restorer, lives inside of me."

~~~~~~~~~~

(9) *I declare to* (the individual's name) *that you have victory over strongholds rooted in despair, darkness, doubt and unbelief because, at the cross, Jesus triumphed over the gods of the sun, moon and darkness so that you can be free from their yokes of injustice.*

In the name of Jesus Christ, I shut your gates to the ruling territorial spirits over the darkness of false lights; I break their demonic chains of bondage; and I lift their wicked yokes of darkness. *Selah!*

Jesus Christ, the Light of the World, is your Source for faith and glory: "I am the light of the world. Whoever follows me will never walk in darkness, but will have the light of life." (John 8:12)

He says to you, (the individual's name), I Am your King of Glory. (Psalm 24:10)

I impart Jesus' Yoke of Light and trust Him to shine upon you: "The LORD bless you and keep you; the LORD make his face shine upon you and be gracious to you; the LORD turn his face toward you and give you peace." (Numbers 6:24–26)

♥ *Now the recipient affirms:* "As the Good Shepherd's lamb, I affirm that Jesus, my King, my Light of Glory, lives inside of me."

~~~~~~~~~~

(10) *I declare to* (the individual's name) *that you have victory over strongholds rooted in rebellion, pride and death because, at the cross, Jesus triumphed over the insurrection of satan and fallen angels so that you can be free from their yokes of injustice.*

In the name of Jesus Christ, I shut your gates to the ruling territorial spirits over rebellion, pride and false protectors depicted as jackals and cobras; I break their demonic chains of bondage; and I lift their wicked yokes of death. *Selah!*

Jesus Christ, the Lamb of God, is your Redeemer who takes away your sin: "The next day John saw Jesus coming toward him and said, 'Look, the Lamb of God, who takes away the sin of the world!'"(John 1:29); "Our Redeemer—the LORD Almighty is his name—is the Holy One of Israel." (Isaiah 47:4)

He says to you, (the individual's name), I Am your Living Redeemer. (Revelation 1:18)

I impart Jesus' Yoke of Eternal Life and trust that you will be an overcomer through the blood of the Lamb: "They overcame him [the dragon] by the blood of the Lamb and by the word of their testimony; they did not love their lives so much as to shrink from death." (Revelation 12:11)

♥ *Now the recipient affirms:* "As the Good Shepherd's lamb, I affirm that Jesus, my Redeemer, my Living God, lives inside of me."

~~~~~~~~~~

I close the session by asking the Lord to fill the believer with His Spirit and to seal all the gates through the blood of Christ. After thanking the Lord Jesus for victory, I sometimes end with a passage that recounts His faithfulness, such as Psalm 44:1–8:

We have heard with our ears, O God; our fathers have told us what you did in their days, in days long ago. With your hand you drove out the nations and planted our fathers; you crushed the peoples and made our fathers flourish. It was not by their sword that they won the land, nor did their arm bring them victory; it was your right hand, your arm, and the light of your face, for you loved them. You are my King and my God, who decrees victories for Jacob. Through you we push back our enemies; through your name we trample our foes. I do not trust in my bow, my sword does not bring me victory; but you give us victory over our enemies, you put our adversaries to shame. In God we make our boast all day long, and we will praise Your name forever. Selah.

~~~~~~~~~~

Together we all proclaim,
Thanks be to our Lord Jesus Christ
"we have escaped with our lives as a bird from the hunter's snare.
The snare is broken and we are free!" (Psalm 124:7)

Chapter 15

New Beginnings

By day the LORD went ahead of them
in a pillar of cloud to guide them on their way
and by night in a pillar of fire to give them light,
so that they could travel by day or night. (Exodus 13:21)

Miriam sang to them: "Sing to the LORD, for he is highly exalted.
The horse and its rider he has hurled into the sea." (15:21)

Glorious and majestic are his deeds, and his righteousness endures forever.
He has caused His wonders to be remembered;
the LORD is gracious and compassionate. (Psalm 111:3–4)

Our God is a God of fresh beginnings. He has written on my heart that He is the Lord Who restores by wondrous ways. Special times are set aside for celebrating His glory; festivities, ceremonies, rites of passage, and other notable occasions help to keep our hope alive.

God knew His people would benefit by commemorating momentous events of victory. The Lord's triumph over Pharaoh was historically and phenomenally miraculous. Because He desired His Passover (passing over them) to be forever remembered, the Israelites were instructed by Moses to honor being spared from the angel of death.

In the first month of each New Year (by the Hebrew calendar), Israel was to observe the Feast of Passover and the Feast of Unleavened Bread. Like all Hebrew holidays, these events were "a shadow of things that were to come" (Colossians 2:16–17; Hebrews 10:1), and both contained rich prophetic symbolism designed to foreshadow glorious truths about Jesus Christ. All tasks the Israelites undertook on the night of the Passover prefigure acts of obedience for those who embody the church, the redeemed of the new covenant. Always and forever, the shed blood of the lamb would be Israel's salvation from death and preparation for the Lamb of God Who, centuries later, would come to sacrifice His life for the world's sin (John 1:29).

"Father, What Does This Mean?"

Moses, on the night of the Passover, obediently counseled his people regarding the Lord's commanded preparations for a successful journey out of Egypt (Exodus 12–13:16). Generations later, Jesus, in fulfillment of Scripture, taught His disciples to do the same. God's people *then* and *now* are to:

Set their hope for deliverance upon the death of a male lamb without defect.
Set our hope for deliverance upon the death of Jesus, the Lamb of God, the perfect substitute (John 1:29).

Have faith for salvation by God's grace through the lamb's blood.
Have faith for salvation by God's grace through the Lamb's blood (Ephesians 2:8).

Apply the blood of the lamb to their doorposts to be protected from death and freed from slavery.
Believe that the blood of Christ protects us from death and frees us from slavery to sin (Romans 6:23).

Share the lamb with their nearest needy neighbor.
Share Jesus with our neighbors and the world (John 1:7).

Break none of the lamb's bones and roast it whole over the fire.
Believe that the Savior died in the spiritual fire of the cross, but that none of His bones were broken (19:36).

Eat the lamb and its inner parts.
Receive Jesus and His body; all parts of the church have value (1 Corinthians 12:12).

Eat a salad of bitter herbs to remember the bitterness of slavery.
Remember the cross as when Christ suffered for sin's bitterness (11:24–26).

Eat unleavened bread at Passover; yeast represents sin, and this was when they were to be separated from sinful Egypt.
Receive Jesus as our sinless substitute and not be conformed to the world (Mark 8:15; John 1:29; 1 Corinthians 5:7).

In the morning, burn any part of the lamb that remains.
Believe the Jesus' grave was empty on Resurrection morning (Luke 24:1–8).

Stay dressed so they'd be ready for the journey out of slavery.
Be clothed with the Holy Spirit to be effective witnesses as sojourners no longer under slavery to sin (24:49).

Keep their sandals on their feet so they could leave Egypt quickly.
Keep our feet shod with the gospel of peace, ready for heaven "in a twinkling of an eye" (Ephesians 6:15; 1 Corinthians 15:52).

Hold their staff in their hand.
Hold on to Jesus, the Word of God, as our Staff of Comfort and Rod of Authority (Mark 6:8; John 1:14; Ephesians 6:17).

Tell their children about the Passover and what it means.
Tell our children about Jesus, the Passover Lamb, and train them in the ways of the Lord (6:4).

In days to come, when your son asks you, *"What does this mean?"* say to him, "With a mighty hand the LORD brought us out of Egypt, out of the land of slavery. When Pharaoh stubbornly refused to let us go, the LORD killed every firstborn in Egypt, both man and animal. This is why I sacrifice to the LORD the first male offspring of every womb and redeem each of my firstborn sons." And it will be like a sign on your hand and a symbol on your forehead that the LORD brought us out of Egypt with his mighty hand. (Exodus 13:14–16)

What Is the Meaning of "Three Days"?

Recently, before fully waking up from resting, I heard: *investigate the importance of three days.* Since the thought kept running through my mind, I asked Father God, "What does this mean?"

I remembered that Jesus' body was three days in the grave before Resurrection morning. When the Jews asked for a miraculous sign of His authority, they were perplexed by His answer: "Destroy this temple, and I will raise it again in three days" (John 2:19).

"They replied, 'It has taken forty-six years to build this temple, and you are going to raise it in three days?' But the temple he had spoken of was His body. After he was raised from the dead, his disciples recalled what he had said. Then they believed the Scripture and the words that Jesus had spoken" (vv. 20–22).

At the time, no one understood the significance of "three days."

I imagine Moses didn't understand why there were three days (instead of any other number) without light over Egypt during the ninth plague (Exodus 10:22–23). Notably, the total darkness that engulfed the land ushered in the final judgment on Pharaoh—*these three days preceded the liberation breakthrough for the Israelites, foreshadowing the death and resurrection of Christ to free mankind.* Jesus made the symbolic connection in time: "As Jonah was three days and three nights in the belly of a huge fish, so the Son of Man will be three days and three nights in the heart of the earth" (Matthew 12:40).

Wondering whether the Bible mentioned other three-day events connected to Jesus and the cross, I discovered there were many times God employed three days before breaking through what seemed to be an impossible situation. Each occasion contained an amazing symbolic correlation!

The following true stories, all with three-day breakthroughs, encourage me to walk by faith and not by sight. These are reminders of what Jesus, the Passover Lamb, accomplished on the cross when He embraced darkness so that man could embrace light.

- *There were three days after Joseph interpreted the dreams of two fellow prisoners before their breakthrough.*

When Joseph came to them the next morning, he saw that they were dejected. So he asked Pharaoh's officials who were in custody with him in his master's house, "Why are your faces so sad today?"

"We both had dreams," they answered, "but there is no one to interpret them."

Then Joseph said to them, "Do not interpretations belong to God? Tell me your dreams."

So the chief cupbearer told Joseph his dream. He said to him, "In my dream I saw a vine in front of me, and on the vine were three branches. As soon as it budded, it blossomed, and its clusters ripened into grapes. Pharaoh's cup was in my hand, and I took the grapes, squeezed them into Pharaoh's cup and put the cup in his hand."

"This is what it means," Joseph said to him. "The three branches are three days. Within three days Pharaoh will lift up your head and restore you to your position, and you will put Pharaoh's cup in his hand, just as you used to do when you were his cupbearer...."

When the chief baker saw that Joseph had given a favorable interpretation, he said to Joseph, "I too had a dream: On my head were three baskets of bread. In the top basket were all kinds of baked goods for Pharaoh, but the birds were eating them out of the basket on my head."

"This is what it means," Joseph said. "The three baskets are three days. Within three days Pharaoh will lift off your head and hang you on a tree. And the birds will eat away your flesh."

Now the third day was Pharaoh's birthday, and he gave a feast for all his officials. He lifted up the heads of the chief cupbearer and the chief baker in the presence of his officials: He restored the chief cupbearer to his position, so that he once again put the cup into Pharaoh's hand, but he hanged the chief baker, just as Joseph had said to them in his interpretation. (Genesis 40:6–13, 16–22)

The breakthrough insights: After three days, the cupbearer was restored, the chief baker was hung on a tree. This event foreshadows Jesus as the Man of Sorrows Who could identify with all imprisoned people. He hung on the cross for the restoration of the captives so they could become fruitful branches, rooted in the Vine.

Some important background information:

> The office of a royal cupbearer ... was a place of great honor in the King's court. The cupbearer, being in the daily presence of the king, and seeing him at his seasons of relaxation from care, had many opportunities of ingratiating himself into the good-will of the monarch. Thus he obtained many favors which were denied others. Cupbearers were generally eunuchs, and their images are often found on Assyrian monuments. In these representations they hold the cup in the left hand and in the right hand a fly-flap made of the split leaves of the palm. The cupbearer, before serving the king, took the wine into the cup from the vessels, and then poured a little into the palm of his left hand and drank it; so that if the wine were poisoned the king might ascertain it without running any personal risk.[20]

Similarly, God's saints no longer bear the fruit of the old nature but bear the fruit of love; they are the chosen cupbearers to the Lord Jesus. Spiritual cupbearers to the King of kings become willing to face death for His sake.

- *There were three days the Israelites were in the desert without water before their breakthrough.*

> Moses led Israel from the Red Sea and they went into the Desert of Shur. For three days they traveled in the desert without finding water. When they came to Marah, they could not drink its water because it was bitter. (That is why the place is called Marah.) So the people grumbled against Moses, saying, "What are we to drink?"
> Then Moses cried out to the LORD, and the LORD showed him a piece of wood. He threw it into the water, and the water became sweet. There the LORD made a decree and a law for them, and there he tested them. He said, "If you listen carefully to the voice of the LORD your God and do what is right in his eyes, if you pay attention to his commands and keep all his decrees, I will not bring on you any of the diseases I brought on the Egyptians, for I am the LORD, who heals you" (Exodus 15:22–26).

The breakthrough insights: Bitterness became sweet through a branch, a piece of wood, which Moses obediently threw into the undrinkable water. The cross of Christ is more than sufficient for today's bitter waters of disappointment. Jesus, the Righteous Branch, transforms stinking sinners into sweet saints!

- *There were three days for the Israelites to gather the needed supplies before their breakthrough.*

> Go through the camp and tell the people, Get your supplies ready—three days from now you will cross the Jordan here to go in and take possession of the land the LORD your God is giving you for your own. (Joshua 1:11)

The breakthrough insights: After three days of gathering, the Israelites were ready to go across the Jordan River into the Promised Land. This event foreshadows the church now, through the cross of Christ, having been given the provision of the Holy Spirit, Who enables God's people to walk by faith in His kingdom promises.

- *There were three days Nehemiah stayed in Jerusalem before breakthrough.*

> I went to Jerusalem, and after staying there three days I set out during the night with a few men. I had not told anyone what my God had put in my heart to do for Jerusalem. There were no mounts with me except the one I was riding on. By night I went out ... [and] said to them, "You see the trouble we are in: Jerusalem lies in ruins, and its gates have been burned with fire. Come, let us rebuild the wall of Jerusalem, and we will no longer be in disgrace." I also told them about the gracious hand of my God upon me and what the king had said to me. (Nehemiah 2:11–18)

The breakthrough insights: After three days of rest, Nehemiah surveyed the ruin and began the work of restoring Jerusalem's walls and gates. This event foreshadows Jesus' words on the cross: "It is finished!" What He had begun was accomplished; after three days when His body rested in the tomb, His work of restoration began.

- *There were three days Esther and her people fasted before their breakthrough.*

> Esther sent this reply to Mordecai: "Go, gather together all the Jews who are in Susa, and fast for me. Do not eat or drink for three days, night or day. I and my maids will fast as you do. When this is done, I will go to the king, even though it is against the law. And if I perish, I perish" (Esther 4:15–16).

The breakthrough insights: After the three days and nights of fasting, the king accepted and favored Queen Esther. The Jews were saved from death by the king's armor, while Haman, their despicable archenemy, reaped what he sowed.

Christ is the Christian's armor of protection: helmet of salvation, breastplate of righteousness, belt of truth, covering on the feet, shield of faith, and sword of the Spirit. After His death, Jesus fasted from all comfort for three days, then arose to the place of highest honor.

- *There were three days Jonah walked through Nineveh, proclaiming the Lord's warning, before breakthrough.*

> Then the word of the LORD came to Jonah a second time: "Go to the great city of Nineveh and proclaim to it the message I give you."
> Jonah obeyed the word of the LORD and went to Nineveh. Now Nineveh was a very important city—a visit required three days. On the first day, Jonah started into the city. He proclaimed: "Forty more days and Nineveh will be overturned."
> The Ninevites believed God. They declared a fast…. When God saw what they did and how they turned from their evil ways, he had compassion and did not bring upon them the destruction he had threatened. (Jonah 3:1–10)

The breakthrough insights: After Jonah's three-day crusade, the Ninevites received God's word as delivered by the prophet, and they repented. Calvary's love also enables all who will come to the cross to be forgiven and set free from the wages of sin.

- *There were three days Saul was sightless before his breakthrough.*

> For three days he [Saul] was blind, and did not eat or drink anything … but the Lord said to Ananias, "Go! This man is my chosen instrument to carry my name before the Gentiles and their kings and before the people of Israel. I will show him how much he must suffer for my name."
> Then Ananias went to the house and entered it. Placing his hands on Saul, he said, "Brother Saul, the Lord—Jesus, who appeared to you on the road as you were coming here—has sent me so that you may see again and be filled with the Holy Spirit." Immediately, something like scales fell from Saul's eyes, and he could see again. (Acts 9:9, 15–19)

The breakthrough insights: Saul the Pharisee had three days of blindness; after prayer he was transformed into Paul, apostle to the Gentiles. Similarly, apart from Christ all are spiritually blind, living in darkness; the touch of God removes the eye-covering blinders, enabling believers to be filled with His Spirit and to see others with His eyes.

~~~~~~~~~~

Is it coincidental that any of these events were three days? *No!* In every case "three days" points toward one central truth: there never would be any miraculous redemption if Jesus Christ had not been crucified and three days later risen to newness of life.

Looking back, I can see that Tom and I experienced our own "three days" before a breakthrough. In the third week of November 1994, we began the overwhelming and oppressive task of full disclosure. We woke up Tuesday morning full of shame and distress. Three days later, on Thanksgiving morning, I cried out to God for relief and restoration. He began to heal my broken heart by displaying to me a revelation of His tender care; later, His Spirit flowed through me as a river of forgiving grace to my husband.

Tom had another momentous breakthrough in prison. Three days after he was cut off from all outside contact, and on the very day his television stopped working, God penetrated through his depression with an impartation of love. The work of the cross is the way to breakthrough for the saints of all eras.

Remembering and Seeing Christ's Passion

For the redeemed, Jesus is the *Unleavened Bread* and the *Passover Lamb* Who sacrificed His life. On the night He was betrayed, Jesus counseled His disciples to remember that His body was broken and His blood shed for the sins—for the leaven—of mankind. Until He returns, all believers are blessed when they remember and proclaim the Lord's death by partaking of the Lord's Supper (1 Corinthians 11:26).

Pondering the awesomeness of Calvary's love, I asked God to impart into my heart a fervent remembrance of Christ's Passion. This prayer led me to take time to recall some breakthrough moments. Tom and I often have needed God's hand to carry us through humanly impossible situations.

One consequential event in 1973, in which God heard our cries, stands out in my mind. With our church's youth group, we had headed out of Boston to go camping in Maine. Except for one flat tire the journey was uneventful until we entered Baxter State Park. Tom was driving ahead of me, pulling our boat filled with luggage and supplies. The winding road leading to the camping site was barely wide enough for one car. Suddenly an oncoming vehicle came around a bend—Tom, with nowhere to go, had his car squeezed between the other auto and a sheer embankment. When he instinctively swerved, the boat and trailer broached the unprotected edge. Miraculously, as the boat was tipping over the ledge, threatening to take everyone with it, the hitch broke, saving Tom and our youth.

The boat and trailer were stopped just short of the lake below by one evergreen tree. I found a narrow place to park, and everyone in my automobile scurried over to the scene. No one was hurt; all were badly shaken by the near miss. Though I felt instantly relieved, I wondered how we could possibly continue. (Plus, almost everything we needed was now down the cliff.)

While Tom and a young man scrambled down a traversable part of the ravine, fourteen pairs of confused eyes looked to me for hope and answers.

I felt like a fearful Israelite whose Moses had led her to a hard place. I was supposed to be the big person, but dark discouragement was closing in.

I gathered us into a circle, and we cried out to God for help. With wobbly knees and short prayers, we thanked Him for His faithfulness. Peace began to quiet our nerves.

Then we heard shouts from below: of everything in the boat, only the glass on a lantern was broken! There was a fixable crack in the stern, and the motor was intact. Even so—a boat in a bush lacks usability.

Tom was ready to walk back to the park's entrance when a ranger pulled up in a tow truck, saying he could ratchet up our trailer and boat—his confidence came from having attended previous accidents in that exact place. Other good news was that there wasn't a service charge, since we were within the park's boundaries.

After experiencing this miracle of care, the Lord's strong presence followed us throughout the week. The kids' hearts were open to the work of the cross. God blew upon each one with a fresh wind of His Spirit. None of us returned home the same: the Almighty had broken through our walls of self! The Refiner's fire had delivered us from a personal Egypt and our yokes of sin, granting us His forgiving, loving touch.

When I remember the cross, I am *filled* with gratefulness. Because of Christ's sacrificial love for me, I have changed and become a new person. He is truly the God of new beginnings!

From Pain to Gain

When the Israelites departed they carried with them the bones of Joseph, as promised to him by their ancestors centuries earlier. On his deathbed, Joseph had prophesied that Yahweh would come to their aid and deliver them from Egypt. The memory of his parting words kept hope of a better life alive in the core of their being.

Significantly, Jesus gave parting words very similar to Joseph's:

Do not let your hearts be troubled. Trust in God; trust also in me. In my Father's house are many rooms; if it were not so, I would have told you. I am going there to prepare a place for you. And if I go and prepare a place for you, *I will come back and take you to be with me that you also may be where I am.* (John 14:1–3)

God is trustworthy! Believers can read the historical record and *know* He will faithfully fulfill our blessed hope.

When the Lord restores, experiences of pain become experiences of gain. After seeing awe-inspiring victory and realizing that Pharaoh's army and chariots were buried in the sea, each Israelite could say, *"My ears had heard of you [God], but now my eyes have seen you"* (Job 42:5). "I AM WHO I AM" was their God, their Lord in word and deed.

God still changes desert places into fields of glory. The Bible says that the Israelites now feared the Lord and began to trust Him again (Exodus 14:31). With joy they saw that they had been spared, "passed over," by the death angel. After leaving, they had victoriously faced a sea of death and passed over to life. Instead of wearing a sackcloth of grief, God's people were clothed with a garment of praise. He was pleased when Moses and Miriam led the people in a song of celebration (15:11–13):

> *Who among the gods is like you, O LORD?*
> *Who is like you—majestic in holiness, awesome in glory, working wonders?*
> *You stretched out your right hand and the earth swallowed them.*
> *In your unfailing love you will lead the people you have redeemed.*
> *In your strength you will guide them to your holy dwelling.*

God Prepares, Repairs, and Cares!

The Lord's mercy continued His people's journey to the land of their forefathers. He now revealed another facet of himself, *Yahweh-Rophe*, "Our Healer": God would miraculously protect them from the diseases of the Egyptians (Deuteronomy 7:15)! Years later, Nehemiah recounted Father God's wondrous ways:

> Because of your great compassion you did not abandon them in the desert. By day the pillar of cloud did not cease to guide them on their path, nor the pillar of fire by night to shine on the way they were to take. You gave your good Spirit to instruct them. You did not withhold your manna from their mouths, and you gave them water for their thirst. For forty years you sustained them in the desert; they lacked nothing, their clothes did not wear out nor did their feet become swollen. (Nehemiah 9:19–21)

Asaph, whom King David appointed as head of liturgical music, wrote Psalm 78, a song that recounted the signs and wonders of God on Israel's behalf. The song was a reminder for them to remember and to teach their descendants about the Lord's faithfulness. It is also a reminder to all about the importance of learning from the spiritual failures of forefathers.

> They (Israel) did not remember his power—
> the day he redeemed them from the oppressor,
> the day he displayed his miraculous signs in Egypt,
> his wonders in the region of Zoan.
> But he brought his people out like a flock;
> he led them like sheep through the desert.
> He guided them safely, so they were unafraid;
> but the sea engulfed their enemies. (vv. 42–43, 52–53)

God's heart for restoration is to cherish His children right where they are in life. He will seek out, nourish and establish His lambs in His love!

> Suppose one of you has a hundred sheep and loses one of them. Does he not leave the ninety-nine in the open country and go after the lost sheep until he finds it? And when he finds it, he joyfully puts it on his shoulders and goes home. Then he calls his friends and neighbors together and says, "Rejoice with me; I have found my lost sheep" (Luke 15:4–6).

Abba Father adopts us as His beloved children. Wholeness is the natural result of knowing that our heavenly Papa delights in us. Recovery is guidance, recovery is humility, recovery is repentance, recovery is change, recovery is freedom, and recovery is becoming like His Son, Jesus Christ. In Christ, recovery becomes a time of restoration and transformation when all things become new (2 Corinthians 5:17). The Lord covers us with His banner of love and leads us to His magnificent banquet table (Song of Solomon 2:4).

THE WONDROUS WAYS OF GOD

"Open my eyes so I can see what you show me of your miracle-wonders."
(Psalm 119:18 MSG)

The Lord redeems and changes:

Austerity into Abundance!
Brokenheartedness into Breakthrough!
Bleakness into Blessing!
Confusion into Comfort!
Contempt into Contentment!
Despair into Delight!
Despondency into Dancing!
Failure into Favor!
Fear into Faith!
Grave into Glory!
Grief into Grace!
Groaning into Gladness!
Havoc into Happiness!
Hopelessness into Hope!
Misery into Mercy!
Poverty into Prosperity!
Rejection into Rejoicing!
Ruin into Recovery!
Sinners into Saints!
Sadness into Song!
Shame into Splendor!
Suffering into Sufficiency!
Tyranny into Triumph!
Weeping into Wonder!

Part 3

REMEMBERING GOD'S WONDROUS WAYS

Chapter 16

Foresight Through Hindsight

I will remember the deeds of the LORD;
yes, I will remember your miracles of long ago. (Psalm 77:11)

All Scripture is God-breathed and is useful
for teaching, rebuking, correcting and training in righteousness,
so that the man of God may be thoroughly equipped
for every good work. (2 Timothy 3:16)

Moses did a fine job working in God's house,
but he was only a servant; and his work was mostly to illustrate
and suggest those things that would happen later on. (Hebrews 3:5 TLB)

In this section of *Beyond Despair: Tender Care,* I will focus on God's incredible ways of bringing recovery, as demonstrated in both Israel's and my spiritual journey. In this chapter, I will summarize redemptive insights and healing thoughts that lifted my head above the raging tumult that often seemed to surround and envelop me. My prayer is that wounded lambs will be encouraged to know the Good Shepherd hears their bleating cries.

The old adage says that hindsight has 20/20 vision. Learning from life's experiences is valuable; however, Jesus and His disciples taught that we also discover wisdom through His Word and gain foresight through the triumphs and tragedies of His people. Scripture says the experiences of Israel are recorded for us as object lessons, beneficial to anyone who seeks the truth: "They were written down so that we could read about them and learn from them in these last days as the world nears its end" (1 Corinthians 10:11 TLB).

When Adam and Eve chose to defy and disobey God, shame and pain became like twin darts aimed at man's heart. God knew before the foundation of the world that men would fall and need restoration; therefore, He provided His Son as their Tree of Life, the way to remain with Him eternally. Throughout the ages, the Lord has beckoned people to know that Jesus Christ is their only Door of Hope and Gate of Salvation.

God's Spirit reaches out to the hurting through His Word and through lives transformed by His grace. He has always been faithful to raise up ambassadors—like Moses—to speak His truth and to be His welcoming arms of healing and recovery. "Recovery" is regaining one's given status or returning to one's original state. Adam was not originally sinful; God did not create us to be blind, living in despair. Jesus Christ, our Savior, came to restore the spiritually blind by removing satan's shroud of death and scales of deception.

Although every book of the Bible is profitable for us, we have seen that the Exodus account specifically discloses foundational principles of recovery. God delivered His covenant people out of slavery and restored dignity to them. He safeguarded them to the wilderness, where He guided them, covered them, and shined His light into their hearts—not to condemn them, but to free them from their bitter roots and deceptive weeds. He chose to set His affection upon the seemingly insignificant descendants of Abraham and purposed for them to become *"a kingdom of priests and a holy nation"* (Exodus 19:6 KJV).

Recovery Highlights From Exodus

When I cried out to God for help, His Spirit led me to meditate, journal, and reflect on how Israel found renewal. As I obeyed, the first fifteen chapters of Exodus unfolded spiritual principles vital to my well-being. Application of these concepts continues to impart hope to me when I face barriers of hopelessness. Note that not all the issues may be pertinent to you, and they likely have not evolved in your life identically to how either Israel or I experienced them.

In a recap of Israel's deliverance from abuse and slavery, I have highlighted the following: beneficial insights, God's progressive care, healing thoughts, and my responsive heartfelt prayers. The ensuing precepts are a life-giving review of God's restorative ways!

- *[The Egyptians] put slave masters over [the Israelites] to oppress them.... But the more they were oppressed, the more they multiplied and spread.* (Exodus 1:11–12)

The Israelites suffered affliction through slave masters; Christians experience spiritual oppression from unseen forces. When God's people look to Christ, the more they are persecuted, the more they will be blessed.

Healing Thought: Evil does not have the power to destroy my blessings.

Dear Lord, open my spiritual eyes,
and help me to see Your treasures in my hard place.

~~~~~~~~~~

- *One day, after Moses had grown up, he went out to where his own people were and watched them at their hard labor. He saw an Egyptian beating a Hebrew, one of his own people.* (2:11)

If Moses noticed the struggles of his own people, how much more does God know and respond to our difficulties?

Healing Thought: My God grieves and hates the injustice that happens to me.

Thank you, Lord, for noticing and for weeping with me
when bad things happen to me.

~~~~~~~~~~

- *The man said, "Who made you ruler and judge over us? Are you thinking of killing me as you killed the Egyptian?"* (2:14).

Moses was unjustly accused, but God's purposes for Moses were not thwarted; neither were the purposes that God had for His Son defeated by His accusers.

Healing Thought: When I suffer unjustly, Jesus understands, and His purposes for me will not be thwarted.

Thank You, Lord, for understanding and
quietly waiting for me even when I'm so discouraged
that I angrily stop talking with You for a while.

~~~~~~~~~~

- *During that long period ... the Israelites groaned in their slavery and cried out, and their cry for help ... went up to God. God heard their groaning and He remembered His covenant.* (2:23–24)

Though what seemed to man like an endless wait, God was quietly preparing Moses to lead His covenant people out of Egypt. God, Who sees the bigger picture, fulfills His promises in His appointed time.

Healing Thought: God comforts me as I mourn and helps me to release my heart's pain to Him.

Lord, my grief is so intense that I can only groan;
but thank You for hearing the cries of my spirit.

~~~~~~~~~~

- *When they heard that the LORD was concerned about them and had seen their misery, they bowed down and worshiped. (4:31)*

The Israelites were encouraged when Moses told them of God's concern for them. They worshiped Him because hope had been imparted into their hearts when they heard about the miraculous signs and the news of their deliverance.

Healing Thought: God's word imparted prophetically to me is my anchor of hope when I feel like a little boat upon a stormy sea.

Thank you, Lord, for Your encouraging words of hope
during my discouraging times.

~~~~~~~~~~

- *Then Pharaoh said, "Look, the people of the land are now numerous, and you [Moses and Aaron] are stopping them from working" (5:5).*

Like Pharaoh's responses, satan is alarmed when God's people seek a quiet place to worship and restfully enjoy His presence.

Healing Thought: God desires intimacy and a sacrifice of praise in my hard times; He understands when my spirit is willing but my flesh is weak.

Dear Lord, I haven't much to offer to You right now,
but I know my groans and tears are precious to You.

~~~~~~~~~~

- *[Pharaoh said to his slave drivers], "Make the work harder for the men so that they keep working and pay no attention to lies" (5:9).*

Like Pharaoh, the devil employs harsh taskmasters who distort truth, wanting us to believe that what's true is actually false.

Healing Thought: My recovery will be opposed by the lies and duplicity of darkness, but God will bring me justice.

> *Please, Lord, help me to know and embrace truth*
> *even though my emotions are very unsteady.*

~~~~~~~~~~

- *Pharaoh said, "Lazy, that's what you are—lazy!" (5:17).*

The Israelite foremen appointed by Pharaoh's slave drivers were put into a dreadful bind: continue to make the same quotas of brick *without* proper provisions. When they failed, they were slandered. When God's Spirit is not in control of a believer's heart, his flesh comes under the servitude of strongmen like slave drivers.

Healing Thought: God allows territorial spirits, with their lies, name-calling, and expectations, to be exposed for my restoration.

> *Dear Lord, I feel overwhelmed.*
> *Please stir up Your people to remember me in their prayers,*
> *and thank You for delivering me from evil.*

~~~~~~~~~~

- *The foremen said to Moses and Aaron,] "You have made us a stench to Pharaoh and his officials and have put a sword in their hand to kill us" (5:21).*

The angry foremen blamed Moses and Aaron for Pharaoh's vile reaction, believing the lie that "peace at all costs" really works. Likewise, some people will blame God for sin in their life.

Healing Thought: Trying to appease evil is like putting a Band-Aid over a poisonous infection.

> *Dear Lord, I desire Your deep healing in my inward parts—*
> *forgive me when I blame You for my pain.*

~~~~~~~~~~

- *Moses returned to the LORD and said, "O Lord, why have you brought trouble upon this people? Is this why you sent me?" (5:22).*

Moses had forgotten God's forewarning that breaking Egypt's iron grip would be a process; nevertheless, he did well in bringing his complaints to God, Who cleared up his confusion.

Healing Thought: When I turn to God and voice my complaints, He will impart grace to me.

Dear Lord, thanks for caring and allowing me to be real
as I vent my feelings and misgivings to You.

~~~~~~~~~~

- *Moses reported [God's news of their deliverance] to the Israelites, but they did not listen to him because of their discouragement and cruel bondage. (6:9)*

The people grew disheartened when their hopes were dashed, for Pharaoh had increased the cruelty of their servitude. Regardless, even when oppressed people can't hear good news and retain truth, God is faithful to His promises.

Healing Thought: God does not condemn me when I struggle in despairing times. He understands my humanity.

Dear Lord, I'm too tired to pray tonight;
as I sleep, may all the songs broadcast through my radio,
comforting me during the night, also become my prayers offered to You.

~~~~~~~~~~

- *Pharaoh then summoned wise men and sorcerers, and the Egyptian magicians also did the same things by their secret arts: Each one threw down his staff and it became a snake. But Aaron's staff swallowed up their staffs. (7:11–12)*

Christ victoriously swallowed up death by disarming dark powers at the cross.

Healing Thought: I do not need to fear foul spirits, because God is with me.

Please, Lord, swallow up all the serpents of deception
that want to destroy me.

~~~~~~~~~~

- *"Bring your livestock and everything you have in the field to a place of shelter, because the hail will fall on every man and animal that has not been brought in" (9:19).*

God is the Good Shepherd and the Shelter for His flock.

Healing Thought: God is my sanctuary and stronghold in times of trouble.

Lord, thank You for caring about animals and
providing shelter for my family and me.

~~~~~~~~~~

- *Moses summoned all the elders of Israel and said to them, "Go at once and select the animals for your families and slaughter the Passover lamb. Take a bunch of hyssop, dip it into the blood in the basin and put some of the blood on the top and on both sides of the doorframe. Not one of you shall go out the door of his house until morning. When the LORD goes through the land to strike down the Egyptians, He will see the blood on the top and sides of the doorframe and will pass over that doorway, and He will not permit the destroyer to enter your houses and strike you down" (12:21–23).*

We are protected from eternal destruction by our Passover Lamb, Jesus Christ.

Healing Thought: The sacrificial death of Jesus is God's gift of love and life to me.

Dear Lord, help me to remember
Your wondrous deliverance to Israel and to me.

~~~~~~~~~~

- [The Passover] will be like a sign on your hand and a symbol on your forehead that the LORD brought us out of Egypt with his mighty hand. (13:16)

The Israelites would never forget the blood of the lamb saving them from death. Christians are to keep in consistent remembrance that they are sprinkled clean from a guilty conscience only through the blood of Christ.

Healing Thought: I never want to forget I am forgiven, set free by the Lamb of God.

Dear Lord, help me to forgive others
the way You have forgiven me.

~~~~~~~~~~

- *As Pharaoh approached, the Israelites looked up, and there were the Egyptians, marching after them. They were terrified and cried out to the LORD. (14:10)*

The Israelites became fearful by looking at their enemies, but they did a good thing by crying out to God.

Healing Thought: Fear displays a stalking enemy, but faith reveals a steadfast God.

> *Dear Lord, help me to keep my eyes upon You*
> *and trust that You are mightier than my enemies.*

~~~~~~~~~~

- *Moses answered the people, "Do not be afraid. Stand firm and you will see the deliverance the LORD....The LORD will fight for you; you need only to be still." (14:13-14)*

Moses assured the anxious Israelites that their liberation was not dependent on their abilities.

Healing Thought: Like a child who trusts her Daddy, I believe Father God will defend me in all my battles.

> *Lord, help me to know when to resist*
> *or when to rest during times of warfare.*

~~~~~~~~~~

- *For three days they traveled in the desert without finding water. When they came to Marah, they could not drink its water because it was bitter. So the people grumbled against Moses, saying, "What are we to drink?" (15:22–24).*

Wondrously, the Israelites were carried out of Egypt to a desert place where they were called to obey and trust their Good Shepherd. Israel faced a dry desert and bitter waters; God faced hearts that were parched and filled with poisonous thoughts. The season of training for reigning had begun, and God would use each life experience to break through their defense mechanisms.

Healing Thought: God guides me in paths of righteousness because I am His child.

Lord, help me to see that You are my Good Physician
Who restores my soul.

~~~~~~~~~~

- *Then Moses cried out to the LORD, and the LORD showed him a piece of wood. He threw it into the water, and the water became sweet. (15:25)*

A piece of wood sweetened the bitter water for Israel; Jesus, the Righteous Branch, sweetens Christians' bitter experiences through His cross and Calvary's grace.

Healing Thought: Grumbling multiplies my misery. Looking to God multiplies my blessings.

Lord, help me to follow Moses' example of crying out to You for help.
Thank You for changing my bitter heart into a grace-giving heart.

~~~~~~~~~~

- *"If you listen carefully to the voice of the LORD your God and do what is right in his eyes, if you pay attention to his commands and keep all his decrees, I will not bring on you any of the diseases I brought on the Egyptians, for I am the LORD, who heals you" (15:26).*

Man has never been able to attain God's perfection, but Jesus perfectly fulfilled all the demands of the law. My hope for healing rests upon the truth that my Righteous Healer lives inside of me. By Christ's wounds, I am healed.

Healing Thought: The way of Egypt brings disease; the way of God brings me health.

Thank You, Jesus, that on the cross
You bore all my grief of sickness, weakness, and distress.

~~~~~~~~~~

- *Then they came to Elim, where there were twelve springs and seventy palm trees, and they camped there near the water. (15:27)*

This place of trees was a wonderful oasis where they encamped and rested. God is the Oasis for His people in recovery, and in Christ are all the provisions for our restoration. The Lord loves His beloved people by the sweet fruit of His Spirit, He protects them through elders who are like stately palm trees, and He cares for them by the prophets and disciples who minister comfort like refreshing springs.

Healing Thought: God is my Oasis of Hope in times of trouble.

Thank you, Lord Jesus, for leading me to a restorative oasis
and not allowing me to stay stuck in parched and bitter places.

Nuggets of Wisdom

If God had not replaced my stones of deception with His nuggets of wisdom, I would not have been able to maintain health during my hard times. A wounded person can discover treasures for healing by taking a moment to review the wisdom imparted into my heart as I reflected on the Israelites' journey from Egypt to the Oasis. Agreeing with each therapeutic thought is good; even better, ask the Holy Spirit to open your inner senses to grasp these restorative truths. If God has already conveyed these concepts to you, pause to remember the details—the when and how of the impartation. *After pondering, continue to enrich your spirit by proclaiming the following pearls of wisdom:*

- ♥ Evil does not have the power to destroy my blessings.

- ♥ My God grieves over and hates the injustice that happens to me.

- ♥ When I suffer unjustly, Jesus knows, and His purposes for me will not be thwarted.

- ♥ God comforts me as I mourn and helps me to release my heart's pain to Him.

- ♥ God's word imparted prophetically to me is my anchor of hope when I feel like a little boat upon a stormy sea.

- ♥ God desires intimacy in my hard times; He understands when my spirit is willing but my flesh is weak.

- ♥ The lies of darkness will oppose my recovery, but God will bring me justice.

- ♥ God allows territorial spirits, with their lies, name-calling, and expectations, to be exposed for my restoration.

♥ Trying to appease evil is like putting a Band-Aid over a poisonous infection.

♥ When I turn to God and voice my complaints, He will impart grace to me.

♥ God does not condemn me when I struggle with despair. He understands my humanity.

♥ I do not need to fear foul spirits, because God is with me.

♥ God is my sanctuary and stronghold in times of trouble.

♥ The sacrificial death of Jesus is God's gift of love and life to me.

♥ I never want to forget that I am forgiven and set free by the Lamb of God.

♥ Fear displays a stalking enemy, but faith reveals a steadfast God.

♥ Like a child who trusts her Daddy, I believe Father God will defend me in all my battles.

♥ God guides me in paths of righteousness because I am His child.

♥ Grumbling multiplies my misery; looking to God multiplies my blessings.

♥ The way of Egypt brings disease; the way of God brings me health.

♥ God is my Oasis of Hope in times of trouble.

If unbelief or hindrances to understanding seem to block insight to these truths, your struggle or doubt may be an indication that you need further healing. Parched souls need to know God as their Restorative Oasis Who desires His redeemed to become like Him by following His ways. *The Good Shepherd promises to restore the souls of His lambs in His fertile pastures, beside His gentle waters!* Remember 1 Peter 5:6–7:

> Humble yourselves, therefore, under God's mighty hand,
> that he may lift you up in due time.
> Cast all your anxiety on him
> because he cares for you.

Chapter 17

Consider His Goodness and Glory

He lifted the needy out of their affliction
and increased their families like flocks.
The upright see and rejoice,
but all the wicked shut their mouths.
Whoever is wise, let him heed these things
and consider the great love of the LORD. (Psalm 107:41–43)

"After this I will return and rebuild David's fallen tent.
Its ruins I will rebuild, and I will restore it…" says the Lord (Acts 15:16–17)

His divine power has given us everything we need
for life and godliness through our knowledge of him
who called us by his own glory and goodness. (2 Peter 1:3)

The Lord calls and pursues His flock through His glory and goodness, graciously initiating and displaying His favor. God's glory is His goodness—the visible manifestation of heavenly splendor and majesty! "The LORD is good and his love endures forever; his faithfulness continues through all generations" (Psalm 100:5).

Some may wonder: is God "good" like apple pie is "good" (pleasing to the senses)? Is He like a "good man" who does good deeds, or like the "good woman" who is pleasant and enjoyable? The Lord is all this and so very much more: He is faithful, responsible, unfailing, unerring, reliable, dependable, credible, trustworthy, authentic, kind, gracious, and merciful. His character is revealed through His numerous names, such as:

- The Lord our Provider
- The Lord our Healer
- The Lord our Banner
- The Lord our Peace
- The Lord our Shepherd
- The Lord our Righteousness
- The Lord Who is There
- The Lord Who Sanctifies

His love always protects, trusts, hopes, perseveres, and *never fails* (1 Corinthians 13:7–8). Godly people wisely remember the wondrous deeds God has done on their behalf. David extolled,

> Yours, O LORD, is the greatness and the power and the glory and the majesty and the splendor, for everything in heaven and earth is yours. Yours, O LORD, is the kingdom; you are exalted as head over all. (1 Chronicles 29:11)

This same shepherd-king confidently exclaimed that the Lord's goodness and mercy would follow His lambs every day of their lives (Psalm 23:6). For day after day hope, we are wise to daily consider His magnificent love and compassion.

When Jeremiah was in great affliction, he wrote:

> This I call to mind
> and therefore I have hope:
> Because of the LORD's great love
> we are not consumed,
> for his compassions never fail.
>
> They are new every morning;
> great is your faithfulness.
> I say to myself, "The LORD is my portion;
> therefore I will wait for him."
>
> The LORD is good to those whose hope is in him,
> to the one who seeks him;
> it is good to wait quietly
> for the salvation of the LORD.
> (Lamentations 3:21–26)

In profound distress David pleaded, "Give me a sign of your goodness, that my enemies may see it and be put to shame for you, O LORD, have helped me and comforted me" (Psalm 86:17). Jeremiah noted,

> You performed miraculous signs and wonders in Egypt and have continued them to this day, both in Israel and among all mankind, and have gained the renown that is still yours. You brought your people Israel out of Egypt with signs and wonders, by a mighty hand and an outstretched arm and with great terror. You gave them this land you had sworn to give their forefathers, a land flowing with milk and honey. (Jeremiah 32:20–22).

God's glorious presence imparts joy and gladness of heart.

Jesus Christ is the manifestation of God's glory and goodness. "The Lord himself will give you a sign: The virgin will be with child and will give birth to a son, and will call him Immanuel" (Isaiah 7:14). Centuries later, in fulfillment of Scripture, Mary gave birth to Jesus who was called, "Immanuel—which means, 'God with us'" (Matthew 1:23). *Jesus is the embodiment of God's glory.*

John, the beloved disciple, declared, "The Word became flesh and made his dwelling among us. We have seen his glory, the glory of the One and Only, who came from the Father, full of grace and truth" (John 1:14). John personally saw Christ's transfiguration.

> He [Jesus] took Peter, John and James with him and went up onto a mountain to pray. As he was praying, the appearance of his face changed, and his clothes became as bright as a flash of lightning. Two men, Moses and Elijah, appeared in glorious splendor, talking with Jesus. They spoke about his departure, which he was about to bring to fulfillment at Jerusalem. (Luke 9:28–31)

Manifestations of God's Goodness and Glory

Throughout the ages, in countless ways, God has manifested His goodness and glory because He knows how consequential it is for mankind to remember His redemptive love and grace. Besides through the life of Christ, God demonstrated of His character through leaders such as Moses, martyrs like Stephen, His awesome creation, heavenly signs like the rainbow, heavenly visions as described by the prophets, the restoration of His people, and all the changed lives of His precious saints.

As a discouraged leader of unruly Israel, Moses, wanting to see God's glory, asked for a sign of His favor: "How will anyone know that you are pleased with me and with your people unless you go with us? What else will distinguish me and your people from all the other people on the face of the earth" (Exodus 33:16)? In other words, Moses was asking Immanuel, *"Are You with us?"*

God honored Moses' request:

> I will cause all my goodness to pass in front of you, and I will proclaim my name, the LORD, in your presence. I will have mercy on whom I will have mercy, and I will have compassion on whom I will have compassion. But ... you cannot see my face, for no one may see me and live.... There is a place near me where you may stand on a rock. When my glory passes by, I will put you in a cleft in the rock and cover you with my hand until I have passed by. Then I will remove my hand and you will see my back; but my face must not be seen. (vv. 19–23)

In like manner, those who are in Christ are invited to behold God's glory: "Did I not tell you that if you believed, you would see the glory of God?" (John 11:40). Stephen, a deacon in the early church, saw God's glory as he was being murdered for his faith: "Full of the Holy Spirit, [he] looked up to heaven and saw the glory of God, and Jesus standing at the right hand of God. 'Look,' he said, 'I see heaven open and the Son of Man standing at the right hand of God'" (Acts 7:55–56). Jesus personally welcomed him into heaven.

No one will be able to accuse God of not revealing His glory, *"for since the creation of the world God's invisible qualities—his eternal power and divine nature—have been clearly seen, being understood from what has been made, so that men are without excuse"* (Romans 1:20). "The heavens declare the glory of God; the skies proclaim the work of his hands" (Psalm 19:1).

As I gaze out my bedroom window each morning, my soul finds so much comfort in beholding His beauty through nature. I giggle with God's joy as I notice the garden squirrels jumping about like acrobats; I remember God's care by observing the variety of birds thriving throughout the winter months; I recall God's splendor when I gaze upon my red maple tree whose limbs seem to reach up into the heavens; I see God's majesty when my flowers become a palette of color; I find God's peace by lingering in awe at the changing hues of the rising sun; I remember God's faithfulness when I view the rainbow after a morning mist.

The Lord set His rainbow in place as a sign of promise to mankind that He would never again destroy all life through a flood: "'I have set my rainbow in the clouds, and it will be the sign of the covenant between me and the earth'" (Genesis 9:13). I also see the rainbow as the heavenly Father's mantle of light around His Son, Jesus, "the guarantee of a better covenant" (Hebrews 7:22). In the biblical account of Joseph, who wore a multi-colored coat he received from his father, Christ's rainbow-like mantle was prefigured. Ezekiel had a vision of this:

> High above on the throne was a figure like that of a man.... Like the appearance of a rainbow in the clouds on a rainy day, so was the radiance around him. This was the appearance of the likeness of the glory of the LORD. (Ezekiel 1:26, 28)

In the Bible's last chapter, the apostle John records the culmination of God's glory for all who embrace His Son:

> Then the angel showed me the river of the water of life, as clear as crystal, flowing from the throne of God and of the Lamb down the middle of the great street of the city. On each side of the river stood the tree of life, bearing twelve crops of fruit, yielding its fruit every month. And the leaves of the tree are for the healing of the nations. No longer will there be any curse. The throne of God and of the Lamb will be in the city, and his servants will serve him. They will see his face, and his name will be on their foreheads. There will be no more night. They will not need the light of a lamp or the light of the sun, for the Lord God will give them light. And they will reign for ever and ever. (Revelation 22:1–5)

A Clearer Picture of God's Goodness

God chooses to reveal His glory through Israel's redemption: "Sing for joy, O heavens, for the LORD has done this; shout aloud, O earth beneath.

Burst into song ... for the LORD has redeemed Jacob, *he displays his glory in Israel.* This is what the LORD says—your Redeemer, who formed you in the womb: I am the LORD" (Isaiah 44:23–24).

Using a spiritual analogy, Ezekiel recounts God's goodness and love for His beloved Jerusalem (see Ezekiel 16). The passage provides an overview of Jerusalem's history from the time God adopted her as His own child to the time of His glorious reunion with His betrothed at the end of the ages. Because Israel turned against the One Who loved her, the awesome ending to the love story still awaits fulfillment. Amazingly, at all times God has continued to be a faithful Father to Israel, despite her becoming like a rebellious daughter to Him. God will return, rebuild and restore His fallen people.

Israel has suffered for her sin: "Because you did not remember the days of your youth but enraged me with all these things, I will surely bring down on your head what you have done, declares the Sovereign LORD" (v. 43). Each time Israel did not trust in God's goodness and forgot His covenant promises, disaster followed. The wise and loving Father allowed her to feel pain when she chose to walk away from His covering love, but not without pain on His own part. Papa God grieved and mourned when Israel became like the idols she served: "Since my people are crushed, I am crushed; I mourn, and horror grips me" (Jeremiah 8:21).

Even God's wrath shows His goodness, for He has been just and true in allowing His childish ones to reap what they have sown. As to the penalty for sin, however—which is death—Father God, at His appointed time, sacrificed His only begotten Son so that sinful people (*all* of us) would again have a way to live forever with Him. Thank *God*, anyone who trusts in the Lord Jesus Christ does not have to reap all he has sown!

When I consider the allegorical picture of Israel and Judah's ruin and restoration as portrayed by Ezekiel, I see a clearer portrait of God's goodness. It is a promise of hope for all who admit they are needy and feel forsaken. The narrative is full of minute details significant for hope and healing. The symbolic elements beckon for an interpretation; there is more in this text than the obvious moral lesson that sin has consequences.

Like telephone rings that can't be ignored, many questions invade my mind. How did this happen? What were the circumstances that led up to Israel and Judah's downfall? How did she receive inner healing from her emotional wounds? What are the revelations about God that will increase my understanding of His tender ways? Are there vital precepts that can be gleaned from this tragic example?

Taking a closer look, I see the intimacy God desires to have with His people; specifically, in this case, a love that is always seeking the highest good for His beloved Jerusalem. Many will identify with her struggles and strongholds: Jerusalem fell into deep sin because wounded people tend to make sinful choices. People neglected and victimized by their parents usually repeat their forefathers' iniquity; sin will perpetuate and continue until its cycle of connection is stopped and broken through Christ.

There is no pit of darkness that brokenhearted individuals may sink into that is beyond God's reach for their total recovery. It is encouraging to know that God's goodness and glory will ultimately heal Jerusalem's wounded spirit and transform her soul. She has never been, and never will be, forsaken.

Please consider the following highlighted reflections from Ezekiel 16.

Consider Jerusalem's Pagan Heritage

Your ancestry and birth were in the land of the Canaanites; your father was an Amorite and your mother a Hittite. (v. 3)

The Amorites were a fierce people who made Babylon their capital. Like the Hittites, they worshiped the stars and planets, especially the sun and moon; both Ur and Haran had temples dedicated to the moon-god. God called Abram (later Abraham) and his family to break from this pagan idolatry and commit to worshiping only the Lord, "Listen to Me, O Jacob, Israel, the One True God, the Creator: My called [ones]: I am He; I am the First, I also am the Last" (Isaiah 48:12 AMP).

In *The Journey to Wholeness in Christ*, Signa Bodishbaugh shares,

The early pagans followed a lengthy fertility ritual. First, the ruler of a tribe celebrated the rites of spring by having sexual intercourse with the earth, symbolizing his peoples' hopes for the fertility of the earth, and thus, abundant crops. Then young virgins were chosen to symbolize the earth by receiving the seed of the carnal priests in temple ceremonies. Every other man and woman was enjoined to imitate the ritual with the male and female prostitutes of the temple. When children were born from these couplings, they were offered as "holy" sacrifices to the god Molech (the other side of Baal), and were thrown into fires or off cliffs or into a river. Modern excavations have uncovered graveyards filled with pottery vessels containing bones of millions of tiny infants sacrificed to the gods. These are always located adjacent to the temple ruins.[21]

Consider Jerusalem's Abusive Beginnings

On the day you were born your cord was not cut, nor were you washed with water to make you clean, nor were you rubbed with salt or wrapped in cloths. No one looked on you with pity or had compassion enough to do any of these things for you. Rather, you were thrown out into the open field, for on the day you were born you were despised. (Ezekiel 16:4–5)

Consider God's Response

Then I passed by and saw you kicking about in your blood, and as you lay there in your blood I said to you, "Live!" I made you grow like a plant of the field. (vv. 6–7)

God breathed His very life into this dying infant and caused her to grow.

Consider the Effects of Abuse

You grew up and became tall and arrived at full maidenhood; your breasts were formed and your hair had grown; yet you were naked and bare. (v. 7 RSV)

Jerusalem was mature on the outside, but she felt emotionally empty. Her spirit had been wounded and crushed.

Consider God's Covenant Relationship

Later I passed by, and when I looked at you and saw that you were old enough for love, I spread the corner of my garment over you and covered your nakedness. I gave you my solemn oath and entered into a covenant with you, declares the Sovereign LORD, and you became mine. (v. 8)

Consider the Blessings Freely Bestowed on God's Beloved

I bathed you with water and washed the blood from you and put ointments on you. I clothed you with an embroidered dress and put leather sandals on you. I dressed you in fine linen and covered you with costly garments. I adorned you with jewelry...and a beautiful crown on your head. So you were adorned with gold and silver; your clothes were of fine linen and costly fabric and embroidered cloth. Your food was fine flour, honey and olive oil. (vv. 9–13)

Consider God's Affirmation of Jerusalem's Identity

You became very beautiful and rose to be a queen. And your fame spread among the nations on account of your beauty, because the splendor I had given you made your beauty perfect. (vv. 13–14)

Consider Her Prideful Response

But you trusted in your beauty and used your fame to become a prostitute. You lavished your favors on anyone who passed by and your beauty became his. (v. 15)

Consider Her Betrayal of God

You took some of your garments to make gaudy high places, where you carried on your prostitution. Such things should not happen, nor should they ever occur. You also took the fine jewelry I gave you, the jewelry made of my gold and silver, and you made for yourself male idols and engaged in prostitution with them. And you took your embroidered clothes to put on them, and you offered my oil and incense before them. Also the food I provided for you—the fine flour, olive oil and honey I gave you to eat—you offered as fragrant incense before them. That is what happened. (vv. 16–19)

Consider Her Generational Iniquity Leading to Abuse and Murder

And you took your sons and daughters whom you bore to me and sacrificed them as food to the idols. Was your prostitution not enough? You slaughtered my children and sacrificed them to the idols. (vv. 20–21)

Consider Her Spiritual Blindness

In all your detestable practices and your prostitution you did not remember the days of your youth, when you were naked and bare, kicking about in your blood. (v. 22)

She forgot God's goodness and grace on her behalf.

Consider the Soul Ties Joining Her to Pagan Nations

- She joined herself to lust: *"You engaged in prostitution with the Egyptians"* (v. 26).
- She lost part of herself: *"I gave you over to the greed of your enemies, the daughters of the Philistines"* (v. 27).
- She gave herself away and her cravings became insatiable: *"You engaged in prostitution with the Assyrians too"* (v. 28).
- She prostituted herself and was devoured by her desires: *"Then you increased your promiscuity to include Babylonia"* (v. 29).

Consider the Results of Her Sin

- She became weak and lost proper boundaries over her personhood: *"How weak-willed you are ... when you do all these things"* (v. 30).

- She practiced idolatry by worshiping pagan gods: *"You ... made your lofty shrines in every public square"* (v. 31).
- She became unfaithful to the Lord, her spouse: *"You adulterous wife! You prefer strangers to your own husband!"* (v. 32).
- She used her gifts from God to buy the affections of others: *"You give gifts to all your lovers, bribing them to come to you"* (v. 33).
- Her "lovers" became her destroyers: *"Your lovers ... will bring a mob against you, who will stone you and hack you to pieces with their swords"* (vv. 35–42).
- She became double-minded, both loving and loathing her lovers: *" ... your lovers, with whom you found pleasure, those you loved as well as those you hated ..."* (v. 37).
- She engaged in carnal and coarse behavior: *"Did you not add lewdness to all your other detestable practices?"* (v. 43).
- She established a generational stronghold: *"You are a true daughter of your mother [a Hittite], who despised her husband and her children"* (vv. 44–45).
- She walked perversely by ignoring those in need: *"Your younger sister ... was Sodom.... They did not help the poor and needy"* (vv. 47–49).

Consider God's Counsel

Three times God says, *"Bear your disgrace."* He also adds, "That you [Judah], amid your shame and disgrace, may be compelled to recognize your wickedness and be thoroughly ashamed and confounded at all you have done, becoming [converted and bringing] consolation and comfort to [your sisters]" (vv. 54 AMP).

It was not good that those outside of God's covenant were relieved that they were not as sinful as Jerusalem. She lost fellowship with her Betrothed because of her idolatry and immorality. Only confession of her sins and turning from evildoing would restore intimacy with her Husband. Father God's love for Israel never ceased, but His holiness necessitated her repentance.

Consider God's Goodness and Glory

- God gave Jerusalem grace to bear her humiliation: *"I will restore ... your fortunes ... so that you may bear your disgrace"* (vv. 53–54).

- God remembered His previous covenant with Israel and now also established an eternal covenant with her: *"I will establish an everlasting covenant with you"* (v. 60).
- Jerusalem would know her God and be His faithful wife for eternity: *"You will know that I am the LORD"* (v. 62).
- At the cross of Christ, God would provide atonement: *"I make atonement for you for all you have done"* (v. 63).
- Never would Jerusalem feel worthless—she would know she was forgiven and delivered of shame: *"You will remember and be ashamed and never again open your mouth because of your humiliation"* (v. 63).

Concluding Insights

Astonishingly, God kept His heart open to His estranged wife by remembering His covenant promises to her. Faithfully He has waited for His prodigal, Jerusalem, to return home! God's prophet Ezekiel proclaimed:

> This is what the Sovereign LORD says: "Come from the four winds, O breath, and breathe into these slain, that they may live" So I prophesied as he commanded me, and breath entered them; they came to life and stood up on their feet—a vast army.
>
> Then he said to me: "Son of man, these bones are the whole house of Israel". They say, "Our bones are dried up and our hope is gone; we are cut off." Therefore prophesy and say to them: "This is what the Sovereign LORD says: 'O my people, I am going to open your graves and bring you up from them; I will bring you back to the land of Israel.
>
> Then you, my people, will know that I am the LORD, when I open your graves and bring you up from them. I will put my Spirit in you and you will live, and I will settle you in your own land. Then you will know that I the LORD have spoken, and I have done it, declares the LORD'" (37:9–14).

Zechariah shares more about her repentance:

> I will pour out on the house of David and the inhabitants of Jerusalem a spirit of grace and supplication. They will look on me, the one they have pierced, and they will mourn for him as one mourns for an only child, and grieve bitterly for him as one grieves for a firstborn son. (Zechariah 12:10)

God will give to the house of David a revelation that Jesus Christ is their cleansing fountain. Someday one-third of the inhabitants of Jerusalem will repent of their wrongdoing and seek their Messiah's face; they will be purified like refined silver (see Zechariah 13). The fruit of Jerusalem's repentance will be clear to the whole world; she will comfort others like a nursing mother.

Rejoice with Jerusalem and be glad for her, all you who love her; rejoice greatly with her, all you who mourn over her. For you will nurse and be satisfied at her comforting breasts; you will drink deeply and delight in her overflowing abundance. (Isaiah 66:10–11)

Ezekiel 16 remarkably demonstrates that whenever a repentant child of God turns to Him for mercy, He will respond with reconciliation and restoration. Scripture declares this of God's faithfulness:

Whenever anyone turns to the Lord, the veil is taken away. Now the Lord is the Spirit, and where the Spirit of the Lord is, there is freedom. And we, who with unveiled faces all reflect the Lord's glory, are being transformed into his likeness with ever-increasing glory, which comes from the Lord, who is the Spirit. (2 Corinthians 3:16–18)

The Lord promises to the contrite of heart: "I have seen your ways; I will heal you, guide you, and restore comfort to you!" (Isaiah 57:18, paraphrased).

A Closing Prayer

One thing I ask of the LORD,
this is what I seek:
that I may dwell in the house of the LORD,
all the days of my life ,
to gaze upon the beauty of the LORD
and to seek him in his temple.

For in the day of trouble
he will keep me safe in his dwelling;
he will hide me in the shelter of his tabernacle
and set me high upon a rock.
Though my father and mother forsake me,
the LORD will receive me.

I am still confident of this :
I will see the goodness of the LORD
in the land of the living.
(Psalm 27:4–5, 10, 13)

Chapter 18

Pivotal Points of My Restoration

Are you tired? Worn out? Burned out on religion?
Come to me. I'll show you how to take a real rest.
Walk with me and work with me—watch how I do it.
Learn from the unforced rhythms of grace.
I won't lay anything heavy or ill-fitting on you.
Keep company with me and you'll learn to live freely and lightly.
(Matthew 11:28–30 MSG)

In this chapter, I will reflect on pivotal points in my life when Christ exchanged my yoke for His. Earlier we learned about particular key events God initiated to mold Moses into a vessel fit for the King. Would God's purposes for Moses have been fulfilled without his encounter with the fiery bush? Never! The blaze in the wilderness was a phenomenon that transformed God's servant from a dimly burning wick into God's lamp who brought light to the entire household of Israel.

Like Moses and all saints down through the ages, I have experienced decisive events—God's anchoring points that inspired me to walk more closely with Him. Many times I have been like a boat upon a stormy sea; yet Jesus, my Anchor of Hope, kept me afloat. Sometimes I have felt forsaken, even though from childhood I was yoked to Him. Each major event has advanced my understanding of the vastness of my birthright in Christ—a transforming breakthrough that has prepared me for the grand purposes God designed for me. The pivotal points have strengthened and continually, unshakably harmonized me to the Lord.

Everyone who trusts in Jesus Christ for eternal salvation is a living testimony of His goodness. God desires all believers under His lordship to be prepared to give an answer to everyone who inquires about the hope that is evident in their lives (1 Peter 3:15). Christians are called to testify about their marvelous Savior and are commissioned to share the gospel of the kingdom so that all the nations may know Him.

After the Samaritan woman found her Eternal Spring at the well, she testified, "Jesus told me everything I ever did" (John 4:39). As a result, many from her hometown believed in Christ after seeing and hearing the transformed woman witness about her wondrous God-encounter. Paul, a light to the Gentiles, acknowledged that he did not speak with eloquence or his own superior wisdom, yet his preaching powerfully impacted multitudes and eventually altered the whole world for Jesus.

Where did the power of their witness come from? *Both were yoked to the Living Christ!*

King David testified:

> I waited patiently for the LORD;
>   he turned to me and heard my cry.
> He lifted me out of the slimy pit,
>   out of the mud and mire;
>   he set my feet on a rock
>   and gave me a firm place to stand.
> He put a new song in my mouth,
>   a hymn of praise to our God.
> Many will see and fear
> and put their trust in the LORD.
> Many, O LORD my God,
>   are the wonders you have done.
>   The thing s you planned for us...
>   They would be too many to declare.
> I proclaim righteousness in the great assembly;
>   I do not seal my lips,
>   as you know, O LORD.
> I do not hide your righteousness in my heart;
>   I speak of your faithfulness and salvation.
>   I do not conceal your love and your truth.
>   (Psalm 40:1–3, 5, 9–10)

In addition to the events I have already shared, I want to speak about significant "connecting moments" when Christ pursued and I responded. Using Jesus' invitation to come to Him, I will address six amazing segments of His gracious yoke. *He exchanged my dry places for His fertile oasis of care, peace, joy, gentleness, love, and significance.*

Jesus asks, *"Are You Tired? Worn Out? Come to Me."*

The first pivotal point occurred in 1959. By then I had been married several years, had a precious one-year-old son, and a husband who was a full-time student at the University of Minnesota. Even though our monthly rent for married housing was forty-five dollars, including utilities, we were barely making ends meet. Tom worked part-time at a service station; I sold Avon. We'd saved up for schooling, but not enough for both of us to complete college. Our dubious fun was going to Granny's once a week for a delicious dinner.

In the midst of all this, I was restless, bored, and thinking about attending school. *But how?* Our resources were insufficient, and loans weren't readily available. Asking relatives for the money would have been futile.

I did a good thing—I cried out to God—and, to my amazement, He responded! He impressed upon my heart that He was with me and would make a way for me; He also inquired whether I would apply my education to His special service. I responded with a quick yes, and didn't bother to ask what He intended by this. Since I desired to be a teacher, I assumed He meant employment in the field of education.

When I told Tom I wanted to enroll in upcoming fall classes, he was very supportive. That September, we were both in school, paying tuition fees from our meager savings. With childlike faith, we trusted God to provide for future expenses. The next year, we transferred to a smaller state college so our expenditures would be less.

In the fall of 1960, after piling all our belongings into a large open four-wheel trailer, we headed south in our seventy-five-dollar 1951 Chevy Belaire toward our new residence in Mankato. With no protective tarp over our furniture, we were relieved that it didn't rain before we pulled into town. However, after stopping at a four-way light, as we started up again, our rear bumper, which had probably been strained from the trailer's heavy load, snapped off with a loud clang.

Alarmed, Tom made an abrupt stop … which supplied momentum to the trailer. With its cargo fully intact, it coasted past the right side of our car and continued down the parking lane of Main Street. I screamed in dread when I saw all our worldly goods headed on a disastrous path that might include people or automobiles. Unbelievably, even though it was mid-afternoon, nothing hindered its flight! The trailer finally ground to a gradual halt at the curb, stopping short of all the parked vehicles ahead of it.

Tom's sister and her husband, who had been following us, had watched the whole scene in horror. After regaining our composure, grateful but weary, we continued our journey. Thankfully their car was able to pull the trailer to our rented basement apartment a few miles away.

Looking back on the move, we are able to laugh at the bizarre near-miss, but also very grateful for what didn't happen. If the trailer had pulled loose on the hilly highway going into the city, there could have been a tragic accident. We all concluded that the only explanation for our happy ending was God's protection through quick-acting guardian angels.

~~~~~~~~~~

The Lord continued to be faithful. He kept our family healthy, stretched our money, and helped Tom to find work. To my delight, I was offered scholarships and grants after attending the first quarter of college. A used five-dollar LC Smith & Bros. typewriter continued to service our typing needs, and our car had only a few repairable difficulties.

There were many days of exhaustion, and we usually spent Sunday sleeping late. I remember taking tests in a fog, but instead of failing I would exceed beyond all my expectations. I started to trust God as my Wise Shepherd Who would hear my cries of distress and carry our family over the numerous rough bumps we encountered.

On June 5, 1962, Tom and I graduated. Twenty days later, our daughter was born! We borrowed three hundred dollars from my parents to pay for her birth and *all* other debts. While I was in the hospital, Tom and a friend moved our furniture, in his more reliable car, to the town where Tom would be employed as a teacher.

In retrospect, I can see that *I was building a career, but God was building a calling.* The university increased my proficiency and knowledge in communication, psychology, child development, writing, art, music, problem solving, and homemaking—all of which has been a practical aid for pastoral counseling. But most of all, it was what I experienced through daily living that was so profitable: God's kindness, love, and grace molded me into an earthen vessel filled with heaven's treasures.

I am so glad I answered yes to Christ's invitation to come to His spiritual rest. He was able to break through my many doubts by a revelation of His care and provision!

Jesus says, *"Burned Out? I'll Show You How to Find Peace."*

The second transforming episode developed around 1969, but had its beginnings in 1964. After teaching for two years, Tom secured a better paying job with 3M as a salesman for their automotive division. After training in Minneapolis, we moved to New Orleans; Tom sold the company's products in Louisiana and along the coastal areas of Mississippi and Alabama. I enjoyed the extra income, but was lonely living so far from family, and I missed Tom during his frequent out-of-town sales calls.

We found a church we liked, and I kept myself busy with its many activities. My self-serving relationship with Christ was not obvious to me because I performed so well in leadership positions. Deceived by pride, religion crowded out my intimacy with God.

By 1969, our marriage had deteriorated; each blamed the other. I was filled with self-pity and resented Tom for leaving me with so many family responsibilities while he played. My mental list of his wrongs kept growing. Miserable, I sought out our pastor for care. After one discouraging meeting, I wondered about divorcing Tom, but making that choice would have devastated our children, so I continued to busy myself with family, teaching, and church.

Everything finally came to a head when Tom stayed out all night one Saturday with nary a call to me. When he did come home, he refused to talk about it; I was furious and schemed revenge. I wanted to show him how much he had hurt me, so later in the day I suddenly left without telling him.

As I drove away, I felt exhilarated at getting even, but my high didn't last: I had failed to plan where to go. Pride kept me from visiting any friends; I wasn't ready to take down my façade of having it all together. Going to a bar alone would have been sheer terror, so I self-righteously drove to our church.

~~~~~~~~~~

I was the first one in the sanctuary for the evening service. Weary from lack of sleep and exhausted from the discord in my home, I wondered if I would fall asleep during the preaching. That night's guest speaker had to be assisted to the podium. His cerebral palsy hindered his speech, and I couldn't understand him. Though I was restless and wanted to leave, God had another plan: supernaturally, I started to hear every word. The man's voice seemingly became unnoticeable while Christ's voice became prominent. His sermon was simple but powerful; more than three and a half decades later I can still recall the message, about a nameless lad who gave his all to Jesus (see John 6:5–13).

While Jesus taught and healed the sick, the gathered multitude had become hungry by the end of the day. Compassionately, Jesus expressed a need to feed them, and Andrew presented five loaves and a couple fish offered by a youngster. Ignoring Andrew's questioning about obvious inadequacy, Jesus received the offering, and after blessing and breaking the food, He proceeded to supply all who were in need.

The speaker compared himself to the lad's insufficient offering: he had difficulty walking and talking, but he had given his broken life, his all, to Jesus, the One Who had called him to be a minister. What he had to give was inadequate, but in Jesus' blessed hands he was transformed, and his Savior became his adequacy.

I couldn't deny the frailties of this man of God; even so, miraculously, his broken, consecrated life was feeding a multitude—and me. Through him, Jesus spoke to my spirit, and my defensive heart was softened. My own importance became ridiculous, and I repented of my self-serving, disrespectful ways, asking God to change me. I also went forward and asked the speaker to pray for me; peace soon settled my heart. When I returned to my pew, God's still small voice encouraged me to go home and love my husband, assuring me that His grace would be my adequacy. And it was!

~~~~~~~~~~

Throughout the years, while I never forgot the message, I could never remember the preacher's name. I wanted to thank him for his testimony and for planting a divine seed into my heart that will bloom forever. Thirty-five years later, a loving God arranged the details. On May 4, 2004, Focus on the Family's radio ministry aired a previously taped message by Allan C. Oggs, Sr.; I knew instantly that this was the man who had tremendously impacted my life. I cried throughout the program and then wrote a thank-you note to Rev. Oggs, sent through Dr. Dobson's staff and kindly forwarded to Pastor Allan.

I am so glad I answered yes to Christ's invitation to choose His way of peace. He was able to break through my strong will by a revelation of His strength and adequacy!

Jesus Beckons, *"Choose My Yoke and Walk With Me."*

The third anchoring event happened April 19, 1971, when the Lord exchanged my discouragement for His encouragement. I know the exact date because I wrote about it in my Bible.

In the spring of 1970, Tom gained a position as national sales manager with a corporation based in Boston. Our family was excited about the adventure, especially our new home where we'd have a distant view of the Atlantic and be able to enjoy its changing seascape. That fall the children settled in their new schools and I did some substitute teaching. We were glad to discover a Baptist church that had many young families, a place where we could make new friends.

It wasn't long, though, before my high expectations came crashing down with a thud. I felt God had brought us to an ocean of troubles instead of His land filled with milk and honey! For one thing, our son's new neighborhood buddy was of questionable character. The one time we brought him to church, he disrupted the service with loud swearing, and the more I quietly prayed for him, the more brazen he became, so we left early. Later that year, the police caught the two of them stealing bicycles for the lark of it. Not only did they have their own bikes, but they hid the stolen ones in our yard. After that, Tommy was not allowed to hang around "the mischief maker." Naively, we thought this would keep him out of difficulties, but our "saintly son" continued in sneaky rebellion with ease.

Meanwhile, our daughter, Michele, was having her own struggles. In New Orleans she had been sought out by friends, but now she experienced mean teasing from bullies. I felt so sad when the children from a family living down the street completely rejected her. Their son threw stones at her on occasion, and she was not included in their parties even when all the other neighborhood kids were. The abuse spilled over into her classroom; she became known as an "untouchable cootie." She spent most of her vacation days at home using her imagination to have fun.

Tom, traveling extensively but home on weekends, had a favorite pastime of lying on our den floor within reach of the TV dial, madly switching channels. After church he usually raced home to watch endless sports. When football season was over, basketball would consume his time. I used to tell him that yes, he was home, but he wasn't home. No essence! He seemed to me like a hibernating cave bear.

Additionally, his company suddenly decreased his salary to a minimal base with incentives. We had no savings to tide us over until commissions would be realized.

I wish I could say I drew closer to my big God by remembering His care and adequacy, but instead I imagined the worst; dark thoughts assailed me. I felt sick with dread and could not shake off lingering illnesses. Like the murmuring Israelites, I felt forsaken by God and wondered why He had led us to this dry place. I was angry at both God and Tom for not protecting me.

Out of discouragement, I stopped my usual conversing with the Lord; I felt my prayers were hitting a wall and bouncing back. It didn't dawn on me that my avoidance of my Savior was similar to Tom's emotional withdrawal from me—we were both isolating out of depression. For three months at the beginning of 1971, the only words I mumbled to God were, "I'm your servant, use me." And I cried a lot.

~~~~~~~~~~

During this time I was seeking financial relief and decided to do something I would enjoy: I put a notice in the local paper advertising art classes in my home. Since the room I would be utilizing had limited space, I was glad a feasible number of women responded. One, Natalie, caught my attention by bubbling over with joy. She dearly loved God and His Word, and at every class she shared about new things God was doing in her life.

When I compared myself to her, I was puzzled; Natalie, a relatively new Christian, was able to witness effectively, effortlessly to others. Unobtrusively she shared the Word she treasured; I, a believer for twenty-five years, could hardly read my Bible, pray, or talk about Christ. I had never seen anyone in my church (much less an Episcopalian!) so excited about God. When I told her I was teaching about the Holy Spirit in my junior high Sunday school class, she handed me a Don Bashan book called *Face Up With a Miracle*.[22] Although I desperately needed to connect with God, I despairingly disregarded the book on the nightstand beside my bed.

About a month later, I woke up and couldn't stop crying. My eyes fell on the title of Don Bashan's book given to me earlier by Natalie. Knowing

I desperately needed a miracle, I picked it up. Transfixed, I continuously read to the last chapter; then, with the book, I headed for the white throne of the "necessary room." There I read a suggested prayer and asked God to touch my life as He had for Bashan and the saints in the book of Acts. Miraculously, His love surrounded me and His joy filled my heart. When the Lord clothed me with His power, He exchanged my yoke of heavy cares with His yoke of gentleness (Luke 24:49).

> My mouth was filled with laughter,
>   my heart with songs of wonder.
> Let it be said among the nations,
>   "The Lord has done majestic miracles."
> The Lord has done great things for me,
>   and I am filled with joy.
> The Lord restored my fortunes,
>   like streams in the desert.
> I who sowed in tears will reap with songs of joy.
>   (Psalm 126:2–5 paraphrased).

Subsequently, intending to sweep the kitchen floor, I grabbed my broom and joyously danced around, repeatedly shouting "God loves me!" Faith, hope, and love continued to fill me, and instead of speaking critical words over my family, I spoke to God on their behalf.

~~~~~~~~~~

This anchoring event not only changed my life, it also had great impact on my family. The oppression in our home lifted. Michele and I forgave the bullies in her life, praying that God would either change them or move them. Six months later, the three main families whose children had wounded her spirit moved away; Michele then found some special friends. God's precept of blessing our enemies was remarkably written upon our hearts through His chisel of adversity.

Our son was caught stealing again, this time by our neighbors across the street. Knowing they weren't around, Tommy had walked into their unlocked home and "borrowed" a Playboy. After looking at the pictures, he returned it by sneaking quietly back inside, but as he was running out their back door, a policeman who was also their gardener, spotted him and reported the incident to them.

Perplexed and embarrassed, we encouraged them to file charges, hoping our son would learn valuable moral lessons. After his arrest, he apologized and was placed on one year's probation. Gladly and faithfully he attended our church's youth group (which Tom and I led); the episode opened up authentic communication with our son. God's loving hand of correction was upon him.

Tom and I drew closer together, and we prayed for blessings on our finances. He soon earned substantial commission checks that provided an income much larger than the old salary. Again God redeemed an apparent curse and turned it into a blessing. God also led me to a teaching position in the junior high art department.

I am so glad I answered yes to Christ's invitation to be yoked with His power. He was able to break through my discouragement by a revelation of His joy and His Spirit!

Jesus Invites, *"Learn From Me, for I Am Gentle and Humble."*

The next defining moment transpired as a burning-bush experience in the fall of 1971. Since the previous spring, God's love had continued to flow like a river through me to others. His Spirit ignited a spark in my heart that became a fiery passion for me to know my Lord Jesus. The Good Shepherd gave me an unquenchable thirst for His still waters of truth.

Previously, trying to have daily devotions, I would invariably get distracted. Urges to eat, sleep, drink, use the bathroom, or have wandering thoughts or daydreams usually meant I had little success and lots of hidden shame. With my newfound desire, the Lord guided me with ease to consume His Word and understand scriptural principles, drawing me to His wisdom like a deer to a salt lick. When I opened my Bible, I felt like an explorer who had discovered the fountain of youth, only to find myriad endless springs and a bottomless well that fed the fount. Never in my lifetime will I be able to totally comprehend or utilize Christ's immeasurable treasures, but my daily portion is always sufficient!

One morning as I was reading about the call of Moses in the desert, God became like a blazing fire inside of me and spoke to my heart about many things, including a revelation of His calling on my life. For about two hours we dialogued about my future mission and the purposes He had planned. As with Moses, God was calling me to be His ambassador to proclaim deliverance to the captive and to set free the burdened and the battered. Getting from where I was to where He was calling me was more than I could have imagined as a possibility.

After pondering what my Lord had spoken to me, I called my pastor and asked if I could see him as soon as possible. That afternoon, when I told Rev. Glynn about my morning events, he listened intently and told me to write the vision down, put it away, and allow God to bring it into being. He warned me not to strive or attempt to open my own doors because God will always inaugurate everything He has commissioned. He told me I had been blessed with a "charismatic" encounter.

Since I didn't understand the meaning of that word, I looked it up and found that it means a *supernatural visitation* by God. I also learned that numerous times the Bible refers to Moses as a servant of the Lord. I knew

Christ had imparted into my heart the revelation that I was called to be God's servant for distinct purposes. I recorded all I could recall about this anchoring time and saved it in my Bible.

~~~~~~~~~~

Over the years, to my delight, Christ has gently shepherded me and given me the desire and the will to listen to Him! My Lord has implemented the purposes designed for me by opening essential doors. Garden of Grace Ministries was a part of that prophetic word given so long ago, but there is still a portion that waits to be fulfilled. I know God will continue to complete everything He has begun in me: "God, who has called you into fellowship with His Son Jesus Christ our Lord, is faithful" (1 Corinthians 1:9).

I am so glad I answered yes to Christ's invitation to learn His gentle ways. He was able to break through my distractions by a revelation of His prophetic purposes for my life.

Jesus Calls, *"Keep Company With Me, for My Yoke Is Easy."*

The fifth crucial connection was birthed in 1974, when God exchanged my loneliness and fears for His fellowship and intimacy. This pivotal point began with a phone call from an old business friend of Tom's, who announced, "Hey, Tom! I gave your name to the personnel manager of a Minneapolis company seeking someone with your qualifications. The position is tailor-made for you!"

Tom and I then talked for hours. The job involved less travel and looked promising, but we wondered if we really wanted to move again. There were many pros for staying—Tom was doing well in his present position, I loved my teaching job, the family enjoyed living by the ocean, and the thought of leaving our youth group and dear Boston friends was sad. However, we also liked the idea of returning to our Minnesota roots and to family members still in the area. The summer before, while on vacation, we had hastily purchased a cabin north of Minneapolis as an investment; we now wondered if there was any significance to this. Peace came after we prayed and asked God to show us His will; we both sensed His hand orchestrating the whole thing.

Tom, invited to fly out for an interview, was immediately offered the position. He accepted and was to start a month later, so we scrambled to get our house ready to sell. Tom stayed with Minneapolis friends and flew home every third weekend. The children and I stayed behind to finish the remaining two months of the school year.

Since I was accustomed to his weekly business trips, I didn't think the three-week wait between home visits would be difficult for me. However, loneliness would engulf me, especially on weekends; I found little relief through staying busy.

I remember sitting in my den one night, with the children asleep and the house quiet; I felt forlorn, "like an owl in the desert or lonely as a solitary sparrow on the roof" (Psalm 102:6–7 TLB). Soon God reminded me of His presence and asked, "Would you dance with Me?" I ignored His invitation, because I *really* wanted to have Tom next to me, physically, tangibly. I felt like a three-year-old again whose heart ached for her daddy to be home instead of fighting in a faraway war.

Realizing this, I invited Jesus to minister His care to my inner little one. That night God delivered me from spirits of grief and loneliness and healed my separation anxiety. Jesus and I then whirled around the room, keeping step with praise music. Throughout the years, His tender touch has continued to sustain me, and loneliness has never overshadowed me again.

After this very special God moment, I was full of confidence that all would go well with our move. Our church had a going-away party and gave us a plaque with kind parting words and this reference: Ruth 1:16, which I later looked up, "Don't urge me to leave you or to turn back from you. Where you go I will go, and where you stay I will stay. Your people will be my people and your God my God." I truly desired to follow Ruth's example of faith and abide in God wherever He would lead me.

~~~~~~~~~~

In June, we left our house in the care of our realtor and moved temporarily to our cabin on Minnesota's Whitefish chain of lakes. Tom came on weekends and our life was almost idyllic, except for one hitch—our east-coast house was not selling, causing an annoying relocation delay. Because the children needed to be enrolled in school, we finally obtained a bridge loan from a local bank and moved in August. From my perspective, this was not the best arrangement because we would soon be facing two house payments and dual upkeep. My confidence in God's faithfulness began to waver.

I questioned, "If goodness and mercy are following me, why aren't they coming to my aid?" Instead, dread and fear seemed to be my constant companions. Again I foolishly doubted God and wondered why He wasn't living up to my expectations. "Most houses sell in three months," I reasoned, "so where is God?"

Then I did something I have never done before or since: I childishly demanded an answer. With a show-me-now attitude, I opened my Bible and let my index finger land on a verse. Sheepishly, I read,

> "You of little faith, why are you so afraid?" Then He got up and rebuked the winds and the waves, and it was completely calm. (Matthew 8:26)

After this, I heard, softly from within, *Do you think I don't care or notice what is happening in your life? Trust Me!* I asked Christ to forgive my unbelief.

~~~~~~~~~~

Not surprisingly, if God had performed to my expectations, I would have missed a tremendous blessing. Just after Labor Day, a divorced friend from Boston called. With a frazzled voice, Mary asked if she and her children could move into our empty house. She explained that the night before she had awakened to a man standing by her bed. Fearing assault, she screamed, and fortunately the stranger fled. After having her apartment broken into and violated so invasively, emotionally she could not spend another night there or feel safe in the inner city. She told us she felt compelled by God to call us, and that she would gladly make the payments and cover the utilities while she lived there.

Empathetically, Tom and I wanted to help, but we said this probably wouldn't work—we needed to keep the property listed for sale. We also expressed our concerns that she didn't need the pressure of keeping the house tidy so it would show well to possible buyers, *or* the stress of having to quickly move out if it sold right away.

She replied that she would take excellent care of our property and that moving again wouldn't bother her, for she had complete peace from God that this was the direction she was to go. She added, "Maybe we'll have to trust God on this one!"

We told her we would pray and return with an answer as soon as possible. Amazed at the turn of events, we asked God for direction; He gave us the peace to call her with a yes!

It ended up being a win/win situation. A purchase agreement was signed in December by two sisters who didn't want to close on the house until their retirement the following June; Mary and her family were able to stay in our beautiful home for the whole school year. Again, Christ lifted our heavy burdens effortlessly. By His wondrous ways, the Good Shepherd richly provided for each lamb's need!

~~~~~~~~~~

Eventually I allowed God to get to the heart of my frequent financial fears. He showed me that from childhood I had been bound by the words, "I can't afford ..." Unintentionally, I imparted to my children the same pattern of focusing on our wishes and resources rather than the Lord's desires and bounty. The generational stronghold of poverty thinking didn't lose its power to make waves in my life until I nailed those deceptive words, with their structures, to the cross. By revelation I accepted the truth: my God would meet all my needs according to His glorious riches in Christ Jesus (Philippians 4:19).

I also needed to realize there was, at times, a big difference between my wants and my true needs. I wanted God to sell our home speedily so I could avoid facing pesky fears; God saw a root of worry that needed to be exposed to His light. He desired true inner peace for me, not a false truce with anxiety.

To commemorate this pivotal point, I composed a painting that depicts Jesus calming the storm that had threatened to drown everyone in the boat. I could identify with the fearful disciples who looked at Him with awe when He rebuked the wind and waves. Many times I have needed this pictorial reminder about God's faithfulness and power. It hangs on our front foyer wall, as if to greet each arrival with the message, "Jesus cares!"

I am so glad I answered yes to Christ's invitation to keep company with Him. He was able to break through my loneliness and fears by a revelation of His dear, intimate fellowship!

Jesus Pursues, *"My Burden Is Light; I'll Carry You."*

The sixth compass of clarity happened in October 1977, shortly before my fortieth birthday. Tom and I were enjoying a fall weekend at our cabin, and that night, after a full day of playing, we readily fell into deep sleep. However, in the early morning hours, I woke with a jolt, hearing, "Obadiah." Nothing was amiss, so I thought I must be dreaming and went back to sleep, only to hear an audible, distinct, "Obadiah", which woke me again.

This time I sensed God's presence and thought He wanted me to read the book of Obadiah. I rapidly read all twenty-one verses, but remained puzzled; the passage is about the destruction of the Edomites, the descendants of Esau, who would not come to Israel's aid when needed. Interesting, but I found nothing profound for myself. I told the Lord I didn't understand, and that if He had something to tell me, He would have to make His message clearer.

Attempting to go back to sleep, I heard another audible, "Obadiah." This time God's Spirit impressed upon my heart to look up the meaning of the name. I read in my Bible's introduction that "Obadiah" means *servant of Yahweh.* Warmth filled me; I knew God was not only calling me His servant, but that this was the same title given to Moses. I began to comprehend that my many wilderness struggles and desert experiences would be utilized for the restoration of others.

Through my limited lens, I saw I was part of God's end-time church of Philadelphia—His community of brotherly love, able to endure patiently in trying times by trusting Him. The Spirit impressed upon my heart this word of truth:

These are the words of him who is holy and true, who holds the key of David. What he opens no one can shut, and what he shuts no one can open. I know your deeds. See, I have placed before you an open door that no one can shut. I know that you have little strength, yet you have kept my word and have not denied my name. Since you have kept my command to endure patiently, I will also keep you from the hour of trial that is going to come upon the whole world to test those who live on the earth. (Revelation 3:7–8, 10)

~~~~~~~~~~

This milestone marker in my life is analogous to the time Israel miraculously reached the Promised Land by crossing over the dried bed of the Jordan. Joshua instructed twelve men of each tribe to select a river stone lying near the priests holding the Ark of the Covenant, while standing between the river banks. The chosen men each hoisted a rock and then laid their heavy burden at Joshua's feet; Joshua records that the rocks were then made an altar of stones, an everlasting sign, to honor their covenant-keeping God.

> In the future, when your children ask you, "What do these stones mean?" tell them that the flow of the Jordan was cut off before the Ark of the Covenant of the LORD.... These stones are to be a memorial to the people of Israel forever. (4:6–7).

Ordinary stones became rocks of remembrance!

In my heart, Jesus became my Joshua, leading me across the Jordan into His Promised Land. As Christ's bondservant, acutely appreciating our eternal and intimate yoke, I bowed down reverently and left the heavy burden of "me" at His feet. *Like a living stone belonging to God, I became Christ's radiant testimony of remembrance!*

> You come to him, the living stone—rejected by men but chosen by God and precious to Him—you also, like living stones, are being built into a spiritual house to be a holy priesthood, offering spiritual sacrifices acceptable to God through Jesus Christ. But you are a chosen people, a royal priesthood, a holy nation, a people belonging to God, that you may declare the praises of him who called you out of darkness into his wonderful light. (1 Peter 2:4–5, 9)

God disclosed to me the fields that were ripe for Him to harvest. In these pastures, God's harassed and bruised lambs were in need of His tender shepherding. When He revealed their plight to me, I would feel compassion and walk with Him through His open doors. I knew that these God-initiated ministries were portions of the prophetic word I had received in the 1971 visitation. I also realized that He had sent me to college so I could apply my education for His purposes and calling. I did not renew my teaching certification when it became due; I knew God was shutting this door. Through many avenues of training, He has continued to teach me His ways and wisdom; even so, it is through personal fellowship that I am becoming like Him.

I am so glad I answered yes to God's invitation to co-labor with the Holy Spirit to be a witness for Christ. He was able to break through my obscurity as a hidden river stone by a revelation that He will carry me, His beloved bride, proudly over the threshold into a fruitful future!

~~~~~~~~~~

The Lord Jesus desires and welcomes all to come to Him. Anyone who voices, "Yes, I choose to know You" will be God's child, destined to be like Him! (Matthew 22:14). Papa God's grace will carry you through all storms, and your difficulties will not last forever.

> Our God who is full of kindness through Christ will give you his eternal glory. He personally will pick you up, and set you firmly in place, and make you stronger than ever. To him be all power over all things, forever and ever. Amen. (1 Peter 5:10–11 TLB)

A Personal Invitation

"Are you tired? Worn out? Come to Me."
Will you answer yes to Christ's invitation to come to His spiritual rest?
He will break through your many doubts by a revelation of His care!

"Burned out? I'll show you how to find serenity."
Will you answer yes to Christ's invitation to choose His way of peace?
He will break through your strong or passive will
by a revelation of His strength and adequacy!

"Choose My yoke and walk with Me."
Will you answer yes to Christ's invitation to be yoked with His power?
He will break through your discouragement
by a revelation of His joy and His Spirit!

"Learn from Me, for I am gentle and humble."
Will you answer yes to Christ's invitation to learn His gentle ways?
He will break through your many distractions
by a revelation of His prophetic purposes for your life.

"Keep company with Me, for My yoke is easy."
Will you answer yes to Christ's invitation to keep company with Him?
He will break through your loneliness and fears
by a revelation of His dear, intimate fellowship!

"My burden is light; I'll carry you."
Will you answer yes to Christ's invitation to co-labor with Him?
He will break through your obscurity as a hidden river stone
by a revelation that He will carry you, His beloved,
proudly over the threshold into a fruitful future!

Chapter 19

Embracing Your Inheritance

In your unfailing love you will lead the people you have redeemed.
In your strength you will guide them to your holy dwelling. (Exodus 15:13)

Awake, awake, O Zion, clothe yourself with strength.
Put on your garments of splendor, O Jerusalem, the holy city.
The uncircumcised and defiled will not enter you again.
Shake off your dust; rise up, sit enthroned, O Jerusalem.
Free yourself from the chains on your neck,
O captive Daughter of Zion. (Isaiah 52:1–2)

Hope does not disappoint us, because God has poured out his love
into our hearts by the Holy Spirit, whom he has given us. (Romans 5:5)

As a child, I loved stories with happy endings. I repeatedly asked for *Snow White*[23] to be read to me. When the Disney movie was released, the characters continued to dance in my imagination. Many times I fantasized that I was the beautiful princess awakened to life by the love of a handsome prince.

I still enjoy this nineteenth-century German fairy tale, but as an adult I also perceive this story to be a meaningful allegory about God and human nature. In ministry, when I share the comparisons, almost invariably the "little one inside" reminisces and chuckles fondly. *Snow White* tenderly conveys hope to survivors of ominous times that through God's amazing love they also will burst into blossom and inherit His peace.

The story is about a beautiful princess whose parents were royals. All was bliss in the kingdom until the Queen Mother died and the king chose a gorgeous but evil woman to be his new wife. This vain queen regularly consulted a magic mirror that told her she was the fairest of all! Because this was her narcissistic source of worth, she became horror-struck when, one day, the mirror proclaimed that Snow White was *now* the fairest of all.

With a sinister heart, the queen ordered her huntsman to kill her stepchild and bring back her lungs and liver in a box as proof that the deed had been accomplished. Once in the woods, the man warned the young lady of the plot, telling her to run for her life and never return to the palace. Snow White was temporarily safe because the huntsman presented a bear's lung and liver to show the queen that her orders had been obeyed. The wicked stepmother then devoured what she thought were Snow White's organs of breath and blood. (Gruesome!)

Meanwhile, deep in the forest, Snow White discovered refuge in a cottage of seven dwarfs. Their unusual names are a description of their dispositions: Grumpy, Happy, Sneezy, Sleepy, Bashful, Doc, and Dopey. Even though everything in the house was too small for her, Snow White adapted, and the dwarfs became her dearest friends.

However, when the queen again consulted her looking-glass, she discovered that Snow White was still alive and knew where she was hiding. With evil intent, the would-be killer disguised herself as a seller of pretty wares and left to find her rival.

While the little people were away at work, Snow White innocently opened the door to a frail old peddler who offered brightly colored silk lace. Before Snow White realized what was happening, the woman had bound her so tightly with lace bands that she fell as if dead. Believing she had succeeded, the queen ran back to the palace, only to hear from the mirror that the paragon of beauty was still alive.

Not giving up, the queen returned again to the cottage and offered a poisonous comb. Snow White, beguiled by pretty things, allowed the old woman to style her hair. As soon as the toxic tips touched the princess's head, she dropped senseless.

Back at the castle, the queen discovered that her third mission of murder had failed. Now, disguised as a farmer's wife, she went with a luscious-looking apple, half of which was poisoned. Forbidden to open the door to any stranger, Snow White talked with her through a window. The deceptive woman then divided the apple and ate the healthy part. Bewitched, Snow White took a bite from the apple and fell dead. The queen laughed aloud and confidently returned to the palace.

The dwarfs found the princess dead and, after mourning three days, they laid her body in a transparent coffin of glass. They wrote upon it an inscription of her name and added that she was a king's daughter. Even after a long time, she continued to look like a sleeping beauty, showing no signs of decay.

One day a king's son arrived upon the scene. Upon seeing his love for her, the dwarfs gave the coffin to him so he would be able to watch over her. While carrying it away, however, his servants stumbled over a tree stump with their heavy load, causing Snow White to spit up the poisonous piece of apple. Instantly she woke up, fully healthy, and gladly left with the handsome gentleman.

At their royal wedding, the wicked queen recognized Snow White and froze with fear and rage. Palace guards then forced her to wear red-hot shoes and dance to her death.

Meaning for Today?

Consider, metaphorically, the story's characters: The royal parents are like Adam and Eve; the evil queen is like the beguiling, devouring serpent in the royal garden; Snow White is like any child loved by God but traumatized by evil; the huntsman is like any well-meaning person who offers temporary relief; the seven dwarfs are like defense mechanisms that help an abused person survive stressful situations; and the king's son is like Jesus Christ, the Savior and Prince Whose love restores people to life. (The magic mirror could represent a conduit for the spirits of witchcraft.)

Adam and Eve, as rulers of this earth, had a royal heritage, but pride brought death and ruin to their kingdom. When Eve listened to the deceiver, and Adam didn't use his God-given authority to defend his family, enmity entered their marriage. Neither did the king in the fairy tale protect his daughter when he married a wicked woman empowered by magic. The bloodthirsty queen is like a crushing beast that tramples underfoot whatever it wants to devour (Daniel 7:19).

When Adam and Eve chose to live apart from God, they opened the gate to generational curses and family iniquity: a spirit of death entered. Shame and blame penetrated Adam's household, demonic spirits entered his lineage with disastrous results. Who could have imagined the increase of the world's wickedness up to the present time?

Through the ages, hostility, envy, and pride have continued to leave a mark on innocents. Whenever the Lord's people have turned to other gods, a stupor has overcome them. He warned the chosen people:

> When you enter the land the LORD your God is giving you, do not learn to imitate the detestable ways of the nations there. Let no one be found among you who sacrifices his son or daughter in the fire, who practices divination or sorcery, interprets omens, engages in witchcraft, or casts spells, or who is a medium or spiritist or who consults the dead. Anyone who does these things is detestable to the LORD, and because of these detestable practices the LORD your God will drive out those nations before you. You must be blameless before the LORD your God. (Deuteronomy 18:9–13)

Just as Snow White hid in the house of dwarfs, adult children from broken beginnings may become soul-stunted. When a fragile person's true identity feels trapped in darkness, he may survive with anger and negativity like Grumpy, with denial of pain like Happy, with caretaking pride like Doc, with learned helplessness like Sneezy, with tiredness like Sleepy, with fears like Bashful, and with shame like Dopey. Fragmented parts of personhood protectively react to whatever is perceived as overwhelming stress or pain.

I envision the dwarfish dialogue to have been somewhat chaotic: Grumpy bitterly complaining that nothing good ever happens to him; Happy not understanding this, as he always considers himself to be just fine; Doc having an answer for everyone's difficulty; Sneezy interrupting all conversations; Sleepy, living in fog, saying little; Bashful hiding, so as not to be noticed; *everyone* feeling superior to Dopey, who acts foolishly from being shame-driven. In an atmosphere where childish feelings dominate and keep others at bay, healthy conversations and mutual interaction are non-existent. Avoidance of difficult issues is *never* a lasting solution.

The dwarfs' household is like a dysfunctional family whose children have been traumatized and neglected during their formative years. They learn to cope by survival behaviors: some run from difficulties to drugs or alcohol; some withdraw from themselves by blocking out what happened; some split off from their feelings; some become stuck in negativity; some become super-achievers. Most feel like perpetual victims who expect to be relentlessly buffeted by ill winds of stormy emotions and expect others to rescue them.

Defense mechanisms permit survival, but can warp reality; they temporarily protect, but can hinder healing; they are coping tools, but can deceive; they act as release valves, but they can keep a person from adjusting, repenting, changing, and thriving. Avoiding responsibility, staying busy, blaming others, making excuses, minimizing reality, displacing anger, and isolating from others might imprison a person for life. The Bible describes this condition as being "a man of two minds (hesitating, dubious, irresolute), [he is] unstable and unreliable and uncertain about everything [he thinks, feels, decides]" (James 1:8 AMP). Civil war within the soul results in an unsettled state of being.

All use defensive means for protection from internal and external stresses. As a gift from God to help children or vulnerable adults weather stormy seasons, these become like winter's debris when spring blooms in an individual's life. The Lord desires to clear away the matted covering of winter so that His saints will become mature, fruitful plants who provide bountiful blessings to others. The Lord of the Harvest has something greater and higher for His beloved than being small and hidden under yesteryear's dead leaves!

Snow White's dear friends were not big enough to save her. She was a king's daughter, yet she lived in a place not designed for her. Bound by immature emotions, she lacked discernment. Making foolish and impulsive decisions based on what looked good to her, she continually opened the door to deception.

Three times the wicked queen deceived her. Silk lace, lovely comb, succulent apple ... each death blow corresponds to satanic attacks that keep God's child in a paralyzing state of toxic thinking, chained to the past.

Snow White coughed up the poisonous fruit as she was being carried by servants of the prince. Jesus Christ, the Prince of Peace, utilizes the prayers of His saints to break generational strongholds. Like the fairy-tale royal, the Lord Jesus delivers His cherished bride from the venom of evil. A beautiful godly line is birthed whose scarlet sins, through repentance, are covered by the blood of the Lamb. All who embrace His love become white as snow, brand-new people inside (2 Corinthians 5:17). It is written,

> "Come now, let us reason together," says the LORD. "Though your sins are like scarlet, they shall be as white as snow; though they are red as crimson, they shall be like wool" (Isaiah 1:18).

God's loving redemption through Christ's shed blood is an everlasting inheritance that revives the heart. Many, like the huntsman, have tried to stop the devastation with their own remedies, but to no avail. Man's resources do not last, but the Son of Man is able to render us incorruptible and righteous. *God hates injustice.* Eventually, satan and all his cohorts will be banished to a lake of fire. Will he dance to his doom?

Awake, My Beloved!

What is the peril of staying in a shelter made for "little people"? Children are unable to utilize and fully enjoy their inheritance. *God is calling His beloved people to wake up and behold Christ as their bounty of blessings!*

Paul wrote, "When I was a child, I talked like a child, I thought like a child, I reasoned like a child. When I became a man, I put childish ways behind me" (1 Corinthians 13:11). Jesus warns the church about the danger of immaturity that leads to spiritual stupor:

> I know your deeds; you have a reputation of being alive, but you are dead. Wake up! Strengthen what remains and is about to die, for I have not found your deeds complete in the sight of my God. Remember, therefore, what you have received and heard; obey it, and repent. But if you do not wake up, I will come like a thief, and you will not know at what time I will come to you. (Revelation 3:1–2)

The righteous are to live in a household of faith where they will grow to be like Christ.

> A shoot will come up from the stump of Jesse; from his roots a Branch will bear fruit. The Spirit of the LORD will rest on him—the Spirit of wisdom and of understanding, the Spirit of counsel and of power, the Spirit of knowledge and of the fear of the LORD—and he will delight in the fear of the LORD. (Isaiah 11:1–3)

Unless God's Spirit is giving guidance, mortals are easily deceived by their limited perceptions. Man is influenced by outward appearances, false evidence, and hearsay.

God desires all to mature and be fruitful by the fullness of His Spirit. Deborah and Barak were Israelites who lived victoriously in oppressive times. Like others who live by faith rather than feelings, they provide an example to follow. Awakened by God's love, they sang this song of praise unto their Lord:

> When the princes in Israel take the lead,
>> when the people willingly offer themselves—
>> praise the LORD!
> Village life in Israel ceased,
>> ceased until I, Deborah, arose,
>> arose a mother in Israel.
> My heart is with Israel's princes,
>> with the willing volunteers among the people.
>> Praise the LORD!
> The voice of the singers at the watering places—
>> they recite the righteous acts of the LORD,
>> the righteous acts of his warriors in Israel.
> Then the people of the LORD
>> went down to the city gates.
> "Wake up, Wake up, Deborah!
> Wake up, break out in song! Arise, O Barak!
> So may all your enemies perish, O LORD!
> But may they who love you be like the sun
>> when it rises in its strength".
>> (Judges 5:2, 7, 9, 11–12, 31)

God's Embrace Is for All

During my journey of learning, when my mind entertained worry, regret, and grumpiness like chosen friends, I was ensnared in a painful trap of misery. Deceived like Snow White, I lived in a place I thought I could keep under my control. One day, when I was feeling disheartened and wondering why I felt as if I were sinking into a quagmire of doubt, the Lord reminded me that Paul also had observed an internal war.

God's Spirit guided me to read about Paul's restlessness. In one instance he states, *"I don't understand myself at all, for I really want to do what is right, but I don't do it. Instead, I do the very thing I hate."* (Romans 7:15 NLT), then subsequently testifies of his knowledge that Jesus Christ rescued him from his wretched prison of shame, from bondage to sin, and from spirits of fear.

Encouraged, yet identifying with Paul's emotional unrest, I asked my Lord Jesus to also deliver me from being double-minded, from living with constant upheaval. Instead of being governed by deceptive feelings, I desired to be guided by the Holy Spirit.

When I listened, the Lord impressed upon my heart that His faithful love would never fail me, that by His power I would be an overcomer. As I continued to read Romans 8, Jesus imparted these thoughts, reflections, and truths into the core of my being:

Transforming Love
(Feel free to speak your name in place of mine)

When I feel accused and discouragement invades my mind,
Jesus speaks to my heart and says:
*"My Spirit sets you free, Erin, from all condemnation,
because you live in Me!"*

When I look at my many shortcomings
and wonder why I sometimes feel angry toward God,
Jesus speaks to my heart and says:
*"The mind focusing on self produces death.
Let My Spirit control your thoughts!"*

When I question—"Is it really that simple? What do You mean?"
Jesus speaks to my heart and says:
*"Yes, you chose to receive Me as Your Savior;
now, daily be empowered by My Spirit!"*

When I feel powerless as a person with little authority,
Jesus speaks to my heart and says:
*"Erin, when you are led by My Spirit,
you are My child, My ambassador!"*

When I feel like a slave to fear, surrounded by terror,
Jesus speaks to my heart and says:
*"Remember: you are adopted into My family.
I answer your calls of 'Abba, Father!'"*

When I struggle with pain and feel robbed of well-being,
Jesus speaks to my heart and says:
*"As My person who shares in My sufferings,
as a co-heir of Christ, you also share in My glory!"*

When I feel alone and frustrated because so many are suffering,
Jesus speaks to my heart and says:
*"I understand. All of My creation yearns for deliverance.
There will be a day of liberty!"*

When I feel forlorn and impatient because my hope is fleeting,
Jesus speaks to my heart and says:
*"Remember: hope is not seen with your natural eyes,
but with the eyes of your heart. See Me, I am Hope!"*

When I feel bound and not able to voice a prayer,
Jesus speaks to my heart and says:
"When you struggle with knowing how to pray,
My Spirit within you prays for you fervently!"

When I feel no comfort, weighted by thoughts of disappointment,
Jesus speaks to my heart and says:
"I am working your present suffering for good
because you love Me and are called to My purposes!"

When I feel unsure about my future and if I will ever change,
Jesus speaks to my heart and says:
"Erin, all who accept My calling are justified and predestined
to be conformed to the likeness of Me!"

When I feel forsaken and not very loveable,
Jesus speaks to my heart and says:
"Nothing separates you from Me
because I embrace you with My love!"

Thank you, God, for graciously challenging me to change while totally accepting me today. Because You, Jesus, died for my sins and now intercede for me, I have Your Spirit, power, and strength to believe that nothing can separate me from Your affection. Overwhelming victory is mine through Christ Who loves me!

I love You— Erin

Love Letters

Back in the seventies, I went with an old college friend to a Christian camp for five days. The rustic accommodations were nestled in a forest, overlooking a scenic lake. Looking for fun and rest while our spouses watched over the home front, neither of us anticipated overwhelmingly being touched by God.

On the last day, we were asked to find a quiet place where we could commune with God. We were encouraged to write Him a heartfelt letter with our non-dominant hand, then be still before Him and wait patiently for His reply. I awkwardly wrote about my bothersome worries, concluding with "I love you, Jesus." Waiting, I became like a little child sitting on my Abba's lap. I was not disappointed: my expectant heart became quietly filled with "Good News." I recorded something like this:

My Child, Erin Faye,
May I comfort you?
I will never forget you.
When you are sad,

I am close to you.
One day I'll wipe away
every tear from your eyes.
I love you, too! Papa God

Since that event, I have shared with others the value of writing letters under the Spirit's inspiration as an aid for healing.

~~~~~~~~~~

One woman seeking support and prayer had suffered a multitude of emotional effects springing from an abusive childhood. Medicating her pain through addictive behaviors, she found herself in a treatment center for alcoholics at age fifteen. By the time she came for counseling, she was still struggling with self-hatred and oppressive thoughts.

Gradually she became able to see herself as God's beloved child, a new creation in Christ. The new person who emerged was like a beautiful butterfly no longer needing the cocoon of the past! Her former ways have been exchanged for His wings of love and truth. Because of Christ's transformation of her inner person, she was able to write:

Dear Little One,

You need not be afraid or lonely. Jesus is holding you in His arms, and He has all the love, healing power, and care you could ever need. He is not too busy for you. Your life is of utmost importance to Him. After all, He died for you!

He is okay if you are not perfect, and feeling alone does not make you a bad girl. Jesus wants to tell you to keep clinging to Him, and keep following His light. Hold out your arms and reach for Him whenever you are lonely.

Tell people that you need love. Don't be afraid to give love, because you will get it in return. Don't think that you have to put on a show for everyone and make them believe you are completely independent. It's okay to need people, to need love, and to need nurturing hugs. Don't let anyone make you feel unworthy to receive love, because you are a child of God, and you are worthy, and loveable. There is nothing wrong with you and people will love you just because you are you. You are not a loner, or a black sheep, or different, or just the artistic one, or the "only" one who can do a certain thing. There is no shame in what you are, and you don't need to do bad things to get attention.

Your worth is not in what you do, or how much you make or how good your prayers are. You are worthy just because you are you. God formed you in your mother's womb for His purpose and has been with you forever. He will always be by your side. Come and sit on Jesus' lap and talk to him like your brother, father, or best friend.

I will do my best to remember you and take care of you. I will try not to be too rushed and full of activities to take time for how you feel. I will let my toughness erode and let you come out. My feelings are based in beginnings. Don't let me bury you anymore.

The new adult who walks with you

A Prayer for Renewal

Dear Heavenly Father,

This day I give my broken heart to you. I choose to trust Your unfailing love and believe Your truth. Please help me to rest in Your arms. Forgive my unbelief. Recreate in me a new heart that is awakened by Your love. With all my spirit, soul, mind, and with all my strength, help me to love You and others as well as myself.

Thank you, Lord, that You are healing my past and giving me a fresh start. Remind me that You want to be Lord of all of my life, my emotions, my attitudes. I choose to forgive those who have wounded me and been untrustworthy. [Let the Holy Spirit guide you through this process.] Forgive me for my bitter judgments against those who have offended me. I release my resentments and my oppressors into Your hands. Thank you for building trust in me and restoring to me the seasons that were consumed by evil. I am forever grateful!

Your "Snow White"

Other Befitting Petitions

Dear Lord Jesus, help me to trust You in trying times, like faithful forefathers did.

In you our fathers put their trust; they trusted and you delivered them. They cried to you and were saved; in you they trusted and were not disappointed. (Psalm 22:4–5)

Dear Lord Jesus, help me to trust You when I am fearful.

When I am afraid, I will trust in you. (56:3)

Dear Lord Jesus, help me to trust You when I am oppressed.

The LORD is a refuge for the oppressed, a stronghold in times of trouble. Those who know your name will trust in you, for you, LORD, have never forsaken those who seek you. (9:9–10)

Dear Lord Jesus, help me to trust You for my salvation.

> I trust in your unfailing love; my heart rejoices in your salvation. I will sing to the LORD, for he has been good to me. (13:5–6)

Dear Lord Jesus, help me to trust You when I am prosperous.

> I am like an olive tree flourishing in the house of God; I trust in God's unfailing love forever and ever. (52:8)

Dear Lord Jesus, help me to trust You when I am tempted to rely on my imperfect knowledge.

> Trust in the LORD with all your heart and lean not on your own understanding; in all your ways acknowledge him, and he will make your paths straight. Do not be wise in your own eyes; fear the LORD and shun evil. This will bring health to your body and nourishment to your bones. (Proverbs 3:5–8)

Dear Lord Jesus, help me to trust that Your Spirit empowers and fills me with joy, peace, and hope.

> May the God of hope fill you with all joy and peace as you trust in him, so that you may overflow with hope by the power of the Holy Spirit. (Romans 15:13)

A Closing Tribute to a Loving God

Give thanks to the LORD, for he is good.
His love endures forever.
To him who alone does great wonders,
His love endures forever.

To him who divided the Red Sea asunder
His love endures forever.
and brought Israel through the midst of it,
His love endures forever.
but swept Pharaoh and his army into the Red Sea;
His love endures forever.
To the One who remembered us in our low estate
His love endures forever.
and freed us from our enemies,
His love endures forever.
Give thanks to the God of heaven.
His love endures forever.
(Psalm 136:1, 4, 13–15, 23–24, 26)

Harken! The Lord's Rally Trumpet is Blowing!

> All you people of the world, you who live on the earth, when a banner is raised on the mountains, you will see it, and when a trumpet sounds, you will hear it. This is what the LORD says to me: "I will remain quiet and will look on from my dwelling place, like shimmering heat in the sunshine, like a cloud of dew in the heat of harvest" (Isaiah 18:3–4).

Christ's shophar of jubilee is beckoning the whole world to come to His goodness, to fathom that He alone executes great wonders, and to grasp that the King of Glory made the heavens and the earth. Remember: The world was shapeless and chaotic when the Creator spoke to set the boundaries in place and separate the light from the darkness.

And, by His Word, the Lord also replenishes all who come to Him. Tom and I are testimonies of His restoring love! The Redeemer delivered Israel out of captivity, and He will rescue you. God Almighty divided the Red Sea for the salvation of His people, and He will reveal His freedom road to you. God, the Warrior, swept Pharaoh's army into the sea, and He will protect you from satan's destruction. The Good Shepherd guided Israel through the desert, and He will escort you through your wilderness journey.

Jesus Christ reveals that *beyond despair is God's tender care.* The Father of Mercies remembers the disheartened, and He will not forsake you in your utter weakness. To every hurting heart: The Commander of the Army freed the Israelites, and He will fight for your safety. The Provider gave food to every creature, and He will continuously provide for you. The Faithful One brought Israel to the Promised Land, and He will bring you into heaven's bounty of deep intimacy with Him. God chooses to wondrously love you!

> Thus says the Lord, the Redeemer of Israel,
> Israel's Holy One, to him whom man rejects and despises,
> to him whom the nations abhor, to the servant of rulers:
> Kings shall see you and arise; princes,
> and they shall prostrate themselves,
> because of the Lord, Who is faithful,
> the Holy One of Israel, Who has chosen you.
> (Isaiah 49:7 AMP)

Appendix

Scripture referenced in the chapter 8 chart: page 89

(1) "Let us fix our eyes on Jesus, the author and perfecter of our faith, who for the joy set before him endured the cross, scorning its shame, and sat down at the right hand of the throne of God." (Hebrews 12:2)

(2) "Greater love has no one than this, that he lay down His life for his friends." (John 15:13)

(3) "Having disarmed the powers and authorities, he made a public spectacle of them, triumphing over them by the cross" (Colossians 2:15); "Death has been swallowed up in victory." (1 Corinthians 15:54)

(4) "Where, O death, is your victory? Where, O death, is your sting?" (15:55)

(5) "[He] canceled the written code [the law], with its regulations, that was against us and that stood opposed to us; he took it away, nailing it to the cross." (Colossians 2:14)

(6) "Through him [God was pleased] to reconcile to himself all things, whether things on earth or things in Heaven, by making peace through his blood, shed on the cross." (1:19–20)

(7) "We preach Christ crucified: a stumbling block to Jews and foolishness to Gentiles." (1 Corinthians 1:23)

(8) "In him we have redemption through his blood, the forgiveness of sins, in accordance with the riches of God's grace that he lavished on us with all wisdom and understanding." (Ephesians 1:7–8)

(9) "Remember that formerly you who are Gentiles by birth and called "uncircumcised" by those who call themselves 'the circumcision' ... remember that at that time you were separate from Christ, excluded from citizenship in Israel and foreigners to the covenant of the promise, without hope and without God in the world. But now in Christ Jesus you who once were far away have been brought near through the blood of Christ." (2:11–13)

(10) "He himself bore our sins in his body on the tree, so that we might die to sins and live for righteousness; by his wounds you have been healed. For you were like sheep going astray, but now you have returned to the Shepherd and Overseer of your souls." (1 Peter 2:24–25)

(11) "May I never boast except in the cross of our Lord Jesus Christ, through which the world has been crucified to me, and I to the world." (Galatians 6:14)

(12) "It is for freedom that Christ has set us free. Stand firm, then, and do not let yourselves be burdened again by a yoke of slavery." (5:1)

Information

If you would like to know more about the ministry or would like to
invite Erin to speak at your church or conference,
you may do so by using the following information:

You can visit Erin's website at:

www.gardengraceministries.org

Or, you can send a self-addressed stamped envelope to:

Garden of Grace Ministries
P.O. Box 61
Elk River, MN 55330

Fax us:

(763) 241-0391

You may acquire additional copies of this book by contacting:

Erin Worthley
(Same address as above)

Be sure to ask your favorite Christian bookstore to stock

Beyond Despair: Tender Care

by Erin Worthley

Thank you for reading this book.
We would welcome your comments!

Tom and Erin Worthley
(Same address as above)

Endnotes

[1] Jamie Buckingham, *Where Eagles Soar* (Lincoln, Va.: Chosen, 1980), 29.

[2] Frank Lake, *Personal Identity: Its Development* (Clinical Theology Association, 1987).

[3] Robert Okin, U.S. *News & World Report,* "Tyranny of Mind" (5/12/03, 47).

[4] www.thepharaohs.net/Gods/

[5] W. E. Vine, Merrill F. Unger, and William White, Jr, *Vine's Expository Dictionary of Biblical Words* (Nashville, Camden, New York: Thomas Nelson, 1985), 26.

[6] Reader's Digest Book, Great People of The Bible and How They Lived (Pleasantville, NY: Reader's Digest Assoc., 1974), 76.

[7] J. I. Packer, *Nelson's Illustrated Manners and Customs of the Bible* (Nashville: Thomas Nelson, 1997, ©1995), 714.

[8] *The Full Life Study Bible—New International Version,* ® NIV,® Copyright, © (Grand Rapids: Life Publishers International, 1992), Study Notes, 1990.

[9] Frances Frangipane, *The Three Battlegrounds* (Cedar Rapids: Arrow Publications, 1989), 112.

[10] Robert Young, *Young's Analytical Concordance to the Bible*, ® (Grand Rapids: Eerdmans, 1978), 811.

[11] *Vine's Expository Dictionary of Biblical Words,* 587.

[12] www.thesnake.org

[13] James M. Freeman, *Manners and Customs of the Bible* (Springdale, Pa.: Whitaker, 1996), 317.

[14] www.thepharaohs.net/Gods/

[15] Merrill F. Unger, *Unger's Bible Dictionary,* (Chicago: Moody Press, 1985), 392.

[16] Vine's *Expository Dictionary of Biblical Words,* 61.

[17] Ibid., 62.

[18] Young, Young's Analytical Concordance to the Bible, 95, 616.

[19] Freeman, *Manners and Customs of the Bible,* 353–54.

[20] Packer, *Manners and Customs of the Bible,* 194.

[21] Signa Bodishbaugh, *The Journey to Wholeness in Christ* (Grand Rapids: Chosen/Baker, 1997), 238.

[22] Don Bashan, *Face Up With a Miracle* (Northridge, Calif.: Voice Christian Publications, 1967).

[23] The Grimm Brothers, *Grimm Fairy Tales, 19th-Century German Stories* (Robert Godwin-Jones: Virginia Commonwealth Univ., Dept. of Foreign Languages).